Wilfred Oyem, a retired aircraft mechanic, is a first-generation Nigerian immigrant to the United States of America. *Tears of Love* is his first attempt at telling a story in book form.

This book is dedicated to the glory of God, who made the impossible possible, and to the memory of my beloved brother Anthony, whose life was cut short in the prime of his youth by forces of darkness.

Wilfred Oyem

TEARS OF LOVE

AUSTIN MACAULEY PUBLISHERS
LONDON * CAMBRIDGE * NEW YORK * SHARJAH

Copyright © Wilfred Oyem 2025

All rights reserved. No part of this publication may be reproduced, distributed, or transmitted in any form or by any means, including photocopying, recording, or other electronic or mechanical methods, without the prior written permission of the publisher, except in the case of brief quotations embodied in critical reviews and certain other non-commercial uses permitted by copyright law. For permission requests, write to the publisher.

Any person who commits any unauthorized act in relation to this publication may be liable to criminal prosecution and civil claims for damages.

This is a work of fiction. Names, characters, businesses, places, events, locales and incidents are either the products of the author's imagination or used in a fictitious manner. Any resemblance to actual persons, living or dead, or actual events is purely coincidental.

Ordering Information
Quantity sales: Special discounts are available on quantity purchases by corporations, associations and others. For details, contact the publisher at the address below.

Publisher's Cataloging-in-Publication data
Oyem, Wilfred
Tears of Love

ISBN 9798895434437 (Paperback)
ISBN 9798895434444 (Hardback)
ISBN 9798895434468 (ePub e-book)
ISBN 9798895434451 (Audiobook)

Library of Congress Control Number: 2025904646

www.austinmacauley.com/us

First Published 2025
Austin Macauley Publishers LLC
40 Wall Street, 33rd Floor, Suite 3302
New York, NY 10005
USA

mail-usa@austinmacauley.com
+1 (646) 5125767

It is not often that God is credited in the acknowledgements of a book, but anyone who has been where I have been in life cannot but shout His praises from the rooftops. Father, thank You for Your hand in my life and for the wonder of my being.

I am grateful to my wife, Julie, for her patience, loving care and support, and for respecting my need for time and space. To my children, for their invaluable support and encouragement: Nkem, my rock and fortress; Azuka, my strength; Chukwuka, my delight; and Ifeanyi, my joy. And of course, my precious crown jewels and grandchildren, Israel, Ava and Michelle. With you all, I am well blessed and highly favored.

My profound gratitude goes to my senior brother, Joseph Omosor Oyem, for giving me a solid foundation in life by way of education. Thanks to my friend, Dr Francis Edo Olotu, medical director of Christ Hospital, Ondo, Nigeria, for his great positive influence on my life. Thanks also to his amiable wife, Bukie. Both of these have proved that in today's sin-laden world, people still make it to heaven, not only by their words but also by their practical daily life conduct.

My gratitude goes to Chuks Nzei, a true friend who sticks closer than a brother—a thing hard to come by in today's world—and to Patrick Eze Adah and Ayo Dom Osanyinlusi. I am grateful to God for routing my path to cross those of these great friends.

My gratitude also goes to Jenny Collyer, senior lecturer and my course coordinator at college—now retired—for believing in me and for her tremendous encouragement.

Many thanks to my friend Segun M. Fajemisin for his editorial advice and for painstakingly proofreading the manuscript and making valuable corrections.

Thank you all for being part of my life's journey.

Table of Contents

Preface — 11

Prologue — 13

Part I: All That Glitters Is Not Gold — 15

  Chapter 1: Gathering Storms — 17

  Chapter 2: Random Musings of Concerned Students — 27

  Chapter 3: Double Standards — 32

  Chapter 4: Parallel Kingdoms — 37

  Chapter 5: Double-Talk — 43

  Chapter 6: Master Artist — 49

  Chapter 7: Divide and Rule — 56

  Chapter 8: The Devil's Invasion of Britain — 66

  Chapter 9: Organized Indiscipline — 73

  Chapter 10: A Christian PM — 82

  Chapter 11: In the Way of Jeroboam — 93

  Chapter 12: Royal Priesthood — 99

  Chapter 13: I, Me and Myself — 116

Part II: The Effective Fervent Prayer of the Righteous Avails Much, And His Expectations Shall Not Be Cut Off — 125

  Chapter 14: Grand Reunion — 127

  Chapter 15: London Tidbits — 141

  Chapter 16: A Divine Encounter — 144

Chapter 17: Jay's Thesis   *158*

Chapter 18: The Call of Faith   *218*

Chapter 19: The Puzzle of Chequers   *225*

Chapter 20: Mystery Over, But…   *316*

Chapter 21: The Audacity of Faith   *324*

Chapter 22: The Lord Reigns   *341*

Epilogue Mission Accomplished   **349**

Preface

This book was not born out of the desire to write, or to tell a story, or to entertain. As they say, necessity is the mother of invention, just as creativity is born out of challenge. It was the challenge to make my voice heard that necessitated writing this book.

Living in a society that professes freedom of expression gives the impression of inclusiveness where people's opinion should count. However, today's Britain is only slightly better than an authoritarian state, as everyone is fettered by a debilitating political correctness that knows no limit. While every system and organ of state is driven toward this unhealthy gagging, the press has outdone every agency of government, or anything else in society, in fostering this.

As a result, there is an unofficial blanket ban on the publication of any genuine contribution in the form of articles, or even letters to the editor, that are not in line with their avowed template. It is the reason why in the UK, there is a near-pathological fear of writing anything down clearly, in case it is later used against the writer. It is, therefore, foolhardy for anyone to sign his or her name to any document, especially in a country where, for the foregoing reason, there is no written down constitution. Even government officials are crucified for their candid views on any issue.

Issues of rights and liberties are promoted and heightened by the press beyond the limit, such that every aspect of life has become extremely difficult in the UK. The government is afraid of the press and is handicapped in effectively confronting the problems in society. Out of that fear, the government allows all manner of agitation, which has crippled public services and ruined the economy. Public roads, especially in London, have become death traps with silly layouts to favor agitators who never abide by the regulations of their usage. The issue of civil liberties is such that all manner of bad and evil people in the world find sanctuary in the UK. It is, therefore, not surprising that the EU counterterrorism coordinator, Gilles de Kerchove, once warned that the UK has more radicalized people than any other country in Europe.

With the foregoing in mind, I implore the reader to accept whatever little variations are seen in the presentation from the standard convention of literary works in this genre. The characters and names in this book are entirely fictitious, and any resemblance to any living being is a coincidence.

Bible quotations are taken from the New King James Version. Copyright © 1982 by Thomas Nelson, Inc. Used by permission. All rights reserved.

Prologue

In the beginning were spirits, and the spirits were all one, serving one single higher and mighty spirit. They were all good spirits and were all servants of the one high spirit. They had no mind of their own but were completely subject and obedient to the one high spirit. They basked in His glory and were completely reliant on Him. They were called angels.

One day, one of the closest spirits that waited on the higher spirit, one who was His worship leader and cup-bearer, developed a mind of his own and staged a revolt, but got banished in the attempt. Some of the other spirits who were sympathetic to his course followed him to banishment. That was Creation's first Fall. The spirit world became divided into two—the good and the evil. It resulted in the emergence of two parallel kingdoms: the kingdom of light and the kingdom of darkness. And so started the rivalry between the two kingdoms for supremacy over Creation and nature. Since then, both Creation and nature could no longer stand at ease. An unknown phenomenon came into existence which they had to endure. It violated their beauty and their peace. It was named rebellion, and its effect was called violence. Violence has since held Creation and nature to ransom and has become the scourge of humanity.

It became the scourge of humanity only because of Creation's second fall—the Fall of Man. This was orchestrated by the king and ruler of the kingdom of darkness to avenge his fall and expulsion from the kingdom of light—God's kingdom.

Part I
All That Glitters Is Not Gold

Chapter 1
Gathering Storms

There was a day when the sons of God came to present themselves before the Lord and Satan also came among them. And the Lord said to Satan, "From where do you come?"

Satan answered the Lord and said, "From going to and fro on the earth, and from walking back and forth on it."

That was very long ago. Much more recently, in the very early years of the second half of the twentieth century, there was a day when Satan's generals and senior commanders came to present themselves before Satan. It was the annual meeting of the military high command, usually chaired by Satan himself as supreme commander. It was a meeting in which the past year's activities and strategies were reviewed, new policies formulated and tactical operational command units and subunits set up as needed. It was also an occasion for the commendation and decoration of outstanding senior officers and the redeployment of commanders to new posts and assignments. Other rank-and-file officers were usually commended and decorated by individual divisional commanders.

After all the usual protocols and fanfare, the meeting started in earnest. The last issues to be discussed were strategies for the new calendar year and the choice of a location for their operational headquarters.

As part of their new offensive, Satan had asked for suggestions on how to stem the increasing number of believers and Spirit-filled worshippers of God in many parts of the world. He noted that the use of poverty and misfortune in parts of the world, especially among the third world nations, and in particular the Kushites, the Latinos and the Asians, was proving to be counterproductive. In these parts of the world, the more distressed people were, the more they turned to God in their simplicity and purity of heart for hope and meaning in life. And so a new generation of sons and daughters of God were daily presenting themselves to God. They had become a formidable army against Satan's kingdom.

Satan also noted that since their expulsion from God's presence, he and his followers had not had a permanent abode. They had been going to and fro on the earth and walking back and forth on it. They had no rest. So part of their discussion was to find a place, a city and a country where they could make their operational headquarters. They would still be residing in people and things as before, but a nation they could call their own would become the capital of their kingdom and a nerve center for the coordination of their activities.

Satan himself chaired the meeting and tabled the motion for consideration. Beelzebub was the first to speak. Bubbling with enthusiasm, he said, "That is an easy task, Your Majesty. Just wish it, and it is done. Remember Job, and how you did it single-handedly in the distant past? This time around, we don't want you to put your hand in it because you are too soft. We don't need Yahweh's permission to do what we want to do. That way we will not be confined to how far we can go. That was your mistake, which resulted in Job's receiving more blessings than was originally apportioned to him. As a matter of fact, we are too big for this job; I will assign it to one of my lower-ranked lieutenants."

In their world, they didn't like mentioning God, instead preferring the Hebrew name, Yahweh, as well as Jesus' Hebrew name, Yeshua.

Next to speak was Jezebel. "Your Majesty," he said, "I support what the Honorable Chief of Defense Staff said but not fully. I support his suggestion that you leave the whole business completely to us. I don't agree that you made a mistake in seeking Yahweh's permission. The hedge around Job was so formidable that there was no way of penetrating without first removing that hedge. And no one was strong enough to remove it except Yahweh Himself, since He was the One who erected the hedge. If Yahweh's permission was not sought, there wouldn't have been any opportunity to try at all in the first place. That Job gained a double portion of his original blessing was not a failure on your part. It was Job's total commitment and unshakable faith in Yahweh that earned him his double blessing."

"That is very true," said Molech. "The gruesome affliction imposed on Job was beyond a mortal's ability to endure. I don't know how he did it, but one thing I do know is that ninety-nine out of every one hundred of those who claim to believe in Yahweh will balk in less than five minutes if afflicted with ten percent of what was heaped on Job. To the extent that Job suffered untold losses and bodily harm, and also lost his peace and sleep, it was a great success for us. Some deaths are worse than physical death.

"And I am not even talking of spiritual death here—I am talking of the death of all that one has ever cherished in life; of falling from grace to grass; of being forcefully but falsely accused of a soiled relationship with Yahweh by those dearest to you; of suffering loneliness and total separation from those who should apply the healing balm of compassion, sympathy and encouragement; of being prone to doubt yourself; of suffering avid torments of supernatural proportion unheard of since Creation. So as far as I am concerned, the attempt was a huge success.

"But much as drawing from past experiences to guide our future policies and strategies is important, I suggest we forget about Job for now. Instead, we should focus on what His Majesty has proposed, then suggest what to do and discuss how to go about it. And we'd better be very careful that we don't start with failure, thinking it is going to be a walkover. So instead of leaving it to one of our lieutenants, as suggested by the Chief of Defense Staff, we'd better start with a series of serious brainstorming sessions before arriving at anything concrete.

"I do not mean to denigrate my honorable boss, but we know how sophisticated humans have become. As they are advancing in science and technology and are solving social problems, so are the Christians advancing in their onslaught against our kingdom. So we must plan very well and not be unnecessarily euphoric as if we have already won. We are launching a war, not a battle."

"As much as you may be saying the right things," said Rimmon, "you must learn to choose your words carefully before you get ensnared and be accused of being disrespectful."

"I don't see anything he said that is offensive," said Chemosh. "He was only making a suggestion and advising caution. If we are not free to air our opinions and make useful suggestions, then how can we arrive at a consensus? Or why do you think His Majesty chose this occasion to table this matter? He surely has the power and authority to take a unilateral decision and simply command us to do what he wants. But he believes in shared responsibilities;

hence, he has offered us the opportunity to partake in the decision-making process."

"I was actually trying to help him," responded Rimmon. "We know all generals are not the same, as some occupy more senior positions and could use their positions to their own advantage if they perceive they are not being accorded their due respect. Remember that the Chief of Defense Staff has the authority to order us about at will without seeking our consent over an issue if he so wishes."

"We will then end up laying blame on one spirit or the other," said Chemosh, "and spend endless time rationalizing our failures, as is happening now over what happened to Job long ago, instead of depending on collective wisdom."

"Did I hear you say, *collective wisdom*?" asked Rimmon. "Who is wiser than His Majesty? Don't you remember how the scriptures describe him? Son of the Morning, he, who will ascend above the clouds and exalt his throne above the stars. Can anyone make the earth tremble, shake kingdoms and make the world a wilderness? Can anyone do these things without wisdom?"

"Enough of these arguments," said Jezebel. "I don't honestly see the point you are pursuing, Rimmon. And I am speaking as a very senior and experienced commander and Deputy Chief of Defense Staff. If you are after something, wait for the appropriate time, because you are distracting us from the purpose of our meeting. If His Majesty did not want our input, He would not have asked us to contribute ideas."

"I was only trying to correct his use of words," replied Rimmon.

"Sorry, there was nothing in his language that suggests disrespect and whatever you have in mind by hyping the argument should strictly remain in your mind and not be voiced out here," said Jezebel. "We have never been known to argue on any issue in the past, and I will not allow that to happen here—and I am sure I speak for my boss, the Chief of Defense Staff, as well."

"Sure, sure!" said Beelzebub. "You must excuse him, though. Remember that some of us here were not a part of the inner caucus who waited on Yahweh before our expulsion. They don't have the same knowledge that we have. We need to understand where they are coming from and be patient with them." Then, looking in the direction of Rimmon, he said, "Please be free to make your suggestions and ask questions without fear; it is the only way to maximize collaboration and generate the best ideas."

"This has nothing to do with who was who while we were with Yahweh," said Jezebel. "After all, this is not his first appearance in a meeting like this."

"That is not quite true," said Beelzebub. "It is true that he has attended many of our meetings previously, but he was only there as an observer and an errand boy. We were always giving him orders. This is the first time they are being given the privilege to contribute ideas at this level. Enough reason for you to forgive him."

"That is true," said Ashtoreth. "We have always taken orders without making any suggestions or even asking questions, although I must admit that what Rimmon said was neither a suggestion nor a question. But I beg for us to move on."

"Now back to the issue of our offensive," continued Molech. "I want us to consider where to start from. I mean a particular nation."

"What do you mean, a particular nation?" asked Milcom. "Are we not capable of invading the whole world at the same time? After all, we've been doing that for centuries."

"It's not about being able to invade the whole world," said Molech. "That is not in doubt. Instead, it is about something on a much larger scale. It is completely different from what we have ever done. It requires us to learn from past experiences and to follow familiar patterns. Let me explain. We should follow familiar patterns in the sense of starting gradually from a specific area, and allow progress both in intensity and coverage until the whole world is consumed. It is not like a learner driver who starts at full throttle and crashes within a minute. That is not how to fight a war. You don't start a war by launching battle at all sectors simultaneously and deploying all your weapons at once in all sectors. That is a recipe for disaster.

"Every country has its capital or its seat of government; every business has its head office; and every organization, including terrorist organizations, has its headquarters. Even mighty Yeshua, who has the power to cover the entire world at once, started and focused on just one remote spot, and gradually took over the whole world. I think we should follow a similar pattern.

"Secondly, we are tired of hovering around and jumping from pillar to post with no place to relax a bit. We want a country we can call our own, one that we can make our operational headquarters, a country that we can use to rule the world. Their people will become our people and will be used to carry out our purpose throughout the world."

"I don't want to seem to sound alarmist," said Adrammelech, "but we must recognize that we are opposed to all that Yeshua stands for; our kingdom is opposite of His kingdom. His ways are diametrically opposed to our ways. Our war is actually not against humans but against Him; we are only using humans to get at Him. Besides, He owns the whole world from the beginning for He created it. It is therefore not quite correct to say He started from a spot. He deliberately decided to start His earthly mission from one spot, but at the same time, He was all over the place.

"Don't forget that His divine nature makes this possible. Starting from one spot was only an example to humans, who cannot be everywhere at the same time. Also, His mission was not with anger and vengeance as ours is. He is never in a hurry, but time is actually running out for us. So we can't really compare with Him. We shouldn't adopt His method if we are not to work against ourselves. I mean, we probably can start from a particular place, but we should not mention His name or adopt His style."

"You have spoken very well, Adrammelech," responded Molech. "Don't forget, we may need to take permission from Yahweh Himself to get to some individuals or even a whole nation, and He may direct us to Yeshua. So if we can't even mention His name, how are we to go to Him if we need to? Those who cannot bear to mention the names of their enemies can never overcome such enemies. I know we are not trying to defeat Him, as we already know that is not possible. But we will be scoring a major victory by taking more people, made in His image and likeness, along with us to Hades. Everybody wants to expand his kingdom, and that is exactly our mission. Even nations of the earth want to expand their sphere of influence. What do the rest of you think about my suggestion?"

"There is an important issue raised by Adrammelech," said Anammelech, "and that is the issue of time. Time is not on our side, and that means that starting from a point and building up gradually will be against our interest."

"Time, time, time!" Jezebel said. He stood up with both hands clasped together behind him, gazing at the floor, slowly taking a few steps and then stopping abruptly. He swung around to almost two hundred and seventy degrees, raised his head, fixed his gaze directly at Anammelech and asked, "What is time? Have you forgotten what you are—a spirit? Have you forgotten that there is nothing like time in our world—the spirit world? It is why a thousand years is like a day and why a day is like a thousand years. And there is no difference between day and night. These are human factors used to create discord and fear. We apply them when we want to use humans to achieve our purposes. Humans are limited by time and space, but as spirits, we can penetrate walls and travel millions of miles in a jiffy. Don't be taken in by the frequent reference to the end times by humans. Look at me, do I look like a woman?"

"Certainly not," replied Anammelech.

"OK!" said Jezebel. "Yet humans always associate me with a woman, all because I once appeared as a woman. Today, all you hear humans talk about when they want to castigate a woman is in reference to the Jezebelian spirit. Neither man nor woman has ever used that phrase in reference to a man. They don't know that a spirit is asexual, and has neither form nor shape and can take any form or shape at will for any purpose."

"It is because their nature only allows them to see and relate with the physical," assented Beelzebub. "That is why the Holy One took on human nature, for them to be able to relate with Him. Unfortunately, it is also the reason why so many of them don't believe in His existence since He replaced His physical presence with that of His Spirit, whom they cannot see. But this ignorance has greatly played into our hands."

"Yes," cut in Jezebel, "it is for the same reason they think we don't exist because for anything to matter to man and be believed to exist or be relevant, it must be tangible or at least testable. It must be observable and must be repeatable. Anything that does not satisfy these conditions does not exist and is not to be accorded any iota of thought. This is where science and research have blinded man and made him perpetually grope in darkness. This blindness or denial is the most potent weapon in our hands to wreak havoc on Creation."

"You can say that again." Molech chuckled. "The physical and spiritual realms are completely different. Matter, phenomena, logic and philosophy don't exist in the spiritual, the same goes for environmental factors that affect the physical. But man does not know this; he wants testable, observable and repeatable evidence to explain an occurrence. He wants a concrete form that can be touched and felt to acknowledge its existence. Anything short of this is a mystery. It is the reason for logic, philosophy and metaphysics."

"Too true," said Beelzebub, "but since mystery and metaphysics prove nothing and are undependable as they cannot be tested, man is still left in denial. It is a vacuum in the human psyche that man desperately wants to fill in the pursuit of knowledge—elementary knowledge, too elementary for sophisticated man to accept at its face value, unlike little children, who just believe and trust. It is that simple."

"Can you imagine a world as simple as that?" interjected Jezebel. "A world of simple belief and trust? We would have run out of business long ago. Thank goodness for unbelief. There would have been nothing like a mystery. But the mystery is a human language just as time is human language, and like time, the mystery does not exist in the spiritual. Mystery has yoked man and all Creation to us, with time as the driving force.

"All you hear human beings talk about is time management—spend time, save time, waste time, enjoy time. They carry timepieces wherever they go and talk of timescale as if everything were a measure of time. They are so enslaved to time that their blood pressure can almost adequately indicate the level of their time-consciousness. But it is a farce—an illusion. It is like humans referring to our kingdom as the kingdom of darkness. Does that make it the kingdom of darkness? Don't we operate in the daytime? It is a mere allegory, my friends."

"So, my dear Adrammelech and Anammelech," began Molech, "for us, time only exists in the manipulation of human thoughts and individual minds to provoke specific actions with a deadly result. That is linking thoughts to actions to coincide with a specific time for disaster. So, time as a discrete period within a continuum is not a factor in what we are considering. Even Yeshua Himself said no one knows when the end will come. But gullible humans simply love conjectures. Whenever we use time in our discussions, it is for lack of a better word, not in the same vein as humans interpret it."

"It is the spirit of unknowing. That is their greatest problem," assented Jezebel. "It is responsible for all the arguments and frictions that abound in the world. If they were endowed with knowledge as we are, what a simple life and great peace they would enjoy."

"There would still have been contentions over little and irrelevant things," said Beelzebub, "at least after we sold them the bait for knowledge of good and evil."

"That is my point," said Jezebel. "Without that enticement, they wouldn't have had any knowledge and would have simply relied on Yahweh. And that is wisdom. There wouldn't have been rivalries in the quest for knowledge. The pride of superiority would have been eroded. Their state would have been better than that of babies. But having been made aware of the existence of knowledge, they are now seeking more and more of it. Unfortunately, they don't know that there is no limit to knowledge and that the more knowledge they acquire, the more problems exist.

"Check the side effects of many drugs that are supposed to improve health. Wait until the internet goes commercial and you will see the unimaginable problems that will result. These will almost cancel out its benefits. And these are examples of good knowledge. Yet there is outright knowledge deliberately acquired for evil, such as poisons and lethal weapons. Some new knowledge even cancels out some existing useful knowledge considered obsolete by the new generations."

"That is the way we love to have it," said Beelzebub. "It was a masterstroke, well delivered in the nick of time. A one-minute delay would have destroyed our cause, and our kingdom would have been lost forever. And now we have the whole of Creation at our feet, to trample at will. Now humanity has aligned with us to frustrate nature and the Creator Himself."

"Ha ha ha ha!" Jezebel said, "Sweet victory. How much better can it get? Imagine the children of a loving parent aligning with his/her enemies to destroy the very inheritance the parent has willed to them. Unbelievable! The spirit of unknowing is the most powerful force in all Creation. We did it before with freedom of choice; we will do it again with freedom of choice."

"You can say that again." Molech chuckled. "Yahweh Himself sealed Creation with this spirit of unknowing to protect the human species. Because the more you know, the more apprehensive you are. Hence, infants have no fear of most things. It was His original plan. Unfortunately, while that spirit was given a seal of approval by Yahweh Himself, it is actually working for us."

"It would never have worked for us," added Beelzebub, "if humanity had not consented to its working for us. Take away the seed of knowledge we planted in man and see the spirit work against our interests. Because man will no longer be inquisitive for knowledge, and the fear of the unknown will simply vanish, as the unknown world will cease to exist in the human psyche. Because, truly, it only exists in the physical world, in man's mental state."

"Unfortunately," added Jezebel, "Yahweh's rescue package could not annul the damage already done, as the quest for knowledge has already been set in motion thanks to our ingenuity. And like us, man prefers his own self-made pill to Yahweh's healing balm. They call it *dignity in labor*—laboring to acquire knowledge and to improve life. It is supposed to be the pride of self-worth, of achievement. This is a good thing, really, but Yahweh regards any act of self-will as resistance and rebellion. That is what He accused us of. He called it a sin, a sin of pride.

"And with Him, pride is pride even if man perceives it as something positive. Ours was an aspiration—an aspiration for higher goals. Which, come to think of it, should actually be commended. But He called it vaulting ambition. And just for that alone, He drove us out of His presence and withdrew His light from us. Lucky man, at least he has the benefit of repentance, which we never had. Who can then blame us for our anger? We would have done better than man if we had been given a second chance."

"Remember that He never actually gave man a second chance," Beelzebub said, interrupting. "At least not until the voluntary sacrifice of Yeshua. And in all fairness, if there is anything like fairness in our world, if man knew what we knew and still did what we did, there is no way Yahweh would have thought of any rescue package to give man a second chance. In fact, if they had a tenth of our knowledge, they would not be trampling on this golden opportunity and the best gift that ever has been offered. Unfortunately, ignorance has taken them hostage."

"Didn't they say ignorance is no excuse?" queried Ashtoreth.

"That is why it has taken them hostage," responded Molech.

Jezebel, responding at the same time as Molech, said, "That is part of the law—their own law—to nip each other. If it were Yahweh's law, they wouldn't have a second chance, I tell you."

"But they have knowledge of Yahweh's law and still violate it," said Ashtoreth. "How about that?"

"Don't be daft," reprimanded Jezebel. "You heard Beelzebub say just now that Yahweh never gave man any second chance until the voluntary sacrifice of Yeshua. That sacrifice provides the excuse in Yahweh's law for multiple second chances. It allows their ignorance to play itself to the full. And the cup always fills up suddenly when the person least expects the game to be over. Hence, they are always taken unaware."

Chapter 2
Random Musings of Concerned Students

In the twilight years of the twentieth century, a new government had just taken office, headed by a Christian Prime Minister. Their election victory was a landslide, and in the euphoria of that victory, the government embarked on a frenzied modernization agenda that resulted in its losing its focus on the important issues of governance. New laws were made that nullified or liberalized existing laws. Human rights gained unprecedented momentum in the drive against reason and common decency. Law courts became public theaters of the absurd and public institutions became centers of indoctrination and political correctness—an enforced conformist program. Laws jetted out of Parliament like the rapid firing of a machine gun, and these laws debased the public conscience and enthroned unruliness.

Into the new century's final year of the first decade, the dull gray winter sky was turning dark and cloudy. The sleet that had started as a light snow shower was fast becoming a full-blown snowstorm. Bloomsbury was usually a built-up area with mini-parks, fern blossoms and a beautiful tapestry of lush vegetation. Now temporarily stripped of its lushness by the harsh winter, it had become a white seabed of snow. Dotted within it, especially at the northern edge in the Tavistock area, were the buildings of London's first-oldest, and England's third-oldest, university.

The distance from the law faculty's Bentham House in Endsleigh Gardens to the school of public policy, Ruben Buildings, in Tavistock Square, was less than a four-minute walk. But within that short distance, Jay had fallen down twice as he hurriedly trotted over the slippery ground to escape the freezing blizzard.

Before the arrival of the lecturer, it was usual for the lecture theater to be a marketplace of noise, with a cacophony of accents and topics ranging from the exchange of pleasantries to the latest fashion gist, to politics, to the study topic, to West End theaters, to the latest advancement in information technology. But today's was no ordinary lecture. It was about one of those subject areas that is prone to much argument—human rights, a topic within the international relations module. The students were already arguing over the rights and wrongs of some recent incidents that had become news headlines.

One was a millionaire businessman and his brother who had been sentenced to almost six years for fighting off knife-wielding intruders who had broken into their family home. The three intruders had pinned the family to the floor, threatening to kill them if they moved. Somehow the brothers fought back and managed to overpower one of the intruders, while the other two escaped. The one overpowered was said to have had fifty-four previous convictions, yet the prosecution accused the two brothers of having taken the law into their hands by beating him.

The judge on his part said, the beating amounted to 'a very violent revenge attack on a defenseless man.' The students argued variously. Some said the brothers' failure to call the police justified the judge's decision. Some questioned what constituted the legal limit of 'reasonable force' which informed the judge's decision. Others defended the brothers' position of not calling the police by saying that they must have acted on the spur of the moment, and also that they had learned from past experiences that calling the police not only gave the criminal enough time to escape but also yielded nothing, even when the criminal was arrested by police.

Two major points of agreement, however, were their disapproval of the judge's setting the criminal scot-free, and of his having regarded the burglar as defenseless when he was carrying a knife. Most argued that it was a bad precedent that gave criminals freedom to operate at will.

Another was an argument centered on a case in the Irish Republic, where it was reported that three women had gone to court to challenge the law that protects the life of the unborn. The women claimed that it violated their human rights, as it put their health and well-being at risk by forcing them to travel abroad for pregnancy terminations that endangered their health.

Those who reasoned with the women argued that the unborn baby as a fetus is not yet human and, as such, has no individual right as its right is dependent on the mother's right. They argued that the well-being of the fetus is dependent on the mother's well-being, and if the mother were to die, then the fetus would automatically die, but aborting the fetus at least saves the life of the mother.

Their opponents argued that a fetus is already a living being and, as such, has rights equal to those of any human being. They argued that, instead, the women should have sued the men who impregnated them for breaching their human rights, also opining that the women should actually be sued by the state for abusing their own human rights by allowing themselves to be impregnated. The students also accused the women of running away from the consequences of their actions.

All this was going on when Jay reached the lecture block, looking wet and windswept. He hung his coat, drenched and heavy, in the cloakroom adjacent to the lecture hall and limped into the lecture room. It was then that he realized that he had bruised his right knee and elbow. His long-sleeved shirt was torn at the right elbow, with a small strip of shredding hanging loose. His trousers were damp and smeared with blood on the right knee but were not torn. With his hair scattered from wiping off raindrops, and slightly shivering with cold, he looked a sorry sight.

No sooner had he entered the hall, he started shouting in his heavy West Indian accent, his voice retaining its adolescent croak. "Hello! Does anybody know where the first aid box is located on this floor?" Without waiting for any response, he continued in the same breath, "This is a stupid godforsaken country. See what the fucking weather has done to me."

The whole class suddenly went quiet as all eyes turned toward him. As he was shouting, a female student shouted from one corner of the hall, "Can someone get the first aid box, please? He looks injured." She stood up and asked, "What happened?" while walking toward the first aid box.

Another female student, closer to the first aid box, met the first female student halfway as she ran back with the box, and they both attended to his wounds. All the arguments resumed as his wounds were being taken care of. As the two female students walked back to their seats, Kojo, one of Jay's friends, beckoned him to a seat he had reserved for him near where he himself was seated. But Jay merely dropped his bag there and walked to one side of the room to close the windows there. Soon enough, while he was still there, a heated argument started between him and another student. A small group of students suddenly gathered around the area, trying to prevent the scuffle that was about to ensue.

Jay closing the windows that were open angered some students. One of them, Grant Lucas, opened them again. And so started the alternating sequence of opening and closing, until it almost resulted in a scuffle between Jay and Grant.

Jay was cold and wanted to close the windows, but Grant argued that the hall was stuffy because of the large number of students, adding that a few panes needed to be opened to allow in some air. Both resorted to the use of foul language in the course of their altercation. Jay branding those who wanted the windows open as being hot and high on drugs, saying the hall was large enough to absorb the mugginess, while Grant taunted him as inconsiderate and full of shit, someone from the bush who was out to display his jungle mentality. They used all sorts of unprintable words—*bum-bum*, *asshole*, *fool*, *blood clot*, etc.— before they were finally persuaded to keep the peace.

When Jay got back to his seat, Kojo rebuked him for not politely requesting to be allowed to close the windows, instead acting macho.

"Bullshit. I say b-u-l-l-s-h-i-t!" retorted Jay, shouting again. "That is what is spoiling this country. People are dying inside and behaving like Mr. Nice outwardly to please others and to seem to be cool. I ain't cool, man; people from my country ain't known to be cowardly. You want me to end up in the hospital with hypothermia and miss my lectures because I wanna conform? No way, man! If you Africans are ashamed of your culture, we Caribbeans are not. I cannot pretend to be English because I am not, pure and simple."

"Stop shouting, Jay," warned Kojo. "I didn't shout when I spoke to you."

"Don't talk to me if you don't want me to shout," said Jay.

"What is wrong with the English, anyway?" one of the white girls asked.

"English people are cowards, man! They conform too much; they pretend too much," said Jay.

"But the guy who challenged you is your fellow Caribbean," said Kojo.

"No, man, he ain't Caribbean," replied Jay. "These are the brainwashed Caribbeans who think they are superior to everybody else because they were born in Britain." Then, mellowing down, he said, "Well, the only element of being Caribbean in him is his boldness to dare to be different. And I respect him for that." Then, smiling and trying to be friendly, he walked over to Grant, stretching out his clenched right fist to bid him *respect*—a sign of reconciliation.

But instead of Grant's stretching out his own hand to reciprocate the gesture, he blurted out, "Why don't you go shag yourself? You want to infect me with AIDS by giving me your blood-dripping hand? Why not your left hand?"

"Don't be ridiculous. How can you say something like that?" retorted Jay. "I only bruised my elbow and not my hand." With that, a few voices followed, speaking against Grant's unforgiving stance.

When the noise died down a bit, one female student said, "Juvenile students! Thank God for the study of international relations and of human rights. International relations are cross-cultural, as are human rights. Let's hope that, by the time the lecture is over, we will have learned how to respect people's basic rights and relate to each other better."

"Ya, man, that is the point: Respect, man! Simple respect," said Jay. Just then, the lecturer entered the hall, and the hall suddenly went quiet. The lecture started in earnest.

Jay Wilson, a political science student, was a handsome, stoutly built young man with an imposing figure. He was a bel esprit of a man, witty, brilliant, and with a razor-sharp intellect. He was effervescent, ebullient, and confident. Born and bred in Jamaica, he, after completing secondary school, was sent to London, England, for his advanced-level and degree studies. He was quite outspoken and humorous too.

Kojo Antwi Agyei was Jay's close friend whom he had met at college in their A-level years. He was from Obuasi in the Ashanti region of Ghana. He, too, had completed his elementary and secondary education in Ghana, and came to do his advanced-level studies and his degree program in London. With his father being a Baptist minister, he had been brought up in strict Christian discipline. He related everything in life to his Christian belief. He was sparkly and radiated an aura of peace and joy, having the disposition of one firmly in control of any situation. He had organized and led a group of Christian students in fellowship, holding prayer meetings every Tuesday evening and Bible study every Thursday evening on the campus. He majored in economics.

Chapter 3
Double Standards

At dinner that evening, Kojo met Jay in the cafeteria and confronted him for the second time over his behavior in the lecture hall.

"You shamed all black students by your behavior today, Jay," said Kojo. "That drama you caused in the lecture theater was uncalled for. Ever since we met in our A-level classes, I have tried to make you stop this uncultured attitude of might is right, but you are unchangeable."

"Hold it there," interrupted Jay. "What attitude are you talking about?" he asked.

"I mean, your easy resort to intimidation and foul language," replied Kojo. "After all, many students came from other blocks. Some probably have suffered worse ordeals than you but never disturbed the class."

"You know something, Kojo," said Jay, "if you weren't my friend, I would've blown up your goddam head right now. It is cowards like you who subject blacks to a second slavery—out of an inferiority complex. I don't know how to conform. And refusing to die in silence should be a source of pride rather than shame."

"Hey, gentlemen, what's all this about?" queried Robinho, who was at the table with them.

"Ask Bible-basher," said Jay, "who despite experience, has refused to acknowledge that the world is no place for weaklings."

Kojo had a penchant for using Bible quotations to support his views of life, and he always centered his discussions and arguments on biblical principles. As a result, he had been nicknamed 'Bible-basher' by his friends.

Robinho Renato was born and bred in Chiswick, North West London and was the son of Brazilian immigrant parents. He had been a nominal Christian until he met Kojo in their first year at university, where they were coursemates, majoring in economics. Kojo's lifestyle impressed him so much that it transformed him into becoming a serious Christian. He started following Kojo to church regularly. They had been very close friends since then and became friends in each other's circle of friends.

"Hey, talk to me, my friend," Robinho said to Kojo. "What's the problem?" Kojo then explained to Robinho what had happened in the class before the human rights lecture.

"Well," said Robinho, "I am not a student of international relations or of human rights. The incident that you've just narrated happened before your lecture on human rights. Now that you have gained a new insight and better knowledge of human rights, and its application in relating with people. Whose right do you think was being infringed?"

"You are missing the whole point, Robinho," said Kojo. "My argument is not on whose rights were violated but on the correct approach to issues."

"No, Kojo," said Jay. "The simple fact is that you Africans are always afraid to stand up for your rights. When these British buffoons go to your country, you treat them like royalty. You come to their country and they treat you like shit, yet you are apologetic. That is pure cowardice. Nobody can mess with us Caribbeans. See how apologetic the average British is to Asians in all situations, because Asians know how to fight for their rights."

"No, no, no, Jay!" said Matt, who was at the table with them. "I was in the class and saw what happened. It has nothing to do with being British. The point Kojo is making is—"

"Do I expect anything better from a full-blooded Anglo-Saxon?" Jay said, interrupting. "Does the leopard shed its spots?"

"Here he goes again, bullying people into submission," said Kojo. "You can air your opinion for as long as you like, but you will not allow others to complete even one sentence."

"That is really not fair," said Robinho.

"Now listen, Jay," said Kojo, "you are simply a racist. Your greatest problem is your enslavement mindset."

"Mind your language, Kojo," warned Jay.

"There were many black students in the lecture hall," continued Kojo, "but which of them attended to your needs? Those who went in search of the first aid box were white. The one who dressed your wound was white. You didn't even thank them, but they did not take offense. There were white students in the hall, but the one who challenged you was black. So how are the whites treating us like shit? Where is your sense of reasoning and fairness? Where is your education?"

"What education?" asked Jay.

"When it comes to humans," continued Kojo, "the God I serve is color-blind because He made us all. As His children, we have equal rights and therefore should treat each other equally."

"You see," said Jay, "that is precisely my point. Where was God when they were enslaving us? Where was He when they were carting away our material resources? I should be asking you about your reasoning and education. That is why I asked what education is because education reminds us of our history, and history teaches us the way forward."

"Yes, but the way forward is to filter out the spiteful and proceed with the virtuous and the harmonious because two wrongs don't make a right," said Kojo.

"That is only possible in a homogeneous or monolithic society," said Jay. "This, however, is a multicultural society. Although, pluralism recognizes the rights of every group, some groups think it is their birthright to subjugate humanity. The only language they understand and respect is that of confrontation and violence. It compels two wrong people to learn to make a right. That is my point, Kojo. I will only agree with what you are saying, if every one of us acknowledges the supremacy of God as our Father and treats each other as one race and one person. Unfortunately, too many people can't come to terms with God's existence, let alone allow His ordinances the light of day."

"I can see that we are not going anywhere with this argument," said Robinho. "Instead, we are just causing saliva to fly into our food, which could be detrimental to our health. Even the lecture on human rights doesn't seem to have changed anything. But I will still ask those of you who attended the lecture one simple question: How do you apply your knowledge of human rights when solving human problems?"

Matt was the first to volunteer an answer. He said, "It is by knowing what those rights are and applying the necessary policy guidelines to address such problems."

"Ha, ha, ha, ha! Clap for him." Jay jeered as he clapped his hands. "Matthew Saltwater, good boy from Nuneaton in Warwickshire, law student extraordinaire, Anglo-Saxon of the Anglo-Saxons, whose progenitors were the forerunners of the Human Rights Act via the Magna Carta and the originators of habeas corpus. Well done!" He laughed sarcastically again and continued, "So the non-law students, the non-educated or the illiterate don't know their rights because they don't know the necessary policy and the associated guidelines to know their rights? Ignoramus." Matthew Saltwater was white, a final-year law student from Nuneaton, and Jay's current college hostel roommate.

"You are getting the whole thing wrong, Jay," said Matt. "Robinho's question was academic and intellectual. My response is academic and intellectual. If it weren't academic, he wouldn't have asked those of us who attended the lecture or referred to the application of our acquired knowledge. So don't make a fool of yourself."

"I don't care what you say," said Jay, "or how you want to recoat the question, or your response to make it acceptable. Law student my ass."

"We are at the table, Jay, for goodness' sake," Kojo reprimanded.

"Well, you can go under the table for all I care," said Jay.

Everyone, including some other students near them, laughed.

"Everything in this country is based on guidelines and policies," continued Jay. "Even simple things of life are made difficult because of this. That is why there is too much legislation, resulting in too much litigation. All leading to either conformity or confinement."

"It is all political correctness," said Robinho, "to make everyone conform to please some sections of the society."

"You can't correct someone," said Jay, "or else not only do you get attacked by the person, but also society itself attacks you for not minding your business. Any small point of disagreement is construed as discrimination. In Britain, every way a person chooses to live is normal. There are no societal values and no standards to guide the way of life. All legislation is to advance non-interference and freedom of choice, thus dehumanizing society with the ruling class's ignoble ways."

"That is very true," said Kojo. "However, if we take a dispassionate view, we see that government is doing the right thing. It is just that some people or organizations are taking it too far. With a multicultural society, the government has to protect the interests of every section of the community and make sure no one is alienated. But this is now exceeding the boundaries of common sense.

Many cultural groups subtly or openly discriminate against one another without litigation. Asians, Africans, South Americans and people of Middle Eastern origin make fun of each other's culture; they even do this with people from other parts of their own countries. The English often laugh at the Scottish, Irish or Welsh accent, and Londoners even make fun of English Midlands and Northern accents."

"Be warned, Kojo," said Jay. "I think, being almost six years in London has made you a white man in black skin—white heart inside and black skin outside. You think if you think the way they think and agree with their ways of life and do what they want you to do without question, then they will accept you as one of them. Conformist. Keep on living in cloud cuckoo land. One day, you will wake up to find yourself in Pentonville or Belmarsh."

"Why would I find myself in any of those prisons when I am a law-abiding citizen?" asked Kojo.

"London is a mirage, a make-believe world," responded Jay. "Anyone living in London is living a cinema life. It is all double-talk. The more you look, the less you see; the more you try to be good, the more they drive you nuts, such that you won't know when you slip. And any small slip, you are gone—while the known criminals are let loose because the authorities are tired of them as they keep offending and reoffending.

"But for you who are afraid to offend, the state will lock you up because you can't talk. This is a city where you have to cry wolf when there is no wolf; you shout discrimination when there is no discrimination; and you shout being bullied when no one is near you or when you are the one actually bullying others. It is the only way to survive. How can you live in a place and not know what it takes to survive there? You must develop a survival instinct if you want to keep afloat in this sinking boat called London."

"Wow, look at the time," Matt said, interrupting. "I beg to leave; I have more useful things to do. Some of the people who came after us have gone, and here we are talking gibberish." With that, he stood up to leave.

Then Kojo, Jay and Robinho also stood up and left.

Chapter 4
Parallel Kingdoms

At the meeting of Satan's generals, Dagon spoke next: "Sorry to interrupt. My question is rather away from the issue of ignorance and second chance."

"I actually thought you were not here," Milcom said, interrupting, "as you sat there numb like a mere observer."

"I think I am permitted to remain silent until I have something reasonable to say," replied Dagon.

"OK, go on with what you want to say," said Milcom.

"I want to get something clear here," said Dagon. "I think the more one knows, the less apprehensive he becomes. At least his conduct and movement are guided by what he knows. Why then did Molech say the more knowledge one has, the more apprehensive he becomes?"

"This is what I was trying to make you understand, Jezebel, in terms of your argument with Rimmon," said Beelzebub. "At their level, both before and after the expulsion, they didn't know much. Remember that only four of us, that is King Lucifer, you, Molech and me, among those expelled from Yahweh's presence, were archangels. We were the only ones to whom Yahweh revealed all secrets and knowledge. The rest had always operated at the lower levels, taking orders unquestioningly and running errands. And on forming our kingdom after the expulsion, we decided that those of them who had followed us should keep taking orders and running errands as before. They only know whatever little things we want them to know. Remember, we promised never to reveal anything to any of them as a way of preventing what happened in heaven from being repeated here in our kingdom. That is learning from experience, which Molech was emphasizing."

"We should not assume that things are simple just because we know them. They are not so simple to those who do not know. And that is the deceit humans suffer. The so-called educated among them assume they know everything and confuse others with stupid jargon in the name of logic and philosophy. And this is where part of the ignorance I was talking about comes in. Molech, please answer Dagon's question and enlighten all of them a bit, without giving out too much. Just say enough to enable them to be carried along with our deliberations here."

"Thanks, my chief," said Molech. "Please listen attentively, you lot. In answer to Dagon's question, firstly, let me tell you that what you don't know doesn't scare you because, as far as you are concerned, it doesn't exist. And you don't get scared by something that doesn't exist.

"Secondly, you know the scriptures as I do, and the scriptures say, 'The fear of the Lord is the beginning of wisdom.' Man equates knowledge to wisdom, but knowledge is not wisdom—at least, not wisdom per se. Wise action is wisdom, but it is not knowledge. And wise action only comes from the source of wisdom, and that is the maker of an object or a product.

"The object may have a sound knowledge of how it was made and how it is programmed to operate, but its knowledge cannot exceed what the maker wants it to know. If it does, the object will destroy its maker and self-annihilate in an attempt to make itself—because nothing in all Creation has ever created itself. There is only one uncreated Creator, and that is because He is outside of Creation.

"And because an object is limited by its maker, it cannot see what its maker sees. Through diligent search, and sometimes through the least of efforts, it can acquire knowledge that the maker chooses to allow it to know. But it can also, through a diligent search, forcefully acquire knowledge that its maker did not and does not want to reveal to it. This type of knowledge can be extremely dangerous and can lead to major disasters. Can you imagine machines and equipment developing minds of their own? That would be an utter disaster both for the device and its maker. Even humans have been victims of impossible stunts in an attempt to challenge nature.

"Wisdom is beneficial and always provides solutions to problems. Knowledge does not necessarily provide solutions to problems. Sometimes its solution is partial, or it can boomerang to harm or destroy. Other times, it can be outright dangerous and fatal. So, while knowledge and wisdom are revelations, wisdom is a higher-dimension revelation than knowledge. Knowledge can only be beneficial when guided by wisdom, but the opposite cannot be said to be entirely true, since wisdom is at a higher level and is always beneficial.

"Animals do not seek knowledge, but they have the wisdom to act as they were created. It is like singing a song; you can't sing it better than the composer. If you do, it becomes your copyright. The purpose of research is to unearth what is already in existence—that is, acquired knowledge—but wisdom created it—revelation knowledge. Scripture says wisdom is pure, peaceable, gentle, willing to yield and full of mercy and good fruits, without partiality or hypocrisy. The same cannot be said of knowledge.

"Knowledge is relative to the environment or situation. It, therefore, can be either universal or localized. Wisdom, on the other hand, is never localized. Like truth, it is constant and universal. It always offers the right solution to the problem at hand, irrespective of environment or geography. No matter how credible knowledge is, it cannot be wisdom unless it comes as divine revelation from Yahweh. Hence, scripture says that the fear of the Lord is the beginning of wisdom. And we know that human knowledge is often devoid of fear of the Lord. But we have hidden this from man's understanding. It is the only way we can gain followership. It was the way many of you lesser angels sitting on the fence on that day of the great decision joined us.

"The finest distinction between wisdom and knowledge is that wisdom is devoid of pride, while knowledge often goes with pride. And pride is the enemy of the Creator, as it takes His glory. That was our mistake. Don't mind that we have fallen from Yahweh's favor. He gave us all these revelations of knowledge and wisdom before He drove us out, but He did not take them back from us. I mean those of us who were at the level of archangels. Together with Michael, we were the closest to Him and were called the spiritual hosts of righteousness in the heavenly places.

"Did you get that? In the heavenly places. But after He drove us out, He simply replaced righteousness with wickedness. That is how we came to be referred to as spiritual hosts of wickedness in the heavenly places. We don't operate in our original home of heaven anymore, but the fact that we retain the heavenly places is a sign that we still have the power and knowledge He gave us from the beginning— except that we have decided to use it against His original purpose for giving them to us. It is the only way we can avenge our untimely and irreversible expulsion."

"So that is how that title came about!" said Ashtoreth, drawing out the word *about* in a rather measured and pensive way.

"What title?" asked Molech.

"I mean, *Spiritual Hosts of Wickedness in the Heavenly Places*, stated in the scriptures," replied Ashtoreth. "How did our kingdom hierarchy come about then? I mean the various levels since we have other levels."

"OK," said Molech. "Let me give you all a brief synopsis of how this came about. You all know we have four levels—that is principalities, powers, rulers of the darkness of this age and spiritual hosts of wickedness in the heavenly places.

"We merely structured our kingdom according to what we saw in heaven. Since heaven's government is in four layers, we decided to make ours four layers as well. Heaven's government has humans at the lowest rung, followed by nations, then angels, and finally Yahweh Himself at the top. Like Yahweh's kingdom, the kingdoms or nations of the earth also have four layers. Although the question is about our own kingdom, it is good to relate the similarities of the three kingdom— more so when humans, who in this case are the ordinary citizens, are at the lowest rung in all three kingdoms, with the head of each governing council at the highest."

"Sorry to interrupt," said Anammelech, "but where is the church in regards to the earthly kingdom? What level is it on?"

"What church?" asked Molech. Then he answered, "The church does not fall within any level because there was never any church. When Yahweh created all things, there was no church. The church came after the Spirit of Yeshua took His place on earth. Have you forgotten the scriptures? Remember Pentecost.

"Humans are at the same level in both the heavenly and earthly domains because all Creation and both kingdoms are all about humans. And such is the case for our kingdom. Heaven's governing council is made up of three equal and very powerful personalities. Nations have their equivalents—executive and legislative arms—with presidents or Prime Ministers as heads. Heaven has angels as ministers—some senior and others junior. Nations also have ministers—some senior, others junior.

"As it is in heaven, so it is on earth, and so it is in our kingdom. Remember, heaven is spiritual, and our realm is spiritual. So our kingdom has a parallel structure to that of heaven and earth. Our governing council is made up of the spiritual hosts of wickedness in the heavenly places. Only four of us are members, as you well know, with King Lucifer as the head. We operate a monarchical government, so he is the supreme monarch. The next level in our hierarchy is the rulers of the darkness of this age, to which all your senior commanders belong. Then we have ministering spirits—fairy darts—that we send on errands to buffet and torment people on earth. These are *powers*. They are equivalent to heaven's ministering angels—angels that empower the righteous.

"As I said earlier, humans are also part of our kingdom, and they occupy the lowest rung, as with the heaven and earthly kingdoms. But we call them *principalities*. However, not every human being is a principality. We have no power over those who align themselves with Yahweh. The rest belong to us, whether they openly identify with our kingdom or not. So no human can claim neutrality in the war between the two spiritual kingdoms. It is not possible. We call them *principalities* because they are our principal agents on earth, wittingly or unwittingly. They may actually debate or deny this, but they are.

"However, among the principalities are those who have excelled in carrying out our assignments. We promote them to the same position as our errand-ministering spirits—that is, *powers*. These are people in positions of authority—heads of government, heads of multinationals and corporate organizations. Any leader, no matter how small the organization may be, who exceeds our expectations in entrenching our policies and executing our strategies in his or her small enclave is a *power*.

"And so are some church and religious leaders, youth leaders, gang leaders, anarchists, leaders of some pressure groups under nongovernmental organizations (NGOs), terrorist leaders, occult leaders, assassins, murderers and so on. We send our ministering spirits to occupy their heads, or we simply use telepathic means to remotely control their minds to do our bidding, like robots.

"For now, I won't go into the details of the operational responsibilities of these levels. Just know that spiritual hosts of wickedness in the heavenly places are on the level of decision-making and policy formulation. Those of us at this level decide the nature and level of attack inflicted on a nation or a particular geographical region. We sometimes take over the operational command of a whole region of the earth.

"Rulers of the darkness of this age take control of systems, nations and regions. At the level of *powers*, spirits are assigned to individuals, organizations and sometimes nations and systems. Individuals and families are the main targets at the principalities level. Sometimes there is cross-breeding and cross-border invasion by the spirits. The man of Gadara was a victim of an invasion by a combined group of *powers* and *principalities*.

"In effect, we set up the hierarchy to determine at which level each spirit is able to operate. It is not that you didn't know some of these things before, but the added information will enhance your contribution to our discussion here. It is unlike taking orders unquestioningly and implementing policies and strategies whose formulation you were not party to. Any more questions?"

"Yes," said Dagon.

"Ooh!" said Beelzebub. "I didn't know you had such itching ears. That should be enough for now; he has actually almost exceeded what is allowed. Anything else you need to know will be taken care of in the course of our discussion. Let's get on with the issues at hand."

Chapter 5
Double-Talk

As they left the cafeteria and walked along, Kojo said, "Let me warn you for the last time, Jay: Never you refer to me or, for my sake, refer to Africans as being fearful or being cowards. I am not fearful or cowardly. As the son of a Baptist minister brought up under strict Christian discipline, my language and attitude must reflect that discipline. A true Christian is the light of the world. If I am the light, I must not allow the smallest darkness because people are constantly watching to find the slightest slip."

"So?" asked Jay.

"Also, if you truly love Mother Africa as you claim," continued Kojo, "you should go and read the history of Africa. Go and read the history of the Ashantis. I am an Ashanti from Obuasi in Ghana. I told you this before. The Ashantis are a warrior nation and have no fear of anything or anybody. Having the warrior blood in your veins does not make you see everything as an enemy and every situation as a battlefield. That is suicidal."

"You can preach for all I care," said Jay. "Tell me, Kojo, if Africans are not cowards, how come they sold their people into slavery? Of all the nations on earth, it is your country, Ghana, that has the slave port—Cape Coast. Its real name is Slave Coast, which the British, with their double-talk and diabolic sense of humor, metaphorically named Cape Coast. To give the people a false sense of identity and pride, they named the country Gold Coast, a euphemism for black gold—African slaves."

"That is why I said you should go and read your history," replied Kojo. "Because if you had, firstly, you would have known that Cape Coast was not the only slave port in West Africa. There were others, such as Calabar and Badagry in Nigeria, to name a few. You would have known that Stone Town in Zanzibar hosted one of the largest markets for slave trade in Africa."

"None was as big or as important as Cape Coast," said Jay.

"Secondly," continued Kojo, ignoring Jay's defense, "you would have known that it was not the British but the Portuguese—the first Europeans to come to Ghana—who named it Gold Coast. Besides, the name is appropriate because we have gold mines in Ghana."

"Appropriate my foot," replied Jay. "Why couldn't they name other countries by the mineral deposits in those countries?"

"Well, they did not colonize those countries," said Kojo.

"I am talking of the countries they colonized," said Jay. "They should have called Sierra Leone 'Diamond Coast'."

"Again, Sierra Leone is a name that was not given by the British but by the Portuguese," said Kojo. "And be informed that there are many countries named after major landmarks and mineral deposits even today. So forget about names. The fact is that many slaves taken from other African countries used the port of Tema as the exit point, especially those taken from West Africa."

"Absolutely right," said Jay. "That is why rather than refer to Ghanaians, I refer to Africans. I only used Cape Coast as an example of a shipping port."

"Hey, geezers," yelled a voice behind them as they approached the college grounds. It was Avtar Chafda, who ran to catch up with them as they walked along Upper Woburn Place, close to the university grounds. "I've been calling you and no one could hear me," said Avtar. "I hope you haven't been arguing too loudly like this inside the bus."

"What bus?" asked Robinho.

"Oh, sorry! I thought you were coming from your halls of residence," Avtar said.

"Of course we are," affirmed Matt. "We've been walking for about thirty-five minutes now."

"You mean all the way from Camden Road?" queried Avtar.

"Yes!" answered Matt.

"That is about two miles from here," Avtar said, estimating.

"So?" asked Jay.

"What is 'so'?" asked Avtar. "What discussion could have been steaming your blood so hot that you would brave walking in this cold for this long? I mean, I just ran across the road from the library to buy something at the grocery shop there, and I am almost freezing."

"That is because we are not as lazy as you are," said Jay, laughing. "It is the result of a regular walking exercise. It is an opportunity to enhance our calisthenics."

"No, I bet you guys must be high on drugs or are mere scrooges," concluded Avtar.

"Wrong. You are just wrong," said Kojo. "You won't know when you've walked fifty miles if you are in the company of Jay. He will keep you on your toes with his loquacity, such that you will lose touch with the weather and almost with reality."

"Yes, reality," said Robinho. "Reality is lost when you are in the midst of politicians or students of politics."

"Oh yes! Now I get it," said Avtar. "It is the usual argument of how politics is the solution to all problems. What amazes me most is that students of politics and practicing journalists are full of fire and ideas of how to mend a broken society, but when they enter into politics, they lose their passion and focus and do nothing. Or even worse, they exacerbate the situation with their puerile arguments."

"Spectators are the best players; that is what it is," said Matt.

"I actually thought you were discussing the news item from this evening's six o'clock bulletin," said Avtar.

"What news item?" asked Matt.

"Didn't any of you listen to the evening news?" asked Avtar.

"Nope," was the joint response.

"I am just amazed by the judicial system in this country," said Avtar, "and I think the criminal justice system is long overdue for an overhaul. Matt, do you remember the case of the Asian man who was hacked to death with an axe as he pursued a tire thief?"

"Yes. What about it?" asked Matt.

"The case has just been concluded in the thief's favor."

"What! How come?" asked Matt.

"Don't ask me. Ask the justice system," answered Avtar. "The judge said the thief was only defending himself and did not intentionally kill the man."

"I don't think I know the case you are talking about," said Robinho.

"Me either," said Kojo.

"How would you know when the only thing you know or remember is Bible study and prayer meetings?" Jay said, laughing scornfully. "Is it any surprise that it is the two of you who don't know?"

"Yes, you can pretend to know just to mock us," said Robinho.

"Honestly, I know the case he's talking about," protested Jay. "Is it not the one that happened around Poplar in the East End?"

"Yes," said Avtar.

"You see when I talk, you people say I am grumpy," said Jay. "Saying the truth is not grumpiness. This is not the first or the last time that a miscarriage of justice will happen here in this country. It has become the rule rather than the exception."

"How do you know it is a miscarriage of justice?" asked Matt.

"Why did you react the way you did when you heard the news if it was not a miscarriage of justice?" asked Jay.

"My reaction was instinctive," said Matt, "based on the surface information we had. And that is that a thief who confessed to killing a man was set free. If we have access to the case file and analyze the available evidence, we may agree with the judgment. For instance, he could have confessed under duress. The man pursuing him could have been armed. The thief could have tried to frighten the man by raising the axe with no intention of harming him, but things just went wrong somehow. We don't really know what happened. Justice is an intricate and complex matter. It does not follow the impulse of public opinion, but depends on proven evidence and follows tested guidelines."

"Stop lecturing us, baby lawyer," said Jay. "What proven evidence and tested guidelines? These are the types of arguments that have scarred this society. It is lawyers who make simple things complex with stupid arguments. They don't care what happens to society as long as they make their money. They are the majority profession in government; hence, governance is made complex to find loopholes to defend bad legislation and justify the nonperformance of those who govern. As long as there are lawyers, there will be no justice in this world."

"Are you saying miscarriage of justice is universal?" asked Kojo.

"Not exactly," said Jay. "At least not in terms of the mere impulse of a judge to wave off all available evidence, including a defendant's confession of wrongdoing, to set a criminal free, as is so rampant here. With all this, people will be forced to adopt jungle justice for survival. Anyone who lives in a society bereft of any element of humaneness will have to put on a brave face and acquire artificial bravado to survive, even if he is a wimp. And I am not just saying this about a particular person or race, but about anyone who lives anywhere on earth, particularly people who live in this jungle called London."

"The problem with you, Jay, is that you are too passionate about these things," said Matt. "You overemphasize them. You are not the only one living here, you know; you have to adapt or find somewhere else to live."

"Don't shut him up," said Avtar. "He may be too critical and sound a bit melodramatic, but he's simply saying the truth. Judgments like that can criminalize the innocent, who are forced to use any means at their disposal to defend themselves."

"Thank you, Avtar, for being honest," said Jay.

"See where such self-defense landed the man chasing an ordinary tire thief?" said Matt. "What is a tire compared to a life? And the car was not even his."

"It is not the gravity of the offense, but the principle of justice, that is at stake here," said Kojo. "The State must be seen to protect life and property, not protect criminals."

They suddenly found themselves at the front of the main library.

"Dammit!" shouted Avtar. "See how too much talk can make one miss his way? I just followed you people impulsively like a robot to your library, when I am actually going to the science library."

The main library was located at Wilkins Building on Gower Street, about three to four minutes' walk from the science library, which was in Watson Building, on Malet Place.

"You can read in our library, can't you?" Matt asked.

"Nah," replied Avtar. "I have already taken a desk with my things in it at the science library. Besides, I don't want any disturbance, and your argument may occasionally crop up while in the library. This is no time to mess about; my exams are staring me in the face."

"Oh, stop it," said Kojo. "Just say you prefer the science library. Our exams are equally important to us."

By now they were in the foyer of the main library.

"Bye, Avtar," said Matt.

"See you. Bye," said Avtar.

And with that, he left for the science library.

Avtar had been Kojo's roommate in their first year, and the two had been close friends since then. Through their association, they had formed a circle of friends, including each other's friends and acquaintances. Avtar was born and bred in the East End of London, the son of first-generation immigrant Muslim parents from India. He was an athletic-looking young man with a bursting, genial smile and an outgoing manner. He had a knack for much hilarity by making light and fun of whatever came his way.

Chapter 6
Master Artist

It was late Sunday morning, eight weeks later. Schools were closed for the Easter break, but as was normal with the university, students who did not want to travel on holidays were allowed to remain in the halls of residence, but without catering facilities. Many final-year students, including Jay, Matt and Kojo, had stayed behind in their college accommodations. Robinho and Avtar, whose parents lived in the Chiswick and Stratford areas of London, respectively, also stayed behind. Most final-year students preferred staying behind to enable them to adequately prepare for their final exams in May and June.

Robinho and Kojo came out from Camden Town Tube station on their way from church. The spring sun was initially hazy as pockets of shifting clouds cast dull shadows in the sky. But as they walked along Camden Road toward their college homes, the sun gradually brightened. They were thrilled by the rather congruous pattern of light and shade cast along the pavement by the sun, filtering through the foliage of the trees. The tapestry seemed to be in symphony with the whispering wind, which was winging its way through the trees. They looked up at the trees on their side of the road and on the other side of the road. The spring-blossoming foliage of variegated leaves was in clusters from one tree to the next, creating a glorious symmetry of beautiful flowers. To Robinho and Kojo, the shadows, the sound of the wind and the beautiful flowers were an intricate work of a master artist, reflecting the invisible hand of nature, which spoke of a creative, omnipresent God.

"Boy," said Robinho, "this is enthralling. It is exhilarating. It confirms Christ's statement that if humans were to stop praising God, the rocks would burst out in praise of Him. God always leaves His signature on every work of nature."

"I thank God for my being part of this refreshing experience," said Kojo. "So many people are passing by without experiencing it because they can't even see it. To them, it is a mere shadow."

"Yes, because they are spiritually blind," said Robinho. "If this pattern were painted on canvas by a person, you would see the throng who would pay a fortune to see it."

"You know, humans never appreciate anything that is free, especially if it is provided by nature," ruminated Kojo. "They take it for granted and never show any gratitude."

As they drew closer to the halls of residence and passed the bus stop, they saw Jay and Avtar come out from a newsagent ahead of them and walk toward the college halls. They called out and beckoned to them to wait up. Then they hastened their steps to catch up with them.

"All hail the bishop and the auxiliary bishop!" shouted Jay. "I see you are coming from church. I hope you prayed for me, a poor sinner."

"We always pray for everybody, especially our friends," responded Robinho. "So, where did you meet Paki?"

"We met just outside the newsagent," replied Jay. "He was coming from the bus stop when he saw me on my way to the newsagent and called over to me. So we went to the newsagent together, where I bought these papers. But he is going to Max Rayne House to collect a book from a friend."

Kojo and Robinho lived separately in Ann Stephenson House, on the same premises as Ifor Evans Hall, where Jay and Matt shared a room with other students. These residences were recorded as No. 109 Camden Road. Avtar, on the other hand, lived in Ian Baker House, Hertford Place, off Maple Street, about a five-minute walk from the main college campus, some two miles away.

"You call me Paki, you *Equus quagga*?" Avtar said to Robinho. They all laughed.

"You are lucky it is Avtar," said Kojo. "Call an Indian man Paki and you will be roasted alive."

"Leave him," said Avtar. "One of these days, I will Paki him." Then he added, "Well, boys, catch y'all later."

"Meet us in my room," said Jay.

"No, in mine," said Kojo.

"Why are we meeting instead of going to read?" asked Robinho. "Or are we reading together, which will amount to no reading at all?"

"Do you have to read every minute, Robinho?" asked Jay. "All work and no play makes Jack a dull boy. We sure could do with a little rest from bookwork, you know, at least for a couple of minutes!"

"Let's meet in my room, then," said Robinho.

"No, I was the first to offer my room," said Jay.

"You can stay here arguing. I am off," said Avtar.

"Mm, OK, meet us at Jay's place," said Robinho.

So Avtar went separately to Max Rayne House, while the other three young men went to Jay's room, where they met Matt. Matt was lying face-up on his bed, reading, when they walked in. A block of sunlight from the window lay across the floor and part of Jay's bed, with the sundry items on the table bathed in the light like a small company of soldiers. Matt stopped reading and sat up to see them.

"Hi, boys, what's up?" said Matt.

Before anyone could respond, Robinho distracted everyone's attention. Pointing to the sunlit part of Jay's bed, he said, "Just look at that. Isn't it beautiful?" They all looked in the direction of Jay's bed.

"What?" asked Jay.

"Can't you see what looks like an artist's impression of a platoon on your bed?" asked Robinho. "Look at the shadow of the TV with its antenna sitting menacingly like a tank, and at the books lying behind it like military vehicles, while the teacup, the desk tidies and the water bottles all look like soldiers. Boy, with little things of life, God registers His presence everywhere."

"Are you representing God with this caricature?" asked Matt. "Beware of sacrilege."

"That is surely not a caricature," said Robinho. "This shadow is one of the many ways God speaks to us."

"Speaks to us?" Jay laughed. "Are you having a laugh? OK, what is He telling us?"

"Jay, you need spiritual ears to hear God," said Kojo. "That is why I am telling you to give your life to Christ."

"OK, you who have spiritual ears, tell us," challenged Jay.

"Promise to act on what I am going to tell you," said Kojo.

"How can I promise what I don't know?" said Jay.

"He doesn't know," said Matt, referring to Kojo. "That is why he doesn't want to tell us. He pretends to hear from God, but he doesn't."

"OK, I will tell you," said Kojo. "Now, God by that shadow has enlisted both of you into His army. He has in particular appointed you, Jay, a commander in that army. That is the meaning of this artistic work you are calling a caricature."

"Look at this joker," laughed Jay. "Have these shadows any resemblance to what Robinho is describing? Where is my laptop in the shadow?"

"What laptop? Can't you see that your laptop is outside the band of sunlight?" said Kojo.

"Or are you physically blind as well?" added Robinho.

Just then Avtar came in. Robinho put his right forefinger across his lips to hush them. "Shh," he said, gesturing.

"Hey, you came here straight without even dropping your Bibles first?" asked Avtar, laughing at Robinho and Kojo. "You sure want to pass your church blessings to these infidels, I think."

"We don't mind sharing our blessings," said Kojo.

"Avtar," said Robinho, "please take a good look at this shadow and tell us what you think it looks like."

Avtar got closer to Jay's bed and looked at the shadows for a while, then said, "The shadow of the TV looks like an armored car; the three books look like minibuses or a people carrier. I can't really make out what the rest look like—perhaps like backpackers? But why? Got nothing else to do than reading shadows?"

"Thank God you were not here when I made exactly the same observation," said Robinho. "Backpackers are human beings, so they can be taken to be soldiers. Jay and Matt couldn't read the shadows at all, let alone understand their significance."

"Are they significant?" asked Avtar. "And if they are, how? In what way are they significant?"

"They send a message; they speak to us; they reveal things," replied Robinho.

"Have you gone crazy or something?" asked Avtar, laughing, as Jay and Matt joined in the laughter. "I mean, have you become a sorcerer or an interpreter of shadows?" queried Avtar.

"Please ask them," said Jay. "Ask them what in the world is in a shadow."

"No, Avtar, this has nothing to do with sorcery or mysticism," said Kojo. "It is both a revelation and a confirmation—a revelation of the message sent, and a confirmation of the interpretation. Your observation really makes it more poignant."

"Did you say poignant?" asked Matt. "What is poignant about some weird interpretation of a shadow? Supposing the beam has taken a different angle or has been cast from a different direction, do you think the images would still be the same?"

"That is the point," replied Kojo. "It has a purpose, and it is to achieve that purpose that the rays have converged the way they have in order to cast that unique shadow. If you like, take this as a divine heliostat."

"Matt," said Jay, "when it comes to religion, no one can win an argument with Kojo or Robinho, so leave them to wallow in their self-delusion. Too much church has brainwashed them."

"You, too, wallow in your ignorance," said Kojo. "Even if one were to come from the dead, you would not believe anything."

"Or heed any warning," added Robinho. "Well, they say familiarity breeds contempt."

"So, it is because you are coming to warn us that you couldn't get to your hostel first," said Matt. "If I may ask, what are you warning us against?"

"Armageddon of course," laughed Jay mockingly. "What else? You can't trust the modern-day churchman. Some engage in necromancy. Better the devil you know than the angel you don't. I'd rather stick to any of the mainstream churches if I must go to church. There is no hidden agenda there. That much I know from when I used to follow my parents to the Catholic church in my younger days."

"May God forgive you, for you know not what you are saying," said Kojo.

"Amen!" answered Jay, still laughing and joining his palms together prayer style.

"Jay, can I glance through one of your newspapers, please?" requested Matt.

"What newspaper?" asked Robinho. He snatched the two papers from Jay's hand. "We are your guests, you know. The unnecessary argument has kept you from realizing you should make us welcome."

"What welcome?" asked Matt. "Are you not the one who started the argument with your magic shadow analysis?"

"Some people simply have no sense of humor, especially when it has to do with religion," said Robinho.

"I knew you couldn't be serious," replied Jay.

"Make us tea, my friend," demanded Robinho.

"Insult upon injury," said Matt. "Wait for your tea after the battle of Armageddon; you will drink mud." But despite saying that, he stood up and went to make the tea.

"Ooh! That means no tea at all," said Avtar, not knowing the reason Matt had stood up. Then he added, "Well, you've got to show compassion. It is midday already and they have eaten nothing. Remember, they are just coming back from church."

"By the way, why are you just coming from church now?" asked Matt. "I thought you said you start church service at nine in the morning."

"Yes, we start at nine and close at eleven, and need time to travel from church, which I told you is rather far from here," replied Kojo. "Besides, we walked down from Camden Tube station instead of taking the short bus ride, just to enjoy the fresh spring air."

"Matt, I hope you don't intend on starting another argument," warned Avtar.

"Not really, but I can't see myself staying two hours in a church," replied Matt. "I would be bored to death."

"I tell you, there are so many exciting activities that you wouldn't even want the service to come to an end," replied Kojo.

"Please, please, don't start now," said Avtar.

Thank goodness for the electric kettle; the tea was ready in no time. Matt handed each person a cup. While the jokes and laughter were going on, he brought out a loaf of bread from a small chest of drawers by Jay's bed and started sharing it with everyone.

"What are you doing, Matt?" asked Jay. "Why are you sharing my bread with everybody? Don't you know that the era of free lunch is long gone?"

"I don't know about that," said Matt, "but I do know that Jesus gave His body and blood, so we must accompany the tea with bread."

"I ain't no Jesus or Father Christmas," replied Jay. "And we are not in a church either."

"Yes, but you accepted the tea I offered you from my own teabag without hesitation," said Matt.

"Why shouldn't I," replied Jay, "when you gave it to me of your own free will? I never asked for it."

"So are our friends here," said Matt.

"Mm, yummy. This bread is very sweet," said Kojo. "Can I have some more slices, please?"

"Look at this voracious thief," said Jay. "Why wouldn't it be sweet when it is free?"

"Innit?" Avtar laughed.

"Anything that is free is always sweet," continued Jay. "And people always take undue advantage, and overdo it until they regurgitate it, to their chagrin."

"Innit," Avtar laughed again. "But let's be honest; there is nobody who doesn't like free things if given."

Chapter 7
Divide and Rule

"Now give me my papers," Jay said to Robinho. "You've had free bread and tea; you can't have free papers also."

"But you can't read both of them at the same time," Robinho replied. He handed one back to Jay. As he did so, he exclaimed, "This is exactly what we were talking about the other time. I mean the justice system in this country. Just look at this." He showed Jay the front page of the paper as he was handing it over to him.

Jay grabbed the paper and said, "I saw it when I bought it, but have not read it yet." Then he started reading out loud for all to hear. The first article centered on a convicted fundamentalist hate preacher awarded £2,500 damages by the European Court of Human Rights for a breach of his human rights by the police who arrested him.

The second was the story of a thirteen-year-old boy who raped his two younger sisters after watching a sex education film at school. At court, he said he wanted to see what sex felt like after seeing the video. The third article was on a government teaching project encouraging children to think of the July 7th terror attacks in London from the suicide bombers' viewpoint. Pupils were asked to examine the perpetrators' motivation.

"Boy, this is unbelievable," said Jay. "Please, let me quickly glance through the headings on every page and see what else looks like these stories." He opened the second page and read about a disabled man applying for a job as a secret service agent, who was suing MI5 for discrimination for failing to secure the job as a mobile surveillance officer who would be trailing suspects. Farther down on the same page, he read of two Iraqis accused of executing two British soldiers being granted legal aid by the British Legal Services Commission with British tax money to defend themselves at their trial in Iraq by Iraqi authorities. They wanted their trial to be in Britain by British authorities because they were not sure they would get a fair trial in Iraq.

Jay moved on to the next page. There was nothing sensational. He flipped through every page and read the stories that caught his fancy. One was the tragic story of an eight-month-old toddler who drowned when his buggy was blown by a gust of wind into the sea while his father, who was with him at the time, was busy kissing his mistress. Another was about solicitors who charged the National Health Service £800 an hour for representing angry patients. Another was of a local council that spent £6,000 kitting their lawnmowers with satellite navigation systems, with the explanation that it was to prevent gardeners from getting lost in the long grass. The last was the story of a youth who had attempted to stab a police officer with a knife. The presiding judge dismissed the case on the grounds that raising the knife in front of the officer was no proof of an intention to use it.

Jay grabbed the second newspaper from Robinho and started reading. The front-page headline announced that £5.4 million had been paid to prisoners who were let out early, about halfway through their sentences, to prevent overcrowding in the prisons. The government claimed it was compensation for the prisoners' loss of free boarding and lodging. On the second page was an article about schools bringing forward plans to teach four- to five-year-olds about sex, and of a particular Church of England primary school in Hatfield, East Sussex, that had declared a "Transgender Day" to help pupils explore their sexuality.

Jay flipped through the rest of the pages and read three more articles. One was on Britain being the cocaine capital of Europe, with seventy-five thousand children using the drug. The second was about the number of young people doing absolutely nothing, which was soaring to almost a million. They were not in employment and not in education or training, just roaming the streets. The final one was about a local council advising young people to have sex to keep healthy.

"Kojo," said Jay, "when I tell you that this is an unreal world, a world where you have to shout wolf when there is none, you don't believe me. Look at what we've got now. We were joking about Armageddon a few minutes ago. Can there be a greater Armageddon than this?"

"Boy! I didn't know that it had gotten this bad," said Kojo. "I think that society has gone completely bonkers. That is what happens when a society shuts its door against God."

"Like Jay has been saying," said Avtar, "if we are so free, then where is the freedom when children are being shown bad films at school in the name of sex education? Where is the freedom in that? Where is public morality, for God's sake?"

"Ask me," said Robinho. "They will leave the things they should be teaching children and start teaching them the wrong things. That boy who raped his two sisters would probably not have done so if he had not watched those videos at school. A lot of GCSE students don't know the geography or history of this country. They don't know parts of London. They don't even know the name of the Prime Minister or their local MP. Tell them to sing the national anthem and they can't. But they know everything about sex. They know everything about their government-imposed rights. They know all about the social benefits but don't know personal responsibility. Who really ever thinks good of this country? I think something is seriously wrong with the policymakers."

"You can't really blame the policymakers or the government," said Matt. "The people would have protested if it wasn't what they wanted."

"That is a very good point, Matt," said Kojo. "And this is what baffles me most about the UK. The people here are only united in the negative things of life. People will brave all weather conditions, including a bitterly cold winter, to protest against any good program coming to any community. They will climb trees, dig tunnels, scale impossible walls and do all sorts of stunts to protest against new roads expansion of existing facilities, or job creation programs. But when it comes to the fundamental issues of life, they either acquiesce or actively promote the negative."

"Has any protest ever changed the government's position?" asked Avtar. "Didn't you read about the massive protest in 1989 when the council tax was introduced? Or the recent outcry for a change of the Olympic logo? Did the authorities budge? The government does not care about protests. And we all know that governments here, from central to local government, don't care about the people; they only pay lip service to freedom of choice and freedom of expression. Life in this country is always a no-win situation. Conform or get out; that's government policy."

"It only happens where private indiscipline colludes with collective exclusiveness," said Robinho. "And it is often the bane of societies bereft of any religious culture. There are no standards to measure or check human behavior. It is very unfortunate."

"In all honesty," said Jay, "the problem lies squarely with the English people, or let me say the white British people."

"You can't say that, because everybody is doing the same thing," said Matt.

"That is true," said Jay. "But other people are following the white people, either by choice or by coercion. The whites are the largest ethnic group in Britain and have the most members of Parliament. They make the laws of the land. They are the custodians of the cultural heritage of the British way of life, as it were—the values and norms of society that enhance individual well-being, the integrity of the human person, and the welfare of the community, the society and the state.

"With all this, they become the sole determinants of what is allowed in society, and what is integrated into society's core values. No foreigner can come to a land and dictate what happens in that land. He has to follow the way of the people of the land, either willingly or by legislative coercion. If irresponsibility and indiscipline are the way of the people, then everyone will be coerced into it. That is what is happening here. Any time there is a word for rectitude, it is a word from settlers, not from indigenes. It is the indigenes who will kill the world.

"Any truth or fact they don't like, they term *vague predictions* or *spurious assertions*, saying these will have *catastrophic consequences*. It is incongruous with the picture painted of Britain in my country."

"It is the same picture in my country and, I dare say, in many third world countries," said Kojo. "And I think it was a correct picture when their forefathers served God and manifested the love of God wherever they went. But when the new generation of pleasure seekers under the cover of freedom and human rights voted God out of life's equation, the result was the absurdity so wantonly manifested today. And because the British press keeps bamboozling the outside world with their gall-laden freedom, the world still views it through the lens of their forefathers' good legacy. But such won't be the case for long. What is hidden is already coming to light."

"I don't agree with your viewpoints," Matt protested. "White people are not the problem with this country. If our forefathers' legacy impacted the world positively, then there would be only one pointer to the present decay in our society. It is immigration. And you are now blaming us for our kindness in welcoming people with open arms. You are blaming us for offering people equal rights and opportunities, ensuring that no one is discriminated against in the scheme of things. You are blaming us for shifting from a monocultural society to a multicultural one to ensure the integration of settlers.

"We now have people of different nationalities, different religions, different cultures, different perceptions and different ways of life. And we have been kind enough to allow them the freedom to live the way they choose. And what have they done? They have abused our generosity and polluted our culture with their bad manners and evil mentality, from their scourge of underdevelopment. And you are now blaming us for all that? Is that fair? Are you paying evil for good?"

"You think you are smart," said Jay, "by shying away from the truth and trying to put us on the defensive. We are talking of the legislative system in which immigrants play no part in policy formulation whatsoever. You also talk of integration; I'd prefer assimilation, and that is, the settlers should assimilate the British culture instead of the British integrating all manner of foreign cultures. Didn't they say that when you are in Rome you should behave like the Romans?

"The truth is that, rather than your line of argument, the settlers actually assimilated the British way of life, and not the other way round. If it were the other way round, there would have been discipline; there would have been morality and ethical standards, which are very visible in the culture of the immigrants. Instead, those who immigrated here were legislatively coerced into throwing away their time-tested life-giving values.

"Tell me, which of the stories that we read in the newspapers portray the cultural values of ethnic minorities? None. If you want me to teach you your history, I will. Britain has always had bad children, but the difference is that your forefathers always ensured that there was no place for them in the land. So they shipped most of the bad people to other countries. That way, they rid the society of its flagitious members."

"So are you saying that nationals of these other countries are all criminals?" asked Matt.

"Not by any stretch of the imagination," responded Jay. "Apart from being a minority there, the criminal justice system in those countries has enough of an element of deterrence to discourage reoffending. They have structures that effectively reform offenders and equip them with lifelong skills. Such skills are crucial to their reintegration into the community and to their transformation as useful citizens after release.

"It is this absence of penal servitude as a bedrock for the rehabilitation of offenders that has made a mockery of the British penal system. That is why in the UK, you hardly find anyone who has been transformed on release from prison. Instead, they are more hardened than ever and would do everything possible to return, to have everything free. You don't empathize with offenders at the expense of the victims in the name of any rights. It is an inverted justice."

"Hmm, that was rather pedagogical," Matt said scornfully, laughing.

"Innit!" shouted Avtar.

"Yes, what we are discussing would have been of less worry if, as Matt said, the government were giving people the freedom to live the way they choose," said Kojo. "Asians and Africans with their solid family bonds and strong cultural affinity would not have so easily gotten sucked into these social problems. Asian children still fare relatively better. Go to an African home here; you will see that the children born or raised here are no different from anyone else. With the exception of very few homes, there is no respect for elders, no respect for public property, no moral principles and nothing sacrosanct that reflects their home community. The Entente cordiale between western liberalism and African conservatism has been obliterated. All the people have synergized into one community marked by libertarian waywardness by copying all the negative attributes of each community. There is no community cohesion. Everyone has his own agenda. The common denominator is rebellion."

"It is divide and rule, man—divide and rule," said Jay. "That is what they used to colonize the world. And they are using it here to destroy community cohesion. It is the only way the leaders can effectively take advantage of the people."

"I don't know how they think," said Kojo. "The other day, a public figure called for street lights to be permanently switched off to reduce global warming. Are streetlights responsible for global warming? Look at the present rate of crime and imagine what would happen if all street lights were to be switched off. I sometimes wonder if some of the leaders even think before they speak. Yet the press will not see anything wrong in such proposals unless they came out of Africa."

"This is not about Africa," said Robinho, "I think an evil spirit has taken over Britain, judging from our reading of today's papers and our reflections on the judicial system. Evil things are happening at such a rate that should cause concern, but instead, this is taken as normal. In fact, the establishment is driving the speed of these abnormal changes, and that is the real problem."

"This is what I have been saying," said Jay. "The society is changing for the worse through self-deceit. And that is the worst thing that can happen to a people."

"I don't think it is as much a matter of self-deceit as turning their backs on God," said Robinho.

"What is the difference?" asked Kojo. "Nothing results in self-deceit as much as turning your back on God."

"Self-deceit is responsible for the best and the biggest in the world," said Jay. "Self-glorification, innit? First this, first that; best this, best that; world-class this and world-class that; largest this and largest that. Ha ha ha ha," he laughed with a drily mocking hilarity.

"Anyway, they are not alone," interrupted Kojo. "Every nation glories in its achievements, no matter how small."

"Yes, in their achievements, but not in their outright lies and inflated pride," said Jay. "The statistics are there for all to see, very impressive—all for the wrong reasons, with the wrong programs, wrong policies and wrong approach."

Matt stood up from where he was sitting and walked to the door, possibly to stretch his legs. He faced the room and placed his right hand at the top edge of the door, then placed his left hand on his hip with his right knee bent slightly to rest his right foot on top of his left foot. "I don't want to argue about self-deceit, but I do want Jay to tell us one area that exists in this country that does not exist in his country," he challenged.

"Matt, is your new posture for defense or for an attack?" asked Kojo.

"What posture?" asked Matt.

"I mean you're standing up to virtually block the doorway," said Kojo.

"It is neither," said Matt. "I have a right to stretch my legs, don't I?"

"Of course you do," said Kojo, "but there is no telling what your intentions are. Maybe you are uncomfortable with Jay's assertions and want to physically confront him."

"Innit," shouted Avtar. They all laughed.

"Even that is deceit," said Jay. "*Innit* is part of the conformist credo so commonplace in British life. It is denying you the opportunity to air your own view by indirectly saying, *Don't you agree with me?* before you even have time to consider what is being said. Such words as '*absolutely*' in response to a statement or question, or phrases such as 'I said it, didn't I?'; 'It makes all the difference, doesn't it?' and 'Take it or leave it' are all part of the conformist nomenclature. They are spoilers' phrases to bully and intimidate people into submission. They spoil the society."

"And the irony," added Kojo, "is that many of these phrases have crept into the daily language spoken by Africans in Africa with glee. Home-based Africans speak Anglo-American jargon and use Anglo-American accents better than those domiciled in Britain or the United States. Some even prefer unhealthy western cuisine to their healthy local menu."

"That is the part of westernization that must be resisted," said Jay. "It is part of the wholehearted but wrong assimilation of anything west as always the best. It is colo par excellence to pretend or want to seem to have lived in the west as if that adds any value to your life." Jay always used the word *colo* for colonial mentality or *neocolonialism.* "It is evidence of an inferiority complex to acculturate foreign habits in your own land. It portends a bad omen for third world countries. Before long, western lifestyles will envelop the world, and that to me is the beginning of Armageddon. It is the deracination of all the races into a unitary hybrid of one true evil race."

"Jay, I perceive you are suffering from ACXS," said Kojo.

"What is that?" asked Matt.

"Acute Caucasian xenophobic syndrome," replied Kojo. They all burst into prolonged laughter.

"Kojo, you must be mad to think like that," said Jay. "I have no problem with the white race. I only have a problem with people who, irrespective of their skin color, prefer evil to good but want everyone to think their evil ways are the right ways."

"The Arabs will resist anything that comes against their culture," said Robinho.

"There are western-indoctrinated Arabs who are dancing to the western tune," said Jay.

"No matter," said Kojo. "Don't forget that the West and the East are forever at war. In the last century, there was a war between the western and eastern political blocs. In the present century, it is between the west and the Middle East in terms of culture and lifestyle. Something intractable must be between the West and the East that passes understanding and underscores their sworn everlasting enmity."

"There is nothing intractable there," said Jay. "It is mere arrogance by the west to forcefully impose its ignoble lifestyle as a universal ideal under the guise of democracy, which the Arabs are resisting. And we are all affected one way or the other. Now every international traveler, irrespective of status, is subjected to extra hours of indignity and restlessness until he or she is safely out of both entry and exit points."

"It is not about lifestyle or democracy," said Matt. "It is religious extremism."

"Jay, I am disappointed," remarked Kojo. "I thought you were intelligent. How can you reason that way? That is trivializing the whole problem of terrorism."

"Terrorism is the language of the west. Their opponents don't see themselves as terrorists," said Jay. "And I am tempted to think that religion is only being used as a subterfuge. Whatever friction exists between Islam and Christianity or Judaism is aimed at getting at the west since Christianity is perceived as the religion of the west, the west is seen as sympathetic to Judaism. But as we know in this country, Judaism is nonexistent, and Christianity is dead and buried—and has long ceased to be a western religion."

"Sorry, boys," said Robinho, "all this has little or nothing to do with the decadent state of our country. Bad leadership, abnormal occurrences and a general shift of society toward evil are something to worry about. These things are the consequences of a nation turning away from God. This is what we should be talking about."

"Tell me about it!" shouted a voice from the door, along with a simultaneous knock on the door frame and entry. Matt had already moved away from the door and was back on his bed.

Entering the room now was Matt's friend and coursemate, Levy Chandler, a young white man from Sutton Coldfield in the West Midlands. Light-hearted, easy-going and jocular, he mostly burst in unannounced and without any formalities. "What's up, boys? Why are you gathered as if a corporate meeting is in session?" he asked.

"You are up, boy—for sale," laughed Avtar. "For ninety-nine pence."

"Who would buy this, even for one penny?" Jay said, laughing. "Who would spend his hard-earned money buying trouble for himself?"

Chapter 8
The Devil's Invasion of Britain

At the satanic meeting, Molech was still advocating for an operational headquarters. "As I said earlier," said he, "it is necessary for us to focus on a particular spot and start our offensive from there. I am actually thinking that somewhere in Europe would be a good starting point."

"I think we should first agree on whether or not to start from a particular nation," said Ashtoreth, "before deciding which nation to start from. Do we all agree to start from a particular place, or should we continue operating as we currently do?"

There was a chorus of yesses to start from a place.

"Molech, can you give us reasons why you want us to start from Europe?" asked Beelzebub.

"Of course, yes, I can," replied Molech. "And in doing that, I want to specifically pick a country instead of making a general reference to Europe. It could be any European country, but I prefer to choose Britain because of its advantages over other countries. Means of communication is very important in any war. Here I am talking of message dissemination tools—language, the press and people. We all know that the English language is very widely spoken all over the world. British and American people are very widely traveled. But more important is the number of travelers to the US and Britain, especially immigrants."

"In that case," said Rimmon, interrupting, "I think the United States would serve our purpose better than Britain or anywhere in Europe. They attract more immigrants than anywhere else in the world."

"Thanks, Rimmon, for that," said Molech. "I still prefer Britain. Remember, we want to start from a specific town or city, and I cannot think of any city in the whole world that is as unique as London. I mean London in the

United Kingdom, not London in Canada, the US or anywhere else. The US has great cities, beautiful and alluring, but London occupies a special place in the minds of humans. It is the greatest cosmopolitan city in the world. It is the most culturally diverse and, as it were, is the melting pot of the world.

"In a sense, it is the capital of the world—and everyone yearns to at least visit the capital of the world. It hosts the greatest number of world-renowned centers of learning. And qualifications gained at these centers are almost tickets to jobs anywhere in the world. People from all over the world want to study in London to acquire these qualifications, and inadvertently the British lifestyle and ideology, and take them back to their countries. And since London is the eye of Britain, what I say of London is ditto for Britain. Many world leaders are products of British education, and they spread British mannerisms like measles in their countries.

"Unlike the US, Britain is a colonial master to many nations on earth, and it still has an overwhelming influence on those nations despite many of them gaining independence. There are, far and wide, British-dependent territories and islands on every continent on Earth. British hegemony in the form of neocolonialism is still very much active in many Commonwealth nations. Besides, Britain has the greatest concentration of citizens, indigenous and dual citizens, residents in other individual countries, and their native countries, and these individuals bring into play British thinking and the British way of life in the affairs of those countries.

"The Charter of Human Rights may be a Universal Declaration of the United Nations, but the concept and introduction of any form of peoples' rights actually originated in Britain, centuries before any other nation or group of nations borrowed the idea. That is why the issue of rights in whatever form not only is more pronounced in Britain but also makes Britain a more socially tolerant society. And I will tell you how this tolerance will play into our hands.

"The policy orientation of the British press, especially the BBC, together with the judiciary and the social security system, to mention a few, is based on this tolerance. It is the reason why the penalty for crime in the US takes a more draconian turn than in Britain. Some things considered serious human rights issues in Britain have no place under human rights in the United States. This is the reason why terrorists, benefit seekers and all manner of disfigured minds consider Britain first when seeking sanctuary from their respective native countries or their countries of domicile. It gives London and Britain a magnetic sway over the peoples of the earth.

"The formation and future expansion of the European Union makes it much easier for EU citizens to move freely to and from Britain than to the US, even if this Union were to cease to exist in the future. Tolerance is the best fertile ground for cross-breeding negative ideas and habits. Remember, humans find it easier to copy bad manners than to copy good ones.

"So all the bad habits and negative cultures of travelers and immigrants of EU member states and other nations will be imported into Britain, where freedom makes them blossom. In turn, all the adulterated habits and unedifying cultures of Britain are taken back to all these other nations. Therefore, whatever seeds we sow in Britain will be carried far and wide to all the nations of the earth. As Yeshua started in Jerusalem—to the ends of the earth, so shall we start from Londo—to the ends of the earth. Britain shall be our pollinating agent, ha, ha, ha!

"There are just so many ways in which the British approach to and lenience in human affairs helps our cause—much more than any American approach. I can't exhaust them in this meeting, but I will give just three more reasons for my choice of London over any other city in the world. And these three reasons or institutions, will become our greatest agents and partners in propagating our seeds to the rest of the earth. The first two are the press and the judiciary.

"The press and the judiciary are earthly institutions. You all know that they don't exist in the spiritual because there is perfect order and perfect peace in heaven—which is also the seat of the deepest knowledge and greatest information. And since ours is a spiritual kingdom like heaven, I would say the same goes for our kingdom. Humans, occupants of the earth, however, have to find a way of controlling people and their behaviors—a system that can bring a semblance of order to their *lost* world. It is the best they can do to make up for what they lost in Eden. A physical world needs a tangible physical instrument to gather and disseminate information in a world that relies on time, position and distance. And we know that information is the soul of life, the food that sustains human existence.

"Everyone knows that the press is the mouthpiece and eye of any nation in terms of communicating with and viewing the outside world. Our possession of a nation's press and its judicial system, especially its criminal justice system, is the death knell for that nation. So I can never, ever overemphasize how important the judiciary and the press are to our mission on earth. Since the Fall of Man, no system, no institution and nothing that man has ever conceived or devised is able to help our cause and our mission as much as the press and the judiciary. Unfortunately, this seems less the case outside the west, and part of our present policy is to extend it to the rest of the earth.

"Now, we all know that at present no media outfit anywhere in the world is as powerful as the BBC. It is the most sought-after in the earth and is taken as the most authentic. But actually, we will make it the most biased and most selective news media on all the earth. Prejudice will be its motto. Its news will only be in accordance with its policy of promoting the British culture of freedom and tolerance at all costs. We will make any new powerful press in any other country imitate the BBC's biased view and presentation.

"It would have been very beneficial to humans if freedom and tolerance were not relative terms, if they truly represented the freedom and love that springs from the Source of Creation. And I say love rather than tolerance because tolerance was never in Yahweh's lexicon. Unfortunately, theirs is a misguided interpretation in accordance with our whims. The same goes for their justice system. Human rights will become the cornerstone of their justice system. But we all know that what they interpret as a human right is anything but right. It is an inside-out wrong, an insidious, puerile jurisprudence. So, for us, the British press and the judiciary make up the double-edged sword that will pierce even to the dividing of soul and spirit, and of joints and marrow, blurring the thoughts and intents of the heart to scorch the mind. They will become the flaming sword that turns in every direction to destroy the nations. Ha, ha, ha!

"The third institution is the church. Oh my, my, my, my! The church alone is more than enough reason for us to make Britain our operational headquarters rather than the US. The church and its influence are more pronounced in the US, especially with the exploits of the evangelicals and Pentecostals. American national life is more rooted in Christian beliefs and principles than British national life. This means that it will be easier for us to penetrate the church in Britain than in the US.

"But a greater advantage of the British church to us is the fact that Christianity has existed in Britain for centuries before North America was even 'discovered' by Europeans. In fact, the apparent view of a greater part of the world is that among West Europeans, British missionaries are responsible for the spread of Christianity to almost the rest of the world, except perhaps some South American countries. But it is a simple mistake of not being able to distinguish Irish from British missionaries. Everybody in the world knows that Britain is the only country in the world with a state church and a monarchical head of that church.

"So from my analysis of the British church, the advantage to us is that there are more mainstream conventional churches than there are Pentecostal churches. And we know that it is easier for us to dim the fire of the Advocate, I mean the Spirit of Yeshua, operating in the conventional churches than in the Pentecostal churches. Besides, while the Pentecostals are more of an individual establishment, the mainstream churches are what I would call a unitary conglomerate, with a louder voice and greater impact. The evangelicals among them are just a handful and have no voice. With the government's having a strong sway over the mainstream churches, which thus fall victim to their manipulations, it becomes easy for the government to regulate the Pentecostals to become noisy and lukewarm. Therefore, the church itself will become our advocate. We will make the church Baal's temple and its priests Baal's priests.

"Now, if we can make the British society one that is anchored on the foundations of the church, one that is credited with the spread of Christianity to the rest of the world, one to which an authorized version of the Holy Book is ascribed to their king, of all the kings of the earth, and one to which the rest of the world looks up for direction and for edifying upliftment—if we can make their church more Laodicean, having the appearance of godliness but lacking its powers, and if we can make this people deny even the existence of Yahweh, then it will be easy for the camel to pass through the eye of a needle. And we will have succeeded in accomplishing our mission, because they will fight our fight for us.

"Britain will become a nice place for bad people. They will help spread our message for us and, as the scripture says, will become 'troublesome to all the kingdoms of the earth.' If this is not convincing enough, then I would like to hear the case for a better alternative. Thank you."

"Marvelous, marvelous. Absolutely marvelous!" said Beelzebub gleefully. Everyone clapped in agreement. "Any alternative viewpoints?" asked Beelzebub.

"No!" was the chorused response. So it was unanimously agreed to launch their offensive from London and make Britain their operational headquarters.

Beelzebub called for strategies and operational mechanisms for taking over Britain as their headquarters. After much deliberation, it was agreed that all the senior commanders, including the top echelon of the ruling council, should be withdrawn from their territorial stranglehold and deployed to Britain. Middle-ranking commanders were assigned to take charge of all the command posts in all the regional groupings, subcontinents and continents. Activities in these areas were to be trimmed down, with more than half their forces withdrawn and redeployed to the British sector.

The Gadara Legions spread around the entire earth, as one of the wickedest divisions, were to be withdrawn from their various zones and redeployed to Britain, half of them in London alone. It was agreed that it was essential to maintain uniformity of cultures, and since Britain was part of the west, two senior commanders were appointed to coordinate activities and oversee operations in all western nations. They were to supervise the middle-ranking commanders in charge of various command posts in the west.

This was to ensure that what would be happening in the United Kingdom would be fully reflected in other western nations, albeit to a lesser extent. Two senior commanders were appointed to take charge of British-dependent territories and islands outside mainland Britain, including Northern Island. They were to ensure that exactly what was happening in mainland Britain would happen in the territories and the islands.

They listed a number of techniques that would form part of their strategy in their new operations. Contrary to human expectations, they drew their inspiration from the Bible in designing their techniques and mapping out their strategies. One of their greatest weapons was the use of lies. Beelzebub had said Satan was not called father of lies for nothing, and he vowed to use that fact to the fullest. He cited a scripture that reads, 'I will go out and be a lying spirit in the mouth of all his prophets.'

"That is a spirit taking permission from Yahweh to destroy a king by means of lies," he continued. "That is how potent lies are. The Fall of Man was the result of lies, and when you want to destroy a people, just plant lies in the heads of their leaders. Make them impulsive liars. So, we are going to plant lying spirits in the minds of their prophets—their priests and bishops and their politicians. And their words shall be nothing but lies. They will lead by deception. Remember, deception is a tool of self-defense. We will sow confusion in the hearts of the people so that falsehood and foolish arguments will blur their understanding and prevent them from knowing when their leaders are deceiving them. We will send a deaf and dumb spirit upon the entire populace to make them extremely stubborn in every area of life, stubbornly embracing immorality and unrighteousness and stubbornly rejecting all the good values that edify a society.

"Human rights will become the recourse of all criminals, and the magic phrase that sets them free. It will become an octopus of evil, a web that will clog their sanity and blur their sense of value. By the time we finish with Britain, the people will not know what stung them. Britain will become synonymous with Belial, but their people will not know it."

When he finished, others made whatever little comments they could. They vowed to turn Britain into their kingdom—the Devil's kingdom. At the end of the meeting, Britain was divided into zones, with senior commanders appointed to be in charge of each zone. London, as the capital, was again subdivided into smaller zones, with the more wicked commanders appointed to take over those zones, and with the even wickeder assembly of evil spirits allotted to those commanders. Operations were to start immediately.

All through the meeting, Lucifer had remained silent while listening to everyone's contribution. In the end, he commended them all before bringing the meeting to a close.

Chapter 9
Organized Indiscipline

Radka Smith was an Englishwoman who had grown up in Slovakia with her aunt. Her mother was Slovakian, and her father was English, from Margate in Kent. She had had her elementary and secondary education in Slovakia before returning to her parents in London, where she pursued her degree program. Doing joint honors in social policy and psychology, she was in the same department as Jay, and they were friends. She had borrowed a book from Jay, which she decided to return to him.

Lisa Price, also an Englishwoman, was Radka's friend who had had her primary education in London before leaving for Doha, Qatar, with her parents when her father moved there on official posting. She had had her secondary education in Doha before returning to London for her degree program. She was a single honors psychology student.

Radka was rather tall, standing at 1.75 meters, and was lanky with dark luxuriant hair flowing down over her shoulders. Her face was long and thin with a pointed nose, a small set of sharp penetrating brown eyes, a smallish mouth and a firm pointed triangular chin. She carried herself with much dignity, though she was quite friendly.

Unlike Radka, Lisa was average in height, standing at 1.62 meters with blonde hair, a broader face with a tapered nose, a set of rather blue sensuous eyes and chubby, lightly dimpled cheeks. A bit stout in build, she was attractively vivacious and carefree. Visiting Radka at the time, Lisa wanted to return the book, she offered to accompany her to Jay's hostel. Both lived at Max Rayne House, on the same ground as Ann Stephenson House and Ifor Evans Hall on Camden Road.

They arrived at Jay's place shortly after Levy. After exchanging pleasantries, Radka handed Jay his book. The two young women had made to leave but were held back by Jay, who offered them a can of Diet Coke each after they declined his offer of tea or coffee.

"Jay, that is discrimination, you know," said Levy.

"What is discrimination?" asked Jay.

"The offer of drink to the girls leaving me out although I got here first," said Levy, smiling.

"Well, they came to see me, but you came to see Matt," said Jay, "so blame Matt, not me."

"You just love women, Jay," said Matt, "admit it and stop looking for excuses."

"Who doesn't love women, don't you love them?" asked Jay. "Well, it's normal for me to love them and love them dearly," he added with a chuckle.

"That is how boys ridicule each other," said Levy.

"That is your problem, not mine," said Jay. "Anyway, let's get on with what we were discussing," Jay added.

"What were you discussing?" asked Levy.

"We were discussing the problems in the world, narrowing it down to the problems in our country," said Avtar, "which are assuming alarming proportions. Many factors were adduced, including bad leadership, but Robinho thinks that it is the absence of godliness."

"Whatever problems exist in a society is the fault of both the leaders and the people," said Levy.

"The leaders are to blame because they use evil legislation to make everyone conform," said Avtar.

"Blame whomever you like," said Robinho. "All I know is that bad leadership, abnormal occurrences and a general shift of society toward evil are the consequences of a nation turning away from God."

"If that is true, then people like you should take the blame," said Matt.

"Why people like me?" asked Robinho.

"Are you not a Christian?" asked Matt. "Christians are supposed to pray for their nations and their leaders."

"It is because of our prayers that God's wrath has not fallen on this country," said Robinho.

"If truly our country is in a mess, then we all share the blame," said Levy.

"Sure, we all share the blame if we are all party to what is happening," said Robinho. "Unfortunately, as Avtar said, we are compelled by legislation to toe the government line whether or not we agree with it."

"That makes us all party to it," said Levy, "because we voted for the government, and by that act, we endorsed whatever way they choose to govern us. If we feel they are failing us, we wait for the next election to show them the way out. That is the beauty of democracy. We have the power, not them. Theirs is a ceded temporary power."

"But all the parties are the same," said Avtar. "There is no difference in their policies, only in the method of delivery."

"The truth is that government policies oftentimes," said Levy, "are the result of suggested opinions of high-ranking organizations, big industry leaders, renowned institutes and research centers, trade unions, pressure groups, powerful individuals and so forth. In a way, these all represent the society."

"Ultimately, it is government that takes the final decision," said Kojo. "So politicians ought to know when people's reasoning is wrong."

"That is in a normal situation when the politicians themselves think rationally," said Robinho. "But when the Devil takes over a country, all the leaders reason the same way, and negatively at that, whether they be in politics, academia, or the corporate world, or serve as community leaders. Can't you see that the Devil has taken over this country? That is why the people are following sheepishly."

"Are you able to substantiate that?" asked Matt.

"How can you ask such a question with all that is happening?" asked Robinho. "The way the entire state apparatus is operating is a clear indication that something is seriously wrong."

"Matt, if the news we discussed in today's papers, and the bad court judgments we talked about, are not enough, then I wonder if anything else will make any difference," said Avtar.

"Truly, when the government itself sees evil as normal or positive," said Kojo, "then something is very wrong."

"At least there is a limit at the government level," said Jay. "The more worrisome is on the individual level, which knows no limit. There seems to be an element of lunacy in many people's attitudes these days that makes the evils of yesteryears our new normal."

"Sincerely speaking, I regard society as inherently evil, so I don't normally bother about many bad happenings," said Levy. "But I must confess that things are taking a turn for the worse."

"Yes, because government policies now indicate open rebellion against God," said Kojo. "Crime is treated with such levity that citizens have no fear of doing evil."

"Of course. Why not, when criminals are rewarded in various ways," said Avtar, "like a reduced penalty for a guilty plea, financial compensation for early release from prison and so forth."

"The way government is going," said Jay, "pretty soon people will no longer be able to differentiate between right and wrong."

"Even Parliament is confused," said Avtar. "MPs now want sixteen-year-olds to be free to change their gender without parental consent."

"These are the signs of a government run by the Devil," said Robinho. "Denying the existence of God opens the way for the Devil to operate at will. That is the reason for the unbridled persecution of Christianity in this land."

"As a Christian, what you see as persecution may not really be persecution," said Matt. "You need to give examples and prove your point convincingly for non-Christians to believe you."

"Anyone who sees what is happening and denies Christian persecution exists here must be very dishonest and very delusionary," said Robinho. "Even perpetrators know it exists."

"Truly speaking," said Matt, "what is happening here is happening all over the world."

"Maybe, but not as a deliberate system of government action toward the negative," said Jay.

"When godliness can no longer guide government policies and actions, the country is in trouble," said Robinho. "Without godliness, there are no restrictions on individual behaviors irrespective of state laws; there will be no inhibitions toward lawlessness and evil because man by nature is evil and rebellious."

"That is true," said Avtar. "Too many things are wrong with us as a society, from the benefits system to national planning, to the justice system, to social services—just name it; everything is out of place. And rather than government curbing it, it is actually promoting it."

"It is no fault of government because people will always be people no matter what," said Matt.

"It is government policies in every area of governance that shape both individual and national life," said Avtar. "The few items we read in today's papers attest to that."

"Matt, you need to look at the spate of recent legislation to understand," said Robinho. "Government legislation is turning people into wild animals of some sort. People just behave any way they want without any shame and without thinking of the impact on other people or on society."

"The worst is the trampling of righteousness," said Kojo.

"That is an understatement," said Robinho. "What is happening is a full-blown frenzied persecution of Christianity."

"How?" asked Matt.

"What do you mean, how? Are you blind?" said Robinho.

"Persecution is definitely going on," said Avtar, "but I think it is generally persecution of righteousness rather than of Christianity."

"There is a general persecution of righteousness," said Jay, "but Muslim persecution stems from the fear of radical Islam, which makes the persecution almost purely Christian. The examples I know so far are against Christians."

"Even the new legislations are brought to bear against Christians," said Kojo. "But while some may not like any argument against legislation, one can effectively argue about specific cases."

"What specific cases?" asked Matt.

"A Christian magistrate was forced to resign from his eighteen-year court family panel by the court managers for requesting that his cases on same-sex adoption be screened for other magistrates to preside over because of his religious beliefs," said Kojo. "Why ask of one's religion in job application forms if it is not to be respected?"

"In London, a renowned scientist and director of education for the Royal Society who serves at the Academy of Science in the UK was forced to resign," said Avtar, "for suggesting that rather than see creationism as a misconception, teachers should see it as a cultural world view, then explain why it has no scientific basis to their pupils. One of the anti-creationist lobbyists said, 'Creationism is anti-science. Teaching it to children is a form of intellectual child abuse because it gives them the wrong facts about life.' Who has the right facts about life other than the Creator of life? If humans have the right facts about life, why are there so many problems in life? Which constitutes intellectual child abuse between a forced acceptance of an idea and the freedom of sifting through many ideas and making an informed choice by the individual?"

"In Morden, South West London, a fifty-seven-year-old woman who provides respite care for children with severe learning difficulties entered a contract with her local council employer," said Levy. "The agreement was not to schedule her for any Sunday work as she was part of a ministry team in her local church. But a few months after adhering to that agreement, her managers began pressuring her to work on Sundays and repeatedly allocated her Sunday shifts, threatening her with disciplinary action, despite her colleagues' agreeing to cover such shifts for her. Eventually, she lost her job and her court case for unfair dismissal."

"I read of a female BBC newscaster who was severely criticized by BBC bosses for wearing a chain with a gold cross while on screen," said Lisa.

"In South Shields, Tyne and Wear," said Robinho, "a mother of three was asked by her housing association to remove her Christmas decorations in front of her house in case they offended non-Christians, saying the lights were *offensive to the community*. The light of God is only offensive to a community that prefers the Devil's darkness."

"In Nailsea, North Somerset, a schoolteacher was sacked for visiting a sick pupil and offering to pray for her," said Jay. "What is the offense in offering to pray for someone when there is no compulsion? The target recipient has the freedom to accept or decline such offers."

"In Baldock, Hertfordshire, bells at St Mary the Virgin Church were ordered to stop ringing after one person complained of noise," said Kojo. "This was followed by other such complaints, as was the case for St Dunstan Church in Mayfield village, East Sussex; Saint Peter and Paul Church in Aldeburgh, Suffolk; and St Mary's Church in Fishguard, Pembrokeshire, just to mention a few. Yet no one has complained about the noise of the adhan and iqama calls from mosques."

"That is the selective persecution I talked about," said Jay. "In Kettering, Northamptonshire, a Christian pediatrician who examines potential adoptive parents for medical fitness to adopt was stripped of her membership on the adoption panel for expressing the view that children do best with a mother and father in a committed, long-term relationship. Yet we are not in a police state where one cannot freely express his or her views."

"I read in the papers that in Doncaster, a six-year-old boy was banned from wearing a Christian band in class on health and safety grounds," said Lisa. "The band, which the boy said made him feel that God was always with him, was decorated with the Christian symbol of a fish and worn on his ankle, covered with his sock, but was discovered by a teacher when the boy scratched his ankle. The band was never on display as it was covered, and it posed no risk whatsoever—health and safety or otherwise."

"In Penwortham, Lancashire, householders were handed postcards," said Radka, "that warned carol singers would not be welcome during Christmas because many residents were 'uncomfortable with having groups of strangers at their doors.' Despite the householders' disapproval of the apparent lies concocted against them, the local police strongly defended their position on the matter. In another development, the Advertising Standards Authority, then headed by a former culture secretary, banned a Christian group in Bath from distributing leaflets, claiming God can heal. I know I don't practice Christianity, but one must say the truth."

"Enough!" Matt shouted, yawning and stretching himself. "Looks like you all agree that Christians are being persecuted. I honestly think these are all a case of discrimination rather than persecution and argue as much as we can, there is really nothing we can do about these things. I am hungry; it is lunchtime already."

"OK, let's go for lunch," suggested Levy.

"Where do we go? Nando's?" asked Kojo.

"That's too damn expensive, man!" objected Robinho.

"Should we go to McDonald's or Burger King? Yes?" asked Levy.

"I am definitely not having any of that stuff. I've said bye-bye to junk food," said Jay.

"OK, let's go to Coffee Republic or Subway," suggested Matt.

"No way—same bad stuff," Jay said scornfully.

"Let's go for an Indian takeaway then," suggested Avtar.

"Fuck all," said Jay. "Who wants to be smelling garlic?"

"What do you want, Jay?" asked Kojo. "Have you never eaten Indian takeaway before, or is it that you don't even want to eat at all?"

"Look, there is a Chinese buffet restaurant that just opened, and it's within walking distance," said Levy. "And you know what? Its takeaway service is very cheap."

"How much?" asked Jay.

"Four quid," replied Levy.

"Are you serious?" asked Jay.

"Why not? Yes!" replied Levy.

"That's it!" said Jay. "Let's go and try it."

"Must you dictate for everybody?" asked Kojo.

"Yes. Because I want to be generous today," said Jay. "I am paying for everybody. I want you to have a taste of how alluring benefits are."

"You joker," said Kojo. "You couldn't even dispense with your bread this morning."

"OK, boys," said Jay. "To tell you that I am serious, Lev, hold this money and return my change, please." He brought out two twenty-pound notes and handed them over to Levy. "You will have to buy your own drinks," he said. "I didn't promise that. And if it turns out that lunch costs more than forty pounds, then everyone will have to make up the balance for his or her own. But if the food turns out not to be nice, Lev will refund my money in full because he is the one who suggested this restaurant. So let's go."

"Agreed," said Levy.

"Lev, I hope you are not kidding," Robinho said, "because it is difficult to get a decent meal that cheap in this part of town."

"I am saying the truth," defended Levy. "It is possible they are using it to attract customers and that once firmly established with good clientele, they may raise their prices. Probably so, but for now that is their price."

"It is not actually cheaper than other places," said Kojo. "Four quid is about the average cost of most takeaways around here unless you are comparing it with the elite ones operated by celebrity chefs."

"Show us just one place in the whole of the West End with a takeaway service that is four quid," challenged Levy.

"This area is not entirely part of the West End but is in the Northwest," said Avtar, "so it should be cheaper."

"OK," Jay said, "enough of the argument. Let's go."

And with that, they trouped outside on their way to the restaurant, chatting as they went.

"The weather is just gorgeous," said Matt, as soon as they had emerged outside. "Why don't we walk down to the park from the restaurant?"

"We might as well do," said Levy.

"Let's get our food first before thinking of whether or not to go to the park," said Jay.

On getting to the restaurant, they saw some of their fellow students. On seeing how yummy the dishes were, Jay said, "I am buying an additional portion for the evening."

"See what I told you?" said Levy smiling.

"Why not wait till evening?" asked Avtar. "You haven't even eaten your lunch yet."

"Because I may not want to come out in the evening," replied Jay.

"You mean you are going to eat again in the evening after this?" asked Kojo.

"Why not?" replied Jay. "This is only lunch; I am talking of dinner."

"How are you sure you will be alive by then?" joked Avtar.

"Kill me if you like," said Jay, "but I will refuse to die until I have eaten my dinner."

They all laughed, including some of the eat-in guests. In the end, they all bought an extra portion for their evening meal.

"Are we still going to the park? Or not?" asked Matt.

"How can we go to the park with our extra portions?" asked Kojo. "I am certainly not going with mine."

"Me either," said Jay. "Those who want to go are free to go; I am on my way to my room to enjoy my meal."

"Same with me," said Robinho and Avtar in unison. And so they all went back to Jay and Matt's room, including the women.

Chapter 10
A Christian PM

As they ate, Kojo said, "Seriously speaking, I see elements of dictatorship among many politicians here. I thought democracy was collective leadership by MPs and government cabinet members, but it is like they are just rubber-stamping the PM's personal agenda."

"You must understand that there is an element of dictatorship in every democracy," said Levy. "Especially when leaders in their desperation, become demagogical."

"Every leader is a dictator," said Avtar, "except that it is less pronounced in a democracy."

"It depends on the leader," said Jay. "The first executive mayor of London displayed his dictatorship blatantly. That is why a major national newspaper referred to him as *the most odious man in Britain,* and a fellow MP called him a Nazi apologist."

"Let's not talk about that man," said Lisa. "He is no better than any of the worst dictators. He is a man who publicly confessed his desire to kill an ambassador by crushing him in his car with a crane for not paying the congestion charge. Leaders are supposed to guard their pronouncements."

"That is one man who was power-hungry," said Radka. "Every billboard, every London transport and every square of public space advertised the mayor of London. Every London newscast started and ended with *the mayor of London.* All that was left was to have his statue in every public place. He even opened his own embassies in foreign countries."

"He was one hellish rebellious arriviste," said Levy.

"But Londoners liked him," said Matt.

"Indeed. Maybe that is why he lost the last election by a landslide," said Levy.

"At least he did not play hide-and-seek as the Prime Minister did," said Kojo. "The previous Prime Minister is someone I simply couldn't understand. Here was a Christian Prime Minister who had a grand opportunity to turn things around, but instead exacerbated the problems through copious anti-Christian legislations."

"What opportunity are you talking about?" asked Matt.

"The previous Prime Minister was supposed to be a Christian, who should have brought his Christian values into government," said Kojo.

"Now I know you don't like the man at all," said Radka. "Do you want him impeached? You have inferred that this is a godless nation. How then do you want him to impose godly principles on a godless people and expect to still be PM the next day?"

"A true Christian who knows what is at stake would rather resign than compromise his Christian principles," replied Kojo.

"It is easy for you to say that because you don't know the allure and glamour of public office," said Jay. "There is no temptation as great as public office. It is the spiritual graveyard of many Christians who venture into politics."

"I personally think that any wise leader would do well to stay away from any form of religious fanaticism," said Matt. "This is more important now that a religiously motivated terrorist war is raging around the world. Besides, a leader of a multifaith country cannot impose the doctrines of any particular faith on the people. That would be to deny the freedom we cherish."

"No one is talking of religious fanaticism," replied Kojo, "or of imposing any doctrine on anyone. I am talking of the natural order of things, which is the basis of all religions."

"The problem is with you, Kojo," said Jay, "for failing to understand the society you live in, despite all my efforts to educate you on this. Forget about the various faith groups and nonfaith groups in this country, and about the natural order of things. I make bold to say none of these exist here because they are not relevant even if they exist. Nature is the same everywhere. But when it comes to society, leaders make the difference; they change societies to please themselves. People's lives are altered to reflect the interests of their leaders.

"Ants and other insects have their natural order of things. Lesser animals of various species have their natural order of things, not *Hom sapiens*, especially in the British Isles. That is why there is so much argument over everything, no matter how trivial."

"That is the more reason why a Christian Prime Minister priding himself on his strong Christian conscience and moral philosophy should set the tone for the moral renaissance of the society," countered Kojo. "He often spoke of family, community and social responsibility—of compassion, soul, duty and love. These should have crystallized into a moral benchmark for the society."

"I think the man tried his best," said Levy. "It is not easy to govern. You can't satisfy everybody. The best you can do is to strike a balance by making some trade-offs, especially in a fast-changing world."

"I agree with you, Lev," said Lisa. "How do you resolve the clash between the traditionalist and the modernist onslaught on society? The only way forward, I think, is the sensitive application of the ethical values of all religions and traditions in a modern, accommodating way. Note that the keyword is *sensitive*. Call it compromise if you like, but we should be sensitive to each other's feelings. That is what I think he did."

"I don't think you people really understand the point Kojo is making," said Robinho. "It is not about projecting Christianity or any religion above anything else. It is about at least maintaining the existing moral standard instead of facilitating its demise. And morality is both a natural thing and a key doctrine of all religions, not that of Christianity alone."

"Has there ever been any moral standard?" asked Jay. "Not since I came here, at least. But in fairness to the man, I must say he was against a stone wall. The fact that his principal spin doctor was a self-confessed atheist ensured that his own spin machine closed him down on God. Add that to a hostile media that is the archetype of libertine modernism, and you will understand what I mean."

"The simple truth is that the man is an iconoclast," said Robinho. "Why should he surround himself with people who are acutely unreligious and avidly controlling? They see any allusion to God or to moral principles as offensive and patronizing."

"Did you expect him to base his appointments on sentiments rather than on merit?" asked Matt. "He had to appoint those who can deliver. Besides, every section of the community has to be represented in his appointments."

"As I said before, a society of liberal moralism, to put it mildly," reiterated Jay, "is very difficult if a leader seeks to translate his religious beliefs into concrete actions. Remember the name-calling he was subjected to by the press for his Christian undertones: *new moralist, sanctimonious, calculating hypocrite*. And he was accused of having a preachy manner, of standing on higher moral ground, and of playing God. This is a country where the press expects a leader to be very ashamed of his religious faith. Even his party is anti-Christian and overtly apoplectic to any reference to God."

"I don't believe in half measures or mere rhetoric," said Kojo. "I understand he postulated a new socialism—socialism that sees the society as a community of people belonging to one race and one family, where everybody is their brother's keeper. A true Christian perspective, I must say, but it is effusive and lacks godly principles. It amounted to taking the shine out of the Christian doctrine and projecting it as a mere vain expression. A true brother's keeper should be able to tell a brother when he is going off the tracks, not applauding him both when he is right and when he is wrong."

"You don't have to be a Christian or be religious to have such views as he had," said Levy. "They are natural and idealistic. They are the language of every politician, and we all know that idealism is different from reality." He drowned the last words in laughter.

"It is not a laughing matter," protested Robinho. "A man who often vaunted the convergence of the values of democratic socialism and those of Christianity should have taken the bold step to stamp such concept into the social psychology of the nation. It would have avidly implanted the clear understanding of what is right and what is wrong in the public mind."

"He can embark on a moral crusade," countered Lisa, "but he cannot personally execute the daily tasks enunciated in such a crusade. He has to respect the constitutional requirements by appointing a minister to execute the programs."

"Ministers more often than not dance to the tune of their masters," said Levy. "If an agenda contrary to Christian principles has already been set, there is little or nothing the minister can do."

"It is not really about an appointed Secretary of State or minister, or who the Prime Minister is," said Robinho. "The problem is that anybody can claim to be a Christian, especially if they can act and speak like one outwardly. Some of them go to church on Sundays and make reference to the Bible, but that is where it ends. A true Christian will live the Bible principles willy-nilly. He hasn't got any choice."

"You are very right, Robinho," said Jay. "There is too much pretense in all the religions. One should not be deceived by goodwill political jargon. On the surface, it is easy to align the values of democratic socialism to those of Christianity, but in practical terms, they are not quite the same. One big difference is that Christianity or Christian socialism goes with responsibility, whereas democratic socialism, especially in the current political milieu, goes without responsibility. The problem with any democratic process is that there will always be vested interests that will pollute the outcome and bastardize both the goodwill and any anticipated standards."

"Come clear, please, and make your case simple to understand," said Radka.

"OK," said Jay, "what I am saying is that when you have a radical with a modernizing agenda galloping with the speed of a conquering army, you shouldn't expect anything to survive in the wake of the rolling tanks. In effect, a politically correct modernizing polity does not gel with conservative Christianity, point-blank."

"Innit," Avtar laughed. The rest joined in the laughter.

"That is the naked truth," complemented Kojo.

"That is exactly what I was saying about hastening the demise of morality," said Robinho.

"The society is not yet ready for any moralizing agenda," said Lisa, "so it would be very difficult for any leader to embark on that now."

"I think you don't still understand what I am saying," responded Robinho. "The first of the erstwhile PM's actions was his approach to the Human Rights Act barely a year after taking office—an Act blown out of proportion of the original UN human rights charter by its protagonists, an Act that has no consideration for a victim or for morality. Once human rights are cited, a judge knows he has no choice but to bow to the defendant's wishes. It is this singular Act that rolled in the wheel of stupidity and insanity.

"Prime Ministers have come and gone, but none has deliberately wiped out moral conduct from the public mind as did the previous PM. Yet he is the one who openly professed Christianity. We didn't expect him to breathe moral rectitude on everyone's neck, but he should not have tampered with the existing time-tested laws that promote good behavior. Within a very short period of time, he abrogated all the legislation that forbade indecent and repulsive behaviors and completely erased the unmistakable line between what is right and what is wrong. All government policy was focused on *rights*, *rights* and *rights*, whether these *rights* were actually right or wrong.

"Under the rolling tank of *rights* and *modernization* came a license for twenty-four-hour liquor store and pub openings despite the destructive effects of alcohol on society. Alcohol is NHS's bottomless pit and the police's overtime-funded drainpipe. There have been concerted efforts to change *Christmas lights* and decorations to *winter lights* as part of the war against Christianity. If I may ask, does the PM's Christianity have no guiding principles?"

"The Christian guiding principle applies only to Christians and not to the larger society," said Matt.

"That may be true," responded Robinho, "but he claims to be a Christian. To be honest, his copious legislation is purely aimed at persecuting Christianity, no matter how much he pretends to be a Christian. Leaders who are overtly garrulous of any personal religious leaning are often pretenders and dangerous."

"All I can see in the erstwhile Prime Minister is a reincarnation of the life and zeal of Saul of Tarsus," said Kojo. "Saul, a Pharisee of the Pharisees, was so zealous for God that he persecuted Christians and wreaked havoc on the church, without knowing that he was the wrong zeal until his Damascus road encounter. May all who think themselves Christian transmute from the poisonous caterpillar Saul to the inspirational butterfly Paul, that they meet Christ and live."

"Your analogy is very strong and rather judgmental," Levy snorted.

"I judge no one, and speaking the truth does not amount to being judgmental," protested Kojo. "Christianity is not misguided zealousness, but understanding the Word of God and living it. The worst tragedy for any Christian is to be on fire for God, only to discover at the very end that it was the wrong fire—that you were actually fighting against God."

"The fact that the law is a respecter of no person," said Lisa, "has made the case for Christians untenable. It is really a matter of understanding."

"Understanding is precisely the point," said Kojo. "We need the government and the society to understand us and accept our way of life. Everybody knows that organizations are set up for specific purposes which are reflected in their mission statements. In the case of religious groups, these purposes are apodictic, immutable and inviolate. These are doctrines and traditions embedded in history, profound and integral to Christian social life and generally accepted in every community as a cohesive force for better living. A good government keen on promoting harmonious coexistence must recognize and respect our differences. Diversity has its own strengths and should be given pride of place in the society. Else all the talk of the gains of multiculturalism is meaningless and should stop."

"You must know that some phrases are selective," said Jay, "used by politicians for their own selfish ends. There is nothing like democratic socialism because socialism is totalitarian and there is nothing democratic about it."

"Government is free to legislate anything it likes," continued Kojo, "but must make exceptions to some legislation. Forcing everybody to do what you want them to do does no justice to the cherished freedom this country prides itself on. It smacks of Gestapo legislation. Faith groups should be exempted from complying with some laws because the society knows the stand of faith groups on issues of a certain nature and will not frown at such exceptions."

"You are being unreasonable now," said Levy. "What is justice if not equally applied, and how do you know that the government's move is not a result of complaints by some sections of the society?"

"But everybody knows the stand of the church, or indeed other faith groups, on such matters," said Robinho. "And society has accepted and lived with them for centuries. And talking about equal application of justice, if justice is to be justice, has what we have now any semblance of justice when cases are being already decided before they get to court, based on the plaintiff's community, whether as an individual or as an organization? Never in the history of the United Kingdom have Christians been so persecuted as they are now. It seems it has become a cardinal offense to be a Christian in the United Kingdom."

"And in a country that has a state church, and under a Christian Prime Minister and a queen/king who is the defender of the Christian faith," added Kojo. "Where is the much talked about religious freedom?"

"Whatever way you look at it, if a law is to be law, it must apply equally to the citizenry," said Matt. "There is no two ways about it."

"My understanding of religious freedom," said Lisa, "is the freedom to choose your religious faith. But any law in any society must be applicable to all and sundry. Why would there be exceptions?"

"I am very disappointed in you, Lisa," responded Avtar. "You are not reasoning like a final-year psychology student. Religious freedom encompasses the freedom of choice of faith groups and their core values and practices. Those practices easily identify them as belonging to that particular group."

"That has not answered my question," objected Lisa.

"The reason why there should be exemptions," said Avtar, "is that they are natural laws; they are not man-made laws. There are consequences for violating natural laws, and we should not be dragged into paying the penalty of minority choice by default."

"If there are consequences for certain actions," said Lisa, "and you don't engage in those actions, why would you pay any penalty? And who says they are a minority choice?"

"Ask our law students here," replied Avtar, "and they will tell you that the law holds you guilty by your act of commission or omission. And so it goes for acquiescence. People have been jailed for merely seeing or knowing of a crime and not reporting it."

"It is only a crime if the government says it is," said Lisa. "Until there is legislation against an act, it is not a crime."

"Aside from legislation, the issue of natural law is open to debate because of cultural differences," said Levy. "We can only talk of natural law if there is a universal standard for human behavior. Unfortunately, that is not the case."

"The concept of natural law is universal," countered Kojo. "Human relationship is based on common moral standards which govern people's behavior for the general good."

"The problem with your definition is that what is moral to you may not be moral to me," said Levy. "While there is that basic concept of morality, what constitutes standard morality varies from one culture to another. In that sense, it is subjective."

"Lev, if we have a Universal Declaration of Human Rights," said Jay, "then why can't we have universal natural laws?"

"The Universal Declaration of Human Rights is the work of the United Nations," responded Levy. "It sets the baseline code of conduct for the internal government of member states. But not every government was a signatory to it. Besides, we have seen that the articles in the Declaration are not even universal in all member states, not even in Europe, as each state has varied its own Declaration by adding clauses to the original articles."

"We are not talking of the additions," said Jay. "At least they all retain the original articles. Those articles were drawn from the natural instinct of humans to view and respond to particular issues and actions exactly the same way irrespective of individual location on earth. They are implanted in everybody's heart. That means they exist."

"I have not said they don't exist," protested Levy. "What I said is that they cannot really be said to be natural since they are not universal. The problem is that once we get addicted to a mindset, we become presumptuous and judgmental. We are inclined to define natural laws in accordance with our own perceptions, which result from our upbringing. That means they are normative. People from conservative backgrounds, especially Christians, base the concept of natural laws on ancient Greco-Judean culture and medieval Christian theology."

"I refuse to accept that explanation," said Jay. "Natural laws are applicable everywhere as nature is not limited to any particular region. It is only people in rebellious countries where there is no boundary to human behavior who will agree with your explanation."

"That is not quite true," said Radka. "We must understand that nature to a great extent is interwoven with the culture of a place."

"Whatever the argument is," said Robinho, "Christians should be accepted as members of the community. They should be made to feel that they belong. This country belongs to every one of us; no one should be made to feel alienated. That is all I am saying."

"I don't think anybody should feel alienated by the laws, natural or otherwise," said Matt. "My point is that if Christians live in this country, they have to obey the laws of the land. Simple."

"C'mon, let's not be unreasonable now," said Kojo. "We all know that the law is an ass that could be driven to wherever the State or the judge decides. It is stupid laws that result in civil disobedience, leading to radicalization and violence. Nobody wakes up in the morning and decides to be a terrorist. It starts with gradual alienation. The government often ignores the warning signs because it thinks it has the means of control to deal with any problems arising from those signs."

"They will listen to other people, not Christians," said Robinho, "because they believe Christians always preach peace and will never resort to violence."

"That is the reason the ex-PM orchestrated the greatest assault on Christian values that this country has ever witnessed," said Kojo. "And the current Prime Minister is following in those footsteps."

"Exactly what values and assault are you talking about?" asked Matt. "Shouldn't everyone have the right to live freely in the community?"

"Matt, first and foremost, let me make it abundantly clear that Christians have absolutely nothing against anybody no matter their state or lifestyle," said Kojo. "Christians love everybody of every community under the sun."

"That is news to me," said Matt rather loudly, shrugging his shoulders. "Christians. Love. Everybody." He punctuated the words in a staccato cadence to let it sink in. "What is all the argument about then?" he asked.

"Hey! Easy, boys, easy! We are not fighting," cautioned Radka.

"I know we are not fighting, but I don't like pretenders who argue for the sake of argument," said Robinho.

"I am not a pretender," said Matt, now tempering his voice. "But I don't like people forcing you to agree with their viewpoints. I also want people to avoid confusing the abbreviation PM with MP because they are two different things. Our democracy does not allow the PM to impose any legislation on the state. Legislation is an Act of Parliament by MPs' majority vote and the PM has no power to veto MPs' votes."

"Matt, that is being mean," said Jay sarcastically. "On the surface, who does not know the difference between the two? But when it comes to the nitty-gritty, how are we sure they are really not the same? Come and tell me about PM and MP—gobbledegook!"

"God save the Queen!" shouted Avtar, as both Radka and Lisa laughed hysterically.

"And BT too. Sorry, TB. Well, they are the same thing." laughed Levy, and everyone joined in the laughter. Even Matt could not hold back from laughing.

"What have British Telecom and tuberculosis got in common anyway?" asked Radka.

"Oh, you didn't get the joke," said Levy. "Ever heard of a backronym? BT and TB are the opposite sides of the same coin. Whether I call you Radka Smith or Smith Radka, I am still referring to you. So BT is the inverted abbreviation of TB; if you like, call it Time Bomb."

"Oh, I get it," said Radka. "Toning B, you cheeky lout."

"Holy Moses!" Jay shouted loudly in his deep baritone voice. They all burst into another round of laughter.

"Where did that come from?" asked Lisa.

"I don't know," replied Jay, shrugging his shoulders. "I was simply exhilarated by both Levy's analysis and Radka's bombshell and didn't know what to say—Eureka or something? Then that phrase dropped right on my lips from nowhere. But now it is beginning to make sense, for if God must save the queen as Avtar said," he said, pausing briefly, "and country"—this, he added as an afterthought—"and Toning B, then He must first send Moses of the burning bush."

The laughter heightened a bit, at the end of which Radka asked, "So what point did Lev's analysis prove?"

"There must be a bush before the burning can take place," answered Jay, still laughing. "That means the PM was first an MP before becoming a PM, so he is an MP and a PM at the same time. The same person, Matt, the same. Got it now? So, never trust political statements or abbreviations. They can mean more than what we hear."

"See how you reason like a simpleton," responded Matt. "It's pointless arguing with you."

"Don't mind them, Matt," said Lisa, trying to cheer him up. "It is only cowards who smudge people's names in their absence."

"No one is smudging the man's name," said Kojo. "To be honest, I like the man's dynamism and outgoing personality—cheerful, open, friendly and easily accessible. It is rare to find leaders with his charisma and qualities. My only point of disenchantment is that he does not understand what Christianity is; if he did, he would not have let Christians down. It is doubtful if Christianity in this country could ever again have the golden opportunity it lost under him."

Chapter 11
In the Way of Jeroboam

"Here we go again," said Matt. "I thought we'd moved on from this argument about the ex-PM. What exactly do you have against him? Go on, spill it out so we can have some peace."

"We have nothing against him as a person," Robinho said, ceding the response to himself, "but we detest his policies, which have compromised Christian principles. No organization deliberately works against the purpose for which it was established. Everybody knows what the church stands for, including its expectations and what is and is not acceptable. Now, Christians cannot wear a cross or possess any Christian symbol at the workplace or in any public place; they cannot pray for anyone, and they cannot exercise or express their faith in any form anywhere, except in the confines of their homes or within the walls of a church."

"If there is no deliberate motive to persecute Christians," said Kojo, "then asking if one could pray for a sick person, or any person, for that matter, should not attract a sack or even a caution for any medical staff. Especially if the person asked took no offense. It is no different from asking someone if he wants tea or coffee. It is a question demanding a choice, and it is antithetical that a society that exalts itself in freedom of choice could take great offense at being offered such freedom. Yet no one has ever been questioned, let alone prosecuted, for the unsolicited offering of a cigarette or alcohol to another person."

"My question is, how is a Christian Prime Minister able to sleep at night with what is happening?" asked Robinho.

"Political leaders have no conscience if you don't know," said Jay. "If they did, there would be far fewer problems in the world. They are pretenders."

"How can you say something like that?" asked Matt. "You are not even a Christian."

"Why can't he say something like that?" Robinho asked impatiently. "He doesn't have to be a Christian to say the truth. Or is that not the plain truth?"

"Robinho, don't worry; I will answer him myself," said Jay. "Matt, I am a black man, and whether of any faith or none, the black person from birth is intrinsically religious and rational, whether or not he or she agrees with this view. There are four fundamental truths about the black person: He or she is theistic irrespective of religious bias; he or she is heterosexual by nature; no matter the odds, he or she regards suicide as foreign; and he or she suffers no gender identity disorder because, being theistic, blacks are satisfied with their gender. It is England that has reconfigured black people's minds here, taking away all the natural goodness in them. No matter how long I stay in this country, I will not allow this tragic metamorphosis, an inside-out ecdysis of the mind."

"Stop making sweeping statements, and speak only for yourself," said Matt.

"As a black person, I know the inherent attributes of black people," said Jay.

"Actually, you should speak for yourself rather than thinking for every black person," said Radka, "because what you just said reminds me of how a judge keen on dismissing a Christian case in the face of overwhelming evidence formulated his own legal jurisprudence by advocating for the state to be thinking for us."

There was a prolonged silence. Then Kojo spoke, "Come to think of it, the judge is right. The state is already thinking for us. That is why we are coerced to conform to illegal legislation. And that is the very root of all the problems in this country. It is why the country has become a nanny state. Even the very basic and simple things in life evade people's ability to think and handle rationally and naturally because the state has taken over every single issue, public or private.

"Every failure is blamed on the system, on the department, on the method, etc. Where individuals are ever blamed, it is the service providers rather than the perpetrators. The government is always quick to protect the perpetrators. Scapegoatism is the only social policy that is succeeding in this country.

"In my country, people are allowed to think for themselves. It is the only way they can take responsibility for their actions. The government does not regulate or interfere with all that happens in society. To a great extent, everyone grows up to have a rational view of life, to know what is acceptable and what is not. Elements of behavior that form the basic fabric of communal existence, the unwritten constitution that defines collective responsibility and sets ethical boundaries—boundaries written in everyone's heart—not something taught in the classroom or read in textbooks."

"No, the state has to think for us," said Robinho. "That is why the present Prime Minister pretentiously referred to Christianity as *the conscience of our country* and his government as *the Good Samaritan*. He thought he was being humorous, but that is a diabolical sense of humor to the extreme. He went on to say, 'The common realm between religion and government is not and cannot be stripped of values, and hence, the Equality Bill is specifically designed to protect religion and belief on exactly the same terms as race, gender or sexuality.'

"I don't know what values he was talking about, because everyone in this country knows that his government and the majority of his party members, from the local council through to the London Assembly and the central government, are the arch-enemies of the Christian faith and Christian conscience."

"I agree with you completely on this one," said Levy, "because most of the local councils that want premeeting prayers outlawed are the government's party-led local councils."

"I wouldn't be surprised if the readmission of the ex-mayor into the party were based on his anti-Christian stance," said Kojo.

"How the duo of a self-confessed Christian PM and his successor, the son of an ordained clergyman, through the instrument of governance, deliberately trampled Christianity with such vile effrontery beats my imagination," said Robinho. "Together they destroyed the moral fabric of the society and torpedoed Christian belief in marriage, conscience and worship. I wonder the type of Bible they read if they read the Bible at all."

"It should not beat your imagination," said Jay. "I was gobsmacked when a TV celebrity called the incumbent a one-eyed jockish idiot. I was genuinely annoyed at the disrespect, but I am not sure if I still disagree with him now.

There is a saying that in the land of the blind, the one-eyed man is king. So don't be surprised."

"Don't insult us," retorted Levy. "Because the majority of us are not blind, whatever connotation you give to blindness."

"What is *jockish*, if I may ask?" asked Kojo.

"Go and find that out yourself, my friend," said Jay, laughing. "Think of north of the border. Well, Lev, it wasn't me but your own citizen who called him a one-eyed whatever. We joked and laughed about BT and TB. Now we know that GB stands for Great Britain, but if for whatever reason someone decides to personalize it as his initialism, for Great Blindness, then why are you cross with me?"

"Gorblimey!" smirked Lisa. "Political relay team GB, from T to G—Toning to Goding. I get it."

"Innit!" shouted Avtar. They all joined in the laughter.

"One-eyed leader. One-eyed leader. One-eyed leader," said Robinho contemplatively. "There is a spiritual dimension to this one-eyed thing," he said. "In the Bible, just like our ex-PM, King Jeroboam had a landslide when ascending the throne. To consolidate his victory, he set up false gods and made false priests from every class of people. He is the only king in the whole of the Bible with the title *who sinned and made Israel sin*, repeated in several passages.

"Even after his death, all the kings who reigned after he were said to have 'done evil in the sight of the Lord, and walked in the way of Jeroboam who sinned and caused Israel to sin.' So his sin became a benchmark of iniquity for all the kings of Israel after him. We are witnessing exactly the same thing here. Like Jeroboam, the previous PM, in his quest for popularity, chose the gods of the earth over the principles of the God of heaven. He forgot that popularity with the world is enmity with God, and so he set a benchmark of iniquity for all the Prime Ministers after him.

"From now on, he will be known in heaven, if not here on earth, as *the man who sinned and made Britain sin*. Mark my words, all the Prime Ministers following him, irrespective of their parties, will not be one-eyed but totally blind—spiritually and in terms of leadership. They will have eyes and will not see. And it will take the genuine repentant submission of a Prime Minister to the church to break this yoke."

"We are all entitled to our opinions," said Matt, "the TV celebrity is entitled to his own opinion. The so-called one-eyed PM is equally entitled to his opinion regarding religion and government. His views are not necessarily representative of everyone in the country. Remember, he ascended the office without an election."

"Sorry if this is a digression," said Lisa, "because I have been thinking of this for a while now. How does a mere oath-swearing ceremony take away one's Christian beliefs? How does it rob a Christian of their faith?"

"A swearing ceremony is more than a contract," said Robinho. "It is a covenant. It is what makes people what they are: husbands, wives, presidents, kings, queens, spiritual leaders and so forth. The official administering the oath is an integral part of the covenant. There can never be a football match without a referee. And the referee's actions have far-reaching consequences on the outcome of the game."

"That is very true," said Kojo. "No true Christian should engage in anything Christ wouldn't do. I know Christ would not officiate in an oath-swearing ceremony that was not righteous, for although He is seen as a friend of all and would not discriminate, He would however show His great love and would tell you the plain truth. He would simply tell you to go and sin no more. As followers of Christ, Christians love everybody irrespective of their choices, but they still tell people the plain truth: do no more what is contrary to Christ's teachings."

"There are lots of unintended consequences of living in England," said Jay, "and compromising your beliefs and values is one of them."

"It is all about rights," said Kojo. "All that seems to matter here are rights, money, alcohol and sex—every government policy and individual discussion is about rights, money, alcohol and sex."

"Yes, because those who are supposed to teach the right things," said Robinho, "are not doing their jobs. Priests here, who should live exemplary lives and teach righteousness, rather see their priestly role as employment, a means to an end. Today's preachers are seeking bread and butter instead of seeking God's face. Those under the poverty oath see it as a mere hobby. So there is no passion for Christ. Paul said, 'Woe is me if I preach not the gospel.' Only those who are called can say that. Until a priest sees himself in this vein, doomed without the fire of the gospel, his gospel will always be worldly. There will be no power, no sparks, and no signs."

"Yes, it is like literature," said Kojo. "Once the itch of literature strikes you, you will never have peace or rest until you put pen to paper and allow the ideas to gush out freely. So is the call of God, an invisible compulsion and a spiritual osmosis that binds you until allowed to flame out from the inward parts. You do not have a choice in it."

"I believe that what is worth doing at all is worth doing well," said Jay. "Either you are in or you are out. That is why I don't go to church. I don't know how to pretend. And it is worse for a priest to pretend. If I decide to be a priest, I will be like Elijah."

Chapter 12
Royal Priesthood

"You don't necessarily have to be like Elijah to be a good Christian," said Kojo. "Once you can read the Bible and let it honestly guide you, you will be all right."

"Are you saying those priests don't read the Bible?" asked Matt.

"What I am saying," Kojo responded, "is that anyone who wants the best in life should read the Bible because it is the constitution for life if only one allows it to guide his or her life. There is no other book like it."

"The sacred text of every religionist is the best book in the world," Lisa laughed. "Yet religion has divided the world more than anything else. Look at Christianity alone. Rather than fight as a family, each denomination is for itself and will not hesitate to malign another denomination if it might increase its membership. Yet they all use the same holy book."

"That is part of the problem with Christianity," said Jay, "but the greatest is acquiescence. The leaders are afraid to speak out. Worse still, they have apologist Archbishops who are rubbishing the church's centuries' time-tested beliefs, sellout bishops and priests who do not know why they are in the priesthood and, therefore, cannot protect their flocks."

"A point of correction, Lisa," said Kojo. "It is not religion that divided the world; it is logic, ideologies, philosophies and doctrines—men's ideas and arguments. That is why Jesus said that anyone who does not accept the kingdom of God as a little child will by no means enter it. None of these are attributes of a child."

"Whatever it is, I just thank God for Muslims," said Jay. "Without Muslims, there would have been a complete erosion of every natural element that makes us human in this country, not least, sanity."

"Why don't you become a Muslim, then?" asked Lisa.

"Belonging to any religion is voluntary," replied Jay, "and comes with conviction. Having been brought up as a Christian child does not put any compulsion on me as an adult to become a Christian, let alone pledge allegiance to any other faith. At present, I don't feel any conviction to belong to any religious group."

"My question I am yet to find the answer to is how Christianity suddenly lost its appeal and stranglehold on the nation," Radka said. The church has suddenly become cataplectic. What happened?"

"Bad leadership—both political and spiritual," said Robinho. "Now, according to recent statistics, only 4 percent of people attend church on any given Sunday. The culture has degenerated into deep moral decay. Vast numbers of people know nothing about the gospel and are living their lives with false hopes or no hope at all."

"The truth is that Christianity never had any grip on British people," said Jay. "From the rebellion of King Henry VIII against Catholicism to the present day, it has never stood its ground. It has always been at the mercy of the state."

"That is not entirely true," said Kojo. "There have been rebellious people here as there are in any other countries, but there have also been those completely fired up by the Spirit of God. But it has never been like this. The situation was not as bad as it is now when I came to this country, recent as it is."

"That is because you have not been observant enough," said Jay. "It was like this before you were born. Let's put Christianity or religion aside because my argument is based not on religion, but on the concept of what constitutes goodness in human nature, what I consider a summum bonum for human existence. These are traits that existed before the advent of religion; religion only came to reinforce them."

"Don't start. We've traveled that route before," said Lisa. "Don't forget the prolonged argument on cultural variations in the interpretation of what is natural and what is not."

"This is not about starting an argument," said Jay. "The majority of people in every nation of the world, including this country, agree with the basic concepts of what constitutes goodness, so it has nothing to do with cultural variations."

"I think there are still firebrand Christians in this country," said Robinho. "It is just that they seem to be in small pockets scattered all over the place, and any impacts are tiny localized pop-up bubbles."

"While still in my country, I used to regard Britain—England in particular—as the cradle of Christianity," said Kojo. "A nation of gentlemen and decent ladies where morality and common decency formed the bedrock of societal values. I used to see it as a nation where Christian values simply percolated into the national consciousness from childhood as a way of life. As a matter of fact, for some unknown reason, I used to ascribe some good scriptures in my subconscious mind to England.

"One such scripture is that which says, 'But you are a chosen generation, a royal priesthood, a holy nation, his own special people, that you may proclaim the praises of him who called you out of darkness into his marvelous light.' Where is the least sign of that now? Where is the light? Where are today's Wesley brothers, the Charles Spurgeons, the William Booths, the Smith Wigglesworths and the Oswald Chambers? Where are the nation's intercessors of today? Where are the prophets who can command the heavens to withhold rain or make the sun stand still in manifest glory of His power?"

Raising his voice, he continued, "How did God-mockers suddenly take over the entire country, from the government to the judiciary, from the press to the people and even to the church? What happened? Britain, who has bewitched you? Who made you choose darkness instead of light? Who made your hearts grow so cold that you are without understanding; that you listen without hearing, that you look without seeing and that you see without perceiving?

"Oh God, I am anguished in my soul to the point of death for Britain. Just look at the Church of England and Anglican Communion. I see it as a reflection of British Christendom. See what it is turning into. See the direction their spiritual leader is heading in—and he happens to be the spiritual leader of the Anglican Communion worldwide."

"There are many Holy Spirit-filled indigenous Anglican Christians in this country," replied Robinho. "But I can see your tears. They are also the tears of God over Britain—*tears of love*. If God were human, His heart would be broken seeing what is happening."

"Very true," said Kojo. "Everywhere you go, you see Church Street, Church Road, Church Avenue, Church Close and other church-related places and names. Those are the works of the British forefathers. Now what you see are dilapidated church buildings and relics of church-related structures and items. You see thriving public houses: Queen's Head Pub, White Lion's Head, Red Lion, Bricklayer's Arm, Thatched House, White House, etc.

"The spirit of dipsomania has taken over the whole place, so much so that even four-year-olds are referred to alcohol clinics. And life-giving children's bedtime stories have disappeared as parents stagger home late from pubs in a drunken state. Until I came to Britain, I did not fully comprehend the import of what it means for sheep to be without a shepherd."

"Kojo, don't mourn for us—mourn for yourself," said Levy. "Remember Shakespeare's 'All the world's a stage.' We all have the freedom to believe what we like."

"Yes, Kojo, you are sounding alarmist now," said Matt.

"Kojo, how do you know the Bible is a true story?" asked Lisa. "And what would you say if someone were to ask you for concrete tangible proof of God's existence?"

"Thanks for your question," said Kojo. "The Bible story is very true. No other book is like it anywhere in the world. Nature itself bears testimony to the truthfulness of the Bible. Nobody has ever doubted that Jesus walked on the face of this earth. Many names of towns and countries mentioned in the Bible still exist today. The rivers and mountains are still there. There are sixty-six books in the Bible written by forty different authors from all walks of life: shepherds, farmers, tent-makers, physicians, fishermen, priests, philosophers and kings.

"The writings span more than sixteen hundred years. Despite these differences, the Bible remains very cohesive and unified. The authors span several generations, but their stories are the same. That proves that they were inspired by a higher authority. All the predictions in the Bible have come to pass from generation to generation. And there is no other book on earth that advocates man's love for fellow man as the Bible does. No other book teaches the way of life as does the Bible. No other book reflects the love of a parent for his or her children as does the Bible.

"God's words as contained in the Bible guide our lives. There is a verse of scripture for every situation in life. Every generation witnesses its timeless truths, and it addresses every issue of life. And whether we agree or not, nothing answers the questions of life as does the Bible. All these things make the Bible unique and enough proof that it is a true story, which makes me believe in the existence of a loving God."

"Historical artifacts and archaeological sites in Iraq and Egypt and the surrounding countries are protected World Heritage sites today because they bear testimony to biblical truths," added Robinho. "The Dead Sea scrolls are the most authentic proof of the Bible stories. Both Palestine and Israel are still on our planet, and the continuing Arab-Israeli conflict as of today started in Bible times. All the predictions about the state of Israel have come to pass."

"What you have both said hasn't answered my question about God's existence," said Lisa. "All you have done is make references. I asked for a practical proof."

"Lisa, the simple answer is England," said Jay. "If God does not exist, then Christianity and all other religions do not exist and so have no history. If Christianity has no history, then England has no history and therefore is nonexistent. But we know England exists, and the fabric of its existence, including its laws, is based on Christianity. Please go and read your history."

"You don't know our history," said Matt, "because if you did, you would have known that England existed long before Christianity came to our shores. Christianity only came to England in AD 597."

"Yes, but when it came, it took hold of everything in the country: the laws and ordinances, the culture and the people's way of life," said Jay.

"Well, when or how Christianity came to England hasn't answered my question about God's existence," said Lisa. "Now, if truly God exists, why all the problems in the world when He has the power to stop them?"

"That is the crux of our discussion, the issue of the problems in the world," said Robinho. "But before I answer that, I will say that one single proof of God's existence is this: man is continually seeking knowledge. Governments, institutions and individuals are all seeking knowledge to improve society and quality of life. They are chasing that perfect state, as it were. You cannot pursue something that does not exist. And if perfection is their aim, then it exists. And if it exists, it has a source. That source is God.

"Now to your last question regarding problems on earth. God made the earth and made laws guiding everything on earth, including man. He gave man dominion over the earth, also giving him freedom of choice. Now man used the freedom to do whatever pleased him, including things that are against

God's laws. In doing that, man created problems for himself. That is why every man-made system has failed."

"But God can use His mighty power to solve the problems," said Lisa.

"Of course, yes," replied Robinho. "And He has the solution already in place, but again with freedom of choice at the disposal of man to apply those solutions. Do what is right and the problems get solved; continue in the wrong, and the solution stays waiting to be activated. In effect, God does not change the conditions of the people unless they first change themselves. It is that simple."

"It is not that simple," said Lisa, "because that does not explain why bad things happen to good people. For instance, good Christians and even God's own priests who have changed themselves for the sake of God, go through terrible ordeals in life. Why can't God protect them from such ordeals?"

"You are right, Lisa," said Kojo. "It is not that simple. We do not and cannot know everything, because if everything were known, there would be no urge to seek God. In a way, the existence of evil points to the reality of God. Jesus in John 16:12 said that He has many things to say, but we cannot bear them now. That means there are many things we cannot understand now, but these things will be made clearer at the time of God's choosing. It could be in the afterlife. The Bible says, 'For now, we see through a glass, darkly; we know in part.'"

"Yes, we don't know all the answers to the puzzles of life," said Robinho. "But if God can assure the apostle Paul that His strength is perfected in Paul's weakness, in his very pains, then there must be a purpose which only God Himself understands. That is why the book of Peter talks of exceeding joy when His glory is revealed in our pains."

"I don't understand," said Lisa. "I mean, how does that answer my question?"

"That is a paradox," said Levy. "The Bible is full of contradictions. How can someone be powerful when he is weak?"

"The Bible seems contradictory to those who merely scan through the pages in the name of reading," said Kojo. "It is very straightforward and easily comprehensible for those who study it and seek God in doing so. The words are spiritual, and you must develop the mind of the spirit to understand it. That is, you must seek God to quicken your understanding when studying it.

"Strength in weakness, as referred to in Paul's case, means that when you are in God, what the world interprets as weakness does not necessarily count as weakness before God. He will come strong for you both in the way you handle the situation and in the way you come out of it. He lives right in your pain, so you are not alone. You draw your strength from His presence in it."

"Meaning…?" asked Matt. "I still don't understand."

"I don't know how else I can explain it," said Kojo. "As I said before, if God were to solve all the problems in the world, then He would no longer be God. The mysteries of life are why God is God. Take these mysteries away and God will cease to exist in people's lives."

"Are you saying the reality of God is found in necessity?" asked Levy.

"That is just one of many ways God becomes real to some people," said Kojo. "But I want you to know that man's finite mind cannot know the deep things of life. We were made for so much more than the things of this world. We have deep hunger and thirsts that cannot yet be satisfied."

"Sometimes God's response is at the moment of His most profound silence," added Robinho. "Silence is what makes God, God. It takes only faith to acknowledge God for who He is. And faith is the unwavering trust in God, even in His silence in the face of one's greatest cry."

"You are making Christianity very difficult to understand," said Matt.

"Only to those taken hostage by the Devil," said Kojo. "Scripture says, 'God uses the simple things of life to confound the wise.' You must have a childlike faith to be a Christian."

"OK, what about science?" asked Lisa.

"What about science?" asked Kojo.

"People believe in science now," said Lisa, "because it has achieved so much. The evidence of science can be proved and is now challenging the concept of God's existence. What is the concrete proof that there is God?"

"I am surprised at you," said Kojo. "You asked the same question only about two minutes ago, and we provided you the answers. We talked of the places mentioned in the Bible that still exist, the Dead Sea scrolls, and—"

"Sure you did," interrupted Lisa, "but I am talking in relation to the challenge of science."

"I see why you were asking for concrete evidence of God's existence," said Radka.

"We thank God for science," said Kojo. "But comparing science to God is the worst mental sickness anyone could ever have. Science cannot equate to God or compete with Him. Science is a product of God's Creation, and therefore cannot measure with Him. The first thing I want you to know is that science is physical, while God is spiritual. Science is knowledge, while God is wisdom. There is a big difference between knowledge and wisdom. You as a psychology student are better exposed to know the difference. God is much more than wisdom, but I use the word in the context of simplifying things.

"God and science operate in two entirely different spheres. God is absolute, while science is not; research goes back and forth. Only recently, a Cambridge University study said that the Earth is probably 70 million years younger than previously thought. But I don't even want to talk of the age of the Earth because the Bible is clear about the age of the Earth, which completely contrasts with the figure given by science.

"Science is subject to man and thus is subject to accidents. God is not. Science is limited because the human mind is finite. God is not. The limitation of science says that two plus two equals four, but God's unlimited power says one can chase a thousand and two can chase ten thousand rather than two thousand.

"God's creations are original, while science is not; science creates from natural elements that are already there, made by God, while God creates from nothing. In fact, it is more appropriate to say that while God creates, science discovers what has been created—and it manufactures rather than creates. And there are still many things in existence created by God, waiting to be discovered by science.

"When God made man and empowered him to subdue the earth, He was in effect telling him to search and discover through science what He already had created; so science is a medium of discovery rather than creative originality. Science starts from the known in search of the unknown, while God knows the end from the beginning. Science expends a lot of resources, time, money, energy, etc.—while God is immediate and expends nothing—simple spoken Word.

"God's creations are perfect, whereas science is not. God has one manual for all His creations; science has multiple manuals for its creations. I could go on and on and on. There is simply no basis for comparing science with God.

Where do you get the raw materials to create the universe? Did science create the universe?"

"Excellent analysis," laughed Jay. "That is one hundred and one out of one hundred."

"Let science tame the weather first," said Robinho. "Science by itself offers no moral guidance or values to govern our lives. All science can do is show us how natural law works, while telling us nothing about its origin. The events described in the Bible took place in real-time and at real locations. Those locations still exist in the places the Bible describes for all to see today.

"Science has not been able to tell us who suspended the planets in space or how they are suspended. Science has not told us the origin of matter, which together with energy is said to make up the galaxies, the planets and the billions of stars—how it all began, all the wonderful things of life and nature. According to the theory of evolution, everything happens by chance.

"According to this way of thinking, all things are ultimately unpredictable and random. Yet science itself holds the likelihood of things actually happening by chance as very remote. The Bible specifically indicates that nothing happens by chance. At any rate, evolution is a mere theory, and theories are not proven facts and, so, cannot be relied on. Whatever way we look at it, nothing answers the questions of life as the Bible does, as opposed to science."

"Kojo, how can you say God creates from nothing?" asked Levy. "How is that possible?"

"Yes, how can you just list the differences between God and science," challenged Matt, "without practical evidence to make it convincing? I mean evidence of an empirical nature."

"Lev, to answer your question," said Robinho, taking over from Kojo, "God creates from nothing in that He simply speaks things into existence by the words of His mouth. He calls things that are not as though they were, and they are truly made."

"C'mon, say something that is more reasonable and tangible," said Levy.

"Why is it difficult for people to believe that God speaks things into existence?" asked Kojo. "Even on the human level, any product is first conceived in the mind, then verbalized in the various stages of development leading to production. There is today a great emphasis on teamwork. How do you communicate ideas and concepts within the team? How does the design process and the production line function without verbal communication?"

"But the raw materials are already there," argued Matt. "Where is God's raw material?"

"God's raw materials are His Word," answered Robinho.

"OK, let's leave that," said Matt. "Answer my question."

"Which?" asked Robinho.

"I am talking to Kojo," replied Matt. "I am asking for proof in the form of evidence to support his analysis of God and science. I want evidence based on facts, not assumptions."

"Facts and truths are not exactly the same," said Kojo. "We are speaking truths, not facts. Facts are research-authenticated, but truths go beyond deductions and evidence. They are the original natural order of things as ordained by the Creator; hence they are constant, ever the same. New findings can contradict facts but cannot contradict truths. And in speaking the tru—"

Kojo was sharply interrupted by Jay, who said, "There is no time for explaining anything to him. If he is not convinced by what has already been said, he will not be convinced by anything new."

"Jesus said, 'An evil and adulterous generation seeks a sign,'" said Robinho. "God has given man power to recreate, and in the success of that, man has now denied God. When a cloud of evil descends on a nation, the people place the creature above the Creator."

"True," said Radka. "There are many hidden facts and truths that cannot be evidenced. Life is too complex and mysterious for one to seek practical evidence of all issues of life. But a lot of people live by the computer acronym WYSIWYG: 'What you see is what you get.' If life is all about what we see, then rich and famous people wouldn't commit suicide. Things happen that defy reason."

"As was said before, faith is the evidence of things not seen," said Robinho. "And without faith, it is impossible to believe in God."

"That won't wash with the public," said Levy.

"Who cares?" said Robinho. "What matters is that the truth is revealed. What will make the two brothers immediately abandon their work and follow a complete stranger as Peter and Andrew did? The same was the case for James and John, who immediately left their father at the stranger's invitation. Does it make sense to immediately abandon your work and your father to follow a stranger in a culture where fatherhood attracts utmost reverence? These are not ordinary incidents, but point to a power greater than the world which the world has refused to acknowledge."

"It will not wash with the public," said Kojo, also responding to Levy, "because faith is too simple for difficulty-oriented British people to believe. They'd rather have faith in magicians, whom they can see physically, than in God."

"Until you know what the purpose of life is, you can never have faith," said Robinho.

"What is the purpose of life?" asked Lisa.

"The purpose of life is to serve God," replied Robinho. "It is to love and be loved. It is to love God and be in communion with Him, and to love your neighbor as you love God or yourself. God created man to be in fellowship with Him. That is His purpose for creating us."

"How can that be the purpose of life? What of happiness?" asked Lisa.

"There can be no happiness without love," said Robinho. "It is love that produces happiness. And love itself does not exist in a vacuum; it exists only in relationships."

"That is just too simple to convince anyone," said Lisa.

"Believe me," said Robinho, "the whole purpose of life is to love God and our fellow man as ourselves because in that is all the peace, joy and satisfaction we all crave. Minus relationship, nothing else satisfies. See, God created us for relationships; hence, He made us in His image and in His likeness so we could relate with Him. And we cannot truly love or relate with Him without extending the same in equal measure to our neighbor. It is love that fosters relationship; it is love that makes forgiveness possible—an important factor in the relationship."

"What of those who don't believe in God and yet achieve great success in life?" asked Levy.

"What the world deems to be a success may not be a success at all," said Robinho, "because it may not necessarily lead to true peace and happiness. Many people are driven by their passions or professions and have great success in their pursuits. But that is seeking their identity, their value and their security in their abilities and achievements. And these can be attained without good relationships. In fact, many successful people are very bad at relationships, and that is why many are miserable. So success on its own cannot be the purpose of life."

"Yes," said Kojo, "because success in one area is not success in other areas. It is only in love, true love, and valuing others as we value ourselves, that we find purpose. True and lasting success is only found in God because God is love. In Him alone do we find contentment irrespective of our state in life. Any other contentment is transitory and hollow."

"God is the Giver of life and of any good gift that goes with it through His love," said Robinho. "Any success or contentment outside a God-centered life results in a strong attachment to the gifts rather than to the Giver of the gifts. And such success is mere pride of life."

"There is something that Christians call kingdom mentality," said Kojo, "which is regarded as a basic concept and philosophy of life required of every Christian because it reflects the true love of God. Kingdom mentality is God's kingdom manifested on earth, with God providing air and food, shelter and clothing, rain and sun, and twenty-four-hour equal opportunities for the good, the bad and the ugly—providing these for the wicked and the merciful alike."

"That is unconditional love, deep-rooted, pure and boundless," said Robinho. "That is how we were meant to love."

"Yes, love is the reason the Son of God became man," said Kojo, "so that we, the sons and daughters of men, can become the children of God. It is love that made Christ die for us. Without the love of God, life is empty, irrespective of what we see on the surface."

Suddenly explosive laughter from Matt and Levy ripped through the air and filled the room. When it abated, Matt said, still with trifles of laughter, "That is the most ridiculous thing I have ever heard. What is the purpose of all the scramble; the rat race; the psychological armor we wear to outwit each other?"

"Good life, man, good life," interrupted Levy, still laughing. "It is to make you feel good and happy."

"Innit!" shouted Avtar with a grin.

"Matt's question reminds me of the former Prime Minister's concept of political life," said Radka. "He summed it up thus: 'Politics: noble causes, ignoble means; the plans you make and the events that turn them upside down; the untold misery and the imperfect attempts to alleviate it. How much triumph, how much tragedy, how much happiness and sorrow, would one accumulate? How many tears, and to what purpose? The purpose of life is to strive, to go through anxieties, to face the ambitions that have to be fulfilled, the dreams that would be dashed.' O how very poignant."

"His definition of the purpose of life is not what God originally intended for us," said Robinho. "Individuals sometimes subvert God's purpose in their lives because of vaulting ambition and vainglory. These are the causes of all the problems. Unfortunately, one leader's ambition affects the whole of society."

"OK, in today's world, is it possible to live a life of righteousness?" asked Lisa.

"Lisa, it is every bit possible to live a life acceptable to God," answered Robinho. "And the joy is that it is never too late. But one should not wait until the last minute, because none of us knows when the heavenly call will come."

"Which is the heavenly call?" asked Levy, laughing in mockery. "That is the Christian belief. From dust I came; to dust, I shall return—so you said. Mother Earth, guys—six feet and it's all over." He laughed more.

"That is your flesh," said Kojo. "There was no life in the flesh until God put the breath of life into it. So when you die, the breath of life, which is your spirit, goes back to tell God what you did with the life He gave you. Remember, God is a Spirit, so He relates with your spirit. God does not judge anyone; it is your spirit that judges you before God. And your spirit does not lie."

"Lisa, yes, living a righteous life is simpler than people think it is," said Robinho. "It is living a natural life that God ordained for us to live. It is an exciting fun-filled life. It is—"

"I want to hear about the fun side of it," Lisa said, interrupting. "Everybody says Christians don't have fun. They are too serious, too sanctimonious, very drab, aloof and sometimes unsociable. They say Christians shun modernism."

"That describes the very opposite of a true Christian life," said Kojo. "What people interpret as fun is not what fun really is. I know there are churches with little or no programs outside of Sunday service and weekday prayer meetings. However, there are many vibrant churches that have many exciting programs with fun-filled activities for all ages. Some programs are such that would be deemed not to be within the scope of the church's traditional framework.

"But they all add to make the church an exciting place to be. In fact, these days some churches go the extra length of teaching financial management, business management, home management, relationship skills and workplace ethics, to mention a few of the topics. They organize outings, funfairs, intellectual discourse and other social events that add value to traditional church teachings. These help to draw people, especially the young, to church. There is nothing drab or unsociable in the life of today's Christians. You just need to be there to know what I am talking about."

"Yes, it is the right place to be," said Robinho. "Living a righteous life does not deprive you of any fun or enjoyment. Oftentimes, indiscipline and recklessness are what people regard as fun. Life is interesting, exciting, joyful and fulfilling when we stay within the boundaries of God's commandments."

"There are problems associated with any form of disobedience," said Kojo, "including disobeying our parents or people in authority. There are different types of fun and various aspects of modern social life. You have the freedom to choose what type you want for yourself. And the easiest part of it is that it is all about your mind. Determine in your mind what you want and stick to it."

"What of peer pressure?" asked Lisa.

"Peer pressure is also a thing of the mind," said Robinho. "You don't follow the crowd; follow your mind. It is within your power not to allow peer pressure to have any hold on you."

"Sometimes social traits of modern life put one at odds with society," said Radka.

"Yes, one would look old-fashioned," added Lisa.

"Depending on the area of social life," said Robinho. "Aligning yourself with negative social traits of modernity can mentally enslave you. You will not be old-fashioned if you keep yourself clean and current. Righteousness does not forbid being decently trendy. No one is more fashionable than today's Christians."

"You know what I mean—typical social expectations," said Lisa.

"Are you meeting another's expectations or your own personal expectations?" asked Kojo. "God is not a Democrat, so there is nothing like popular culture with Him. The only popular culture is obedience. Nothing is more modern than a transforming life in Christ, being changed from the inside-out. Every old thing is gone, including your past sins. You are a brand-new individual, polished, glorious, special and very modern in God's eyes."

"Hallelujah," Matt said mockingly with a giggle.

"If sin will make you unpopular or unmodern, so be it," said Robinho. "Think of your climacteric years. Visit a nursing home and look for any difference between a professor and an illiterate resident. Vegetative life has no glamour, no class difference. Listen to this: 'Eye has not seen, nor ear heard, nor have entered into the heart of man the things which God has prepared for those who love him.' It is equal and opposite for those who disobey God."

"And why it is good to start young," said Kojo, "is that habits die hard. A woman who subjected herself to years of self-abuse following popular culture will resort to plastic surgery in her old age to regain the youthfulness she lost. And we know what plastic surgery does to people. The same goes for an elderly man in an unbuttoned shirt with gold-plated teeth and flashing jewelry, in an effort to recreate the macho image of a lost youth. No chance! Start early and you get used to it. Christ in you, the hope of glory. Don't wait until it is too late."

"You frighten me," said Lisa. "It seems quite hard, and to think you will live it for the rest of your life makes it even harder."

"The good news is that there is nobody who is righteous before God," said Robinho. "No matter how much we try, we can never attain His holiness. Our righteousness is filth to Him. He loves us just as we are—no preconditions. The Calvary cross has reconciled us, and our righteousness is in the abundance of His grace. We only have to surrender—a life of obedience."

"If God loves us as we are, why do we need to change?" asked Levy.

"That He loves us as we are," said Robinho, "means that He has left the door open and is waiting for us to come back to Him just as we are. He made us for Himself, but His Spirit cannot be in us until we welcome Him into our lives. Then the transformation will begin."

"Yes, when we surrender to His will, He imparts His Spirit in us to help us," said Kojo, "because we really cannot live the true Christian life without His Spirit in us."

"I get more confused by all this mention of grace and spirit," said Lisa.

"You can't learn Christianity in a day or a year," said Robinho. "It is a lifelong learning process. Even if we explain this now, you will not understand. Once you give your life to God and join a local church, you will be nurtured and will mature with time."

"And when you start reading the Bible," said Kojo, "you come under the Master's tutelage. He will teach you all truths because He is Truth Himself."

"You must be fooling yourselves to think Lisa can forego her obsessions to become a Christian," said Levy.

"There is nobody whom God cannot accept, no matter the evil or sin committed or how long," said Kojo. "He is eagerly waiting for you to run into His arms."

"She hasn't even said she wants to become a Christian," said Avtar. "She is just being inquisitive."

"I bet that the day Lisa becomes a Christian, I will become a reverend," Matt said, laughing.

"Matt, anybody can change at any time," said Radka. "So be careful what you say."

"I mean it," Matt said, laughing.

"With what I see in the world," said Lisa, "if there is hell, there must be more people going there."

"That is no reason to choose to go there," said Robinho. "And don't have any doubt and be deceived by *it*; heaven and hell are as real as the earth is real."

"I still think there is just too much to give up," said Lisa. "Suppose there is no life after death—all these self-denials would have been in vain. I honestly think I'd rather prefer to remain as I am."

"I said it! I said it!" Matt shouted, giggling.

"Lisa, believe me, there is life after death," said Kojo. "And there is judgment. But even on the assumption there is none, what have you to lose by being good? Not worldly goodness, because none of us is good enough for God. What I mean is goodness that pleases God—goodness in godliness. Either way, you certainly have nothing to lose, but much to gain upon crossing the big divide between life and death."

"You can't say either way she has nothing to lose," said Jay. "She certainly has her pleasures to lose while here on earth if she changes to your type of Christianity."

"Jay, we are not talking to Lisa alone," said Robinho. "What we are discussing here pertains to all of us, and indeed to the wider society. Don't vilify Lisa to make it seem as if she is the reason for our impromptu gathering. God has a purpose for everything. Nobody can force anyone to do what he or she doesn't want to do, or become what he or she doesn't want to be."

"I know every opportunity is an evangelistic mission for you," said Jay, "but you must know that there is nothing in Christianity I don't already know. I will go to church at my own volition, not at anybody's persuasion."

"Well, nobody can claim to know everything," said Kojo. "But even if you know, Lisa openly said she doesn't know. That is why she is inquisitive."

"And that has provided you the opportunity to convert her, has it not?" asked Jay.

"Conversion is a thing of the mind and is individualistic," said Kojo. "The little help we render is to lay bare the facts and truths, and leave the choice to the individual."

"Anyway, Lisa," said Robinho, "Christianity is a pleasure on its own. Christianity gives you a choice of what true freedom and pleasures are—a change you will treasure forever. If you don't belong to a college or a club, you don't know what it is like to be a member. So, until you welcome God into your life, you will never know how easy change comes. The first and most important thing is to give your life to God and see what follows."

"Gosh, it is seven o'clock already," shouted Levy suddenly with a yawn. "What a day this was!"

"True, the day is far gone," said Radka.

"OK," said Avtar, glancing at his watch, "it is time to call it a day." And with that, he left the room.

They all followed suit, with Levy going back to his hostel, and with Kojo and Robinho escorting Lisa and Radka to their hostel before going to their own. Jay and Matt saw Avtar off to the bus stop and waited until he had caught a bus before returning to their room.

Chapter 13
I, Me and Myself

About two weeks later, on their way from the library, Lisa and Radka started discussing a reported finding of the body of an eight-year-old girl who had been declared missing a week before. She was found to have been sexually assaulted before being strangled.

"I don't know why there is so much wickedness in the world," said Lisa.

"Men are simply evil—so evil," said Radka. "What is in that tiny little thing that a man should go into her?"

"It is bad enough to rape someone, but it is entirely another dimension of evil to kill the person," said Lisa.

"Especially an innocent child," added Radka.

"Innocent or not, nobody deserves to die such a violent death," said Lisa.

"I know, but you know how defenseless children are," said Radka. "I wonder why they can't just go away after raping a child. At least their punishment will be less."

"They are afraid the child may recognize them," responded Lisa.

"But they know they will eventually be caught," said Radka.

"No, they always think they will never be caught." Lisa frowned.

"Crimes like this are unforgivable; the perpetrators should rot in hell," opined Radka.

"Poor child; may her soul rest in peace," Lisa prayed.

"The grieving family's life must have been completely shattered," said Radka. "Nothing can replace such a loss."

"Absolutely nothing," added Lisa. "Whatever punishment the criminal is given, if he is ever caught, will not bring the child back."

"A missing child is every parent's worst nightmare until found alive and safe," said Radka.

"I wonder who will give the world justice," added Lisa.

"Only God, perhaps," said Radka.

"God!" exclaimed Lisa. She hesitated and again she said, "God!" and became silent for a short while. "How does God come into this? The world has been like this since I was born. There has never been any justice. Where is God when this type of wickedness is taking place?"

"What do you want me to say?" replied Radka. "That is the only thing I could possibly think. The world can't give justice. Governments have failed the people. All the systems of the world have failed the people. The only recourse is God."

"Do you believe in God?" Lisa asked.

"Yes, I believe in God," replied Radka.

"I am not asking if you believe God exists," said Lisa, "because I already know you do. I am asking if you believe God is interested in what happens on earth. Why is He sitting there doing nothing? I mean, how can there be God, and all these evils take place? Where is His power to protect the innocent, especially children? Where is His judgment?"

"I don't know the answers to your questions," Radka said softly. "Nor was Kojo or Robinho able to address these questions adequately when you asked them. What I hear people say is that God's judgment sometimes comes after one dies."

"That means the criminal is free to kill more and more," said Lisa. "Then what happens to the little child who is killed? She is gone and gone forever. Why did God allow her to be born?"

"None of us knows the mysteries of life," said Radka. "Some are born to die; some are born to be poor and wretched; and some are born to reach for the skies and shine like the stars."

"And some are born to be wicked, while others are born with the milk of human kindness. Why?" asked Lisa.

"There are so many devils in human skin roaming the streets," said Radka, "yet there is no way of identifying them. You can't discern people's minds. They will laugh with you at the same time they want to kill you."

"I wonder where that little girl is now," said Lisa.

"What do you mean, where she is? She is dead," answered Radka.

"I know she is dead," said Lisa. "What I mean is whether she is lying still in her small grave or is in hell or in heaven. Where else can one go when dead?

I ask in the light of what Kojo and Robinho said, assuming what they said is true. In fact, I should first ask if she will be judged because according to them, that determines where the soul goes."

"If there is judgment, I don't think she will be judged," said Radka. "I remember in the Bible, Jesus said something.... ooh, I can't remember how He said it." She flicked her right finger several times, trying to remember. "You know," she said, "whatever little knowledge I have about God was gained during my Bible lessons at secondary school. And I studied it the same way I studied other subjects—to pass my exams. Since I left my mom's country and came back here, I have never gone to church and have never opened a Bible. In fact, I don't have a Bible. Anyway, what He said is something like, 'Anyone who does not change and become like a little child will never enter the kingdom of heaven.' That indicates that children go to heaven when they die, I think."

"Is it because of their innocence?" asked Lisa.

"Maybe," replied Radka.

"That means she must be in heaven now, free from this wicked world," said Lisa. "My heart really goes out to her parents. This is not the first time something like this has happened, but never have I felt so touched."

"There is no one who will not be touched by this type of crime unless the person is not human," said Radka. Then she added as an afterthought, "Anyway, the perpetrators are not human."

"What of the man? Will he be judged?" asked Lisa.

"If there is judgment, he will be judged—maybe here or after his death," replied Radka.

"What would be his punishment after he is already dead?" asked Lisa.

"How would I know? Am I God? Or have I been there?" replied Radka. "I think you are asking the wrong person. Your drilling me will not give you the right answers. I advise that you go to a priest who may provide better answers."

"Sorry," said Lisa. "It's just that life is becoming more and more of a mystery to me. And between you and me, you are better in the sense that you have been a Christian and have knowledge of the Bible. You have been able to shed more light on these matters than I know. Tell me, do you think if the man becomes a Christian and turns away from evil, God will forgive him after all the pains and sorrows he caused?"

"I really don't know, but if what Christians say is true, then he will be forgiven," replied Radka.

"That would not be fair at all; it means there is no justice, here or in heaven," said Lisa.

"Would you rather the man continue with his killing spree, or change and free society from his evil grip?" Radka asked.

"But there are some crimes that are unforgivable." Lisa frowned. "I mean, this child did nothing wrong; she was the one violated—the one supposed to kill as an act of vengeance—yet she was the one killed. How can you fathom that? The world is not fair."

"You've said it all," said Radka. "The world is not fair, not in any area of human affairs. Mind you, Christian forgiveness doesn't go without punishment. From what I was taught in my secondary school Bible class, and according to what Kojo and other Christians have said, if man were to turn to God, he would have to give himself up. He would confess and repent of his evil ways, and he would serve the punishment the courts recommend."

"What of someone who lied or cheated, or mistreated people, or—" She was cut short by Radka's shout of annoyance.

"Lisa, stop asking questions like a kid who knows nothing! It is not all misdeeds for which you need to report yourself to the police or the courts. There are things we do which are not recorded in the statutory books as crimes but that are offenses against God. Stop doing them if you feel guilty, and move on with your life."

"Sorry for bothering you," Lisa said, apologizing once again. "If that child were a youth or an adult like us, do you think God would judge her even though she is a victim?"

"If there is God's judgment," said Radka, "I understand it does not depend on whether you are a victim or a villain. It is not based on one incident, but on the course of your entire life aside from your kindergarten years. It encompasses all the crimes and all the things that constitute sin in the eyes of God that you committed in your lifetime unless you repented."

"You see, this is what I was talking about," said Lisa. "How fair is it that a victim who dies before having the chance to turn to God is judged and punished, while the villain who turns away from evil before his death goes unpunished?"

"Lisa, I don't know. When you meet God, ask Him," replied Radka.

"How and where do I meet God?" asked Lisa.

"Lisa, we are in the same boat because I don't really belong to any religion as such," said Radka. "My secondary school Christianity was very elementary, and I have no answers to the mysteries of life. You have stretched me beyond my religious scope."

"I am sorry, Radka," Lisa said, apologizing yet again. "It's just that I am totally useless when it comes to religion. My parents never went to church once, and neither do I. At least you were once a Catholic, no matter how elementary, and your parents still go to church to date. You quoted some Bible verses a few minutes ago. I don't even know the color of a Bible. So you are far better than me."

"But you know I am not a practicing Christian," said Radka. "I guess we are on the same line on God's moral yardstick. I think I know what is going on. I guess this is an attack of conscience from our discussions almost two weeks ago at Jay and Matt's place. Maybe it will do you some good to see Kojo or Robinho. They would be of tremendous help and will be all too ready to assist if you ask them."

"I really don't know if it is a matter of conscience," said Lisa. "I can't quite place my finger on it, but since that day, I have suddenly taken quite an eager interest in knowing more about life. I don't know where it is coming from."

"Maybe they've bewitched you," laughed Radka. "Christians do have that compelling way of speaking that immediately plays on your psyche and arouses guilt."

"It is not that," said Lisa. "You know Kojo and Robinho are different from the typical Christians we are used to. There is something about them that I can't quite explain. They are never offended. I have never heard them swearing or using any foul language. It even goes deeper than that. There is a simplicity about them that is powerful and guileless. They exude so much confidence and joy, which comes from deep within, that it seems to shatter any gloom wherever they go."

"So you think it is worth having whatever they have?" asked Radka.

"Sure, girl, except for the price," replied Lisa. "It is difficult with so much temptation all around. And there are those who deliberately provoke you to test your will."

"It is all about determination and prayers, like they said," replied Radka. "They soak themselves in prayers every day. I remember one time when Kojo was talking about prayers and I said I didn't know how to pray; he taught me a very simple prayer that would never have come to my mind."

"Have you been praying it?" asked Lisa.

"Praying it?" asked Radka. "What have I ever done that is not known to you? Maybe we prayed it together—in the pub." They both burst out laughing.

"Do you still remember the prayer?" asked Lisa.

"Yes, of course," replied Radka. "Do you want to start learning how to pray? What has come over you, girl?"

"You said you have never prayed it. It is only right to ask if you still remember it," said Lisa.

"I guess you have suddenly become married to Jesus because a little girl was murdered and you are not sure if there is life after death," said Radka.

"Whatever," Lisa smirked.

"OK," said Radka. "Kojo said every morning when I wake up I should pray to God that my presence in any place should bring joy and peace, and solutions to the problems there and that my contact with other people should transform their lives for the better for themselves, for God, and for society. He said if a third of the population would say that prayer every morning and practice it, then society would be a better place for all. Such a simple prayer, yet so rich and very powerful. Not many people think or conceive of such a simple wish."

"Does prayer work?" asked Lisa.

"How would I know? I don't pray," replied Radka. "It probably works for those who genuinely pray."

"But that prayer is really not for him but for others," Lisa admitted.

"I think it is a measure of selflessness," said Radka. "Your blessing others is a measure of how blessed you are, so he often has told me."

"That is very hard and rare in a selfish society like ours," said Lisa, "where the doctrine of 'I, me, and myself' seems to be the anchor for survival."

"Maybe that is why Kojo and Robinho are so peaceful because they are not seeking any gain at someone else's expense," opined Radka. "That is love in action."

"I don't even know how to pray a simple prayer like that," said Lisa. "I thought prayer was just asking God for my needs."

"Me too. I don't know anything about prayers," conceded Radka. "I guess if I put my mind to it, I will learn pretty fast. But for now, I want to enjoy myself to the maximum. They say to make hay while the sun shines. The sun is shining for me right now. I do whatever I want, when I want, how I want, and where I want—woo-hoo, freedom unlimited. That is what I want right now, girl!"

"God, I thought you were supporting Kojo and Robinho in all they were saying that day," said Lisa.

"Sure. One doesn't necessarily have to be a Christian to speak the truth," replied Radka.

"Oh, I see," said Lisa.

"See what?" asked Radka.

But rather than answer, and in a surprised mood as they reached the point where they normally parted ways to go to their respective rooms, Lisa asked, "What are you up to tonight? Any particular club in mind?"

"What?" exclaimed Radka. "We've barely finished talking about prayers, and now you're mentioning clubbing. From being Christ's bride to a club-crawler; it doesn't gel, girl. Sorry, no clubbing until after my last paper."

"Life is sometimes difficult," said Lisa, "in the sense that even when you know the right things to do, it is often difficult to do them. Old habits die hard."

"Because nothing in life worth anything happens suddenly," said Radka. "Change, as indeed everything else, is a gradual process."

"Maybe I need to have a feel for what church is like," said Lisa. "Maybe I need to go to Kojo and ask him to take me to church this coming Sunday. Maybe I need to start the search for the meaning of life."

"Good for you," said Radka. "With all those questions, I knew this was coming. For now, that is off my agenda."

"Yesterday, while taking a seat by a desk in the library, I saw an opened book on the desk," said Lisa. "I don't know who left the book there, but something happened that beats my imagination even now. As I went to sit down, a flash of light leaped from the book, traveled straight across my face, and disappeared. I don't know if it was a reflection of some sort, but I remember it was the momentary flash that attracted my attention to the book. And guess what?

"The first text on the page that caught my eye was a statement by an American astronaut who, on seeing the marvels of the created universe in outer space, said: 'It's very hard to think this must have happened by chance. You realize at the same time that there had to be a Master Designer, a Creator of this planet. And to me that makes life all the more special. That tells me that instead of me being something that just came along in the course of time to live and die, instead of a meaningless existence, I have Someone who cares for me, who has made me and cares about me, Someone I can go to with my troubles, my cares and my joys.'

"This man was on a mission in search of knowledge. In the process, he found the Source of knowledge and of life. For unknown reasons, I just found myself glued to that page for a long time. The more I looked at those words, the more I thought of life, and what it all means.

"Eventually, out of curiosity, I picked up the book and looked at the cover and title. It is a book about astronauts in space who powerfully encountered the God who created the heavens and the earth. I was compelled to read it and spent much time doing so, flipping from the tale of one astronaut to the other. Their accounts were extraordinary and intriguing, and I have been thinking of them since yesterday, especially those first words that attracted me to the book, the words of a scientist in space who, I suppose, is better equipped to assess the existence of other beings and things in the universe."

"There comes a time when we all have to search for the meaning of life," said Radka. "I think I have as much meaning to my life as any normal human being. Right now I am on course for a goal I've set for myself, and I am focused on achieving it—passing my exams and obtaining my degree. I think contentment brings meaning to life."

"You don't understand," said Lisa. "I am contented and have meaning and purpose to my life, but what I felt, thinking about what I read in that book was far beyond mere meaning to my life by achieving certain goals. Something was suddenly nibbling away at my heart—some unanswered questions about life. I tell you, since yesterday I have never felt at ease. My mind has been racing in search of the truth. Was this a mere coincidence? Was it a divine encounter? I cannot tell, but something is happening somewhere in the cosmos."

"Sometimes, things happen that we can't explain," said Radka.

"Yes, but I think this is more than that," said Lisa. "To think that for the first time in my life about two weeks ago I inadvertently gave an audience to a religious discussion definitely means that something beyond the surface is happening. I've never participated in any religious discussion before because I don't allow it. I remember asking about the place of science during the discussion that day. Could yesterday's incident be a direct response to my question—a scientist through a page in a hitherto unknown book speaking to my inner being? Girl, my heart is burning with a series of questions. This is the reason I am asking you all these questions. I think I should go on a mission of discovery."

"With your exams staring you in the face?" asked Radka. "I wish you well on your mission, but please, when conducting your search, go to the right people for correct information. As you can see, I am the wrong person."

And with that, they bade each other goodnight and parted ways to go to their respective rooms.

***

That Saturday night, Kojo received a surprise phone call from Lisa asking if he would come and take her to church the next day. Kojo was so excited that he immediately phoned Robinho. The following day, the two young men arrived early enough at Lisa's place to ensure they were not late to church, in case Lisa was late in preparing. They were surprised to see that she was ready before they arrived at her hostel room.

At church, Lisa sat in between the two of them. They could easily see how thrilled she was to be there. She was very excited and observed all that was going on in rapt attention, not allowing anything or any stray thought to break her focus. She thoroughly enjoyed the praise and worship and was completely mesmerized by the preaching, so much so that, in the end, she wished for more.

From that day, she never looked back, but became hungrier and hungrier for God. She never missed any activity organized by the church, no matter how pressed she was for time. Although the church had given her a Bible on her first day as a welcome gift, Kojo and Robinho had bought her one each of different versions to encourage her. She was soaked in the Word of God, almost at the expense of her exam preparations. And Kojo and Robinho were ever ready to guide her in her voracious quest.

But try as she might, Lisa was unable to persuade her friend Radka to go along with her.

Part II
The Effective Fervent Prayer of the Righteous Avails Much, And His Expectations Shall Not Be Cut Off

Chapter 14
Grand Reunion

After receiving his degree certificate, and having donned the cap and gown, Kojo went back to Ghana. He had the choice to apply for a two-year work permit and seek employment in Britain, but he opted to go back to his country. With a second-class upper division from London's elite premier university, getting a job in his home country was no problem. In fact, he had a choice of three job offers but settled for a capital management outfit based in the Legon area of Accra. Robinho got a job with Goldman Sachs in their London office.

In their own case, after donning their academic gowns, Levy and Matt enrolled at a law school for their one-year law practice course (LPC). Avtar, Radka and Lisa went back in the autumn semester for their master's program. Jay also enrolled for the autumn semester but for his doctorate. He graduated summa cum laude, a first class with a difference, collecting all the prizes as the best all-round student for the year. He was consequently awarded the UCL Graduate Research Scholarship for his doctoral program in international relations.

Three years later, Kojo was in London, having been transferred from Accra by his company to head their newly opened London office. Quickly he reconnected with Jay, whom he had been in contact with since leaving London for Accra at the end of his undergraduate studies. Apart from Jay, the only person he had been in contact with was Robinho.

It was a late spring day, late afternoon; Jay was on a bus on his way to the British Library on Euston Road when a call came through his cell phone. The number on his screen was unknown to him.

"Hello," he said.

"Hello, Jay. How are you?"

"Kojo!" Jay shouted in excitement, recognizing the voice. "It is a local number you are calling from. Are you in London?"

"Yes."

"When did you arrive?"

"Last night."

"Why didn't you tell me you were coming?"

"Wanted to take you by surprise."

"On a visit?"

"Official assignment."

"How long?"

"I am here to stay, boy, even though I don't like it."

"So, it is permanent?"

"Yes."

"Where are you staying?"

"Lancaster Gate."

"Where in Lancaster Gate?"

"The hotel, Lancaster Gate Hotel, by Lancaster Gate Tube station on Bayswater Road—Room 710."

"With your woman?"

"No."

"How is she?"

"She is fine. How about your babe?"

"Cool, man, cool. Slugging it out in the race for survival."

"How's your program going?"

"Cool, man. Actually just on my way to the library. It's been tough, but I am on top of it. Can we meet this evening?"

"A bit tired now. Can we make it tomorrow? Tomorrow is Friday. We could do a lot of catching up, discussing late into the night."

"Not a one-day job, but catch you tomorrow then. What time?"

"Whatever time suits you after six o'clock."

"See ya."

"Cheers."

****

Jay stepped into the reception of the Lancaster Gate Hotel at a quarter to seven the following evening—a beautiful spring evening. He had already phoned Kojo when he got to the Tube station adjacent to the hotel, and Kojo was at the reception lobby waiting for him. They were ecstatic on seeing each other, embracing excitedly. Even after they slowly unlocked from the embrace, their hands remained locked in an unending handshake.

The shreds of their infectious laughter that knitted a web of lost time splashed across the lobby, attracting every eye and gently drawing pleasant smiles from the few faces there. This being their first meeting since the end of their undergraduate days, it couldn't have been less hilarious. They walked to the lift, chatting as they ascended to the seventh floor and walked through the corridor after exiting, heading to Kojo's room.

"You didn't bring Sandra along, or she is no longer … you know wor' I mean," said Kojo.

"No, I didn't even tell her you were around."

"Why?"

"Some other time, boy; today is just for you and me. No one else matters—and no distracting interruptions."

"Are you still together?" asked Kojo.

"Oh yes," replied Jay. "As a matter of fact, I have proposed to her."

"Good. Very good," said Kojo. "You must promise to bring her along next time."

"I promise."

On entering the room, they sat opposite each other, Kojo on the bed, on top of a plain white eiderdown, and Jay on a sofa almost directly in front of Kojo.

"You're looking good, boy," said Jay as he gazed at Kojo, before shifting his eyes, briefly scanning the room as he talked. From the entrance door was a short passageway, to the left of which was a wardrobe and to the right of which was a door to the WC and bath/shower room. The wardrobe had a sliding door with a large top-to-bottom mirror affixed to it.

"The end of the passageway led to a spacious room with a king-size bed, which was shifted to the right with the pillow end to the wall, leaving enough space at the tail end, much larger, as a continuation of the passageway down to the rear wall, which had a large wall-to-wall window with a champagne-colored curtain. Near the right wall after the bed was a reading table with a chair. Almost directly opposite the reading table and by the left wall was another table with a set of four drawers on the left side of it, then a small fridge compartment with a door on the right side. On top of this table rested a 20-inch flat-screen TV at the center, with a tray with tea/coffee set on the right. Standing on the floor between this table and the rear wall was a tall lamp stand with an ivory-colored scalloped shade.

"In between the two tables was a single-seater beige-colored leather sofa. On each side of the bedhead was a small stand-alone bedside table with drawers and enough space between the WC/bathroom wall and the bed on this side, and between the bed and the reading table on the other side, to freely move about. Each of the bedside drawer tables and the reading table had a much shorter lamp stand with a small plain pleated shade. The right side table also had a telephone on it.

"The floor was carpeted with a soft burgundy-colored carpet. Mounted at the midsection of the right wall above the bed was a framed oil painting of a beautiful seaside scene with a number of picnickers dotted on the beach, and directly on the opposite wall was another painting, this of a tranquil vast grazing field with a little shepherd boy leading a herd of sheep. The room was of cream Dulux Diamond Matt emulsion paint.

"Thank you. You are looking good too," Kojo said in response to Jay's pleasantries.

"Thanks once more for sending me your beautiful wedding pictures," said Jay.

"How many times are you going to thank me for that?" said Kojo. "I should rather thank you for the expensive gift you bought for us. Imagine the cost of parceling it."

"No gift of any size could replace my physical presence, which is the mark of true friendship. Unfortunately, it was a very busy time for me. How time flies; it's almost eight months now."

"Eight good months, boy," said Kojo, "and it looks like yesterday. One has to be in the fast lane these days to catch up with time."

"Afua was absolutely gorgeous in her wedding gown," said Jay. "It was really tailor-made to fit."

"First things first," said Kojo. "What do I offer you?"

"What can you offer me—you, a visitor?" asked Jay. "Your presence is more than enough for me, man."

"OK, let's go for dinner. What is your popular choice of restaurant?"

"I don't mind. Anywhere that suits you." Then after a slight thought, he said, "OK, what of Chinatown? It is only about five to seven minutes from here by Tube."

"Where is Chinatown again?"

"Ah, you've forgotten so soon. Remember, Soho, between Piccadilly Circus and Charing Cross Road?"

"Oh yes, I remember," said Kojo, "along Shaftesbury Avenue."

"You got it."

"Do you like seafood?"

"I eat anything as long as it is real food," said Jay.

"Which is real food, the one without meat or fish?" asked Kojo.

"I beg your pardon? I am not a vegetarian," said Jay.

Then Kojo started laughing. "You know," he said, "I really find that very funny because it never crossed my mind. In Africa, we don't have vegetarians. It is abundance that creates selectiveness. With due apology to vegetarians, tell me you will not eat meat if you go a week without food."

"What I find funny is that humans have a way of painting anything relating to them as beautiful," said Jay. "Tell me the difference between an herbivore and a vegetarian. They are the same, man—shrub-eaters. Grass, man. Grass. They want to be seen as better than animals, so they give it a posh name." He repeated the word in his baritone voice: "V-e-g-e-t-a-r-i-a-n!" Both of them laughed a prolonged mocking laughter.

"That is really very funny," said Kojo. "Yes, to Chinatown."

When they stood up to leave, Jay walked to the picture paintings on the wall, admiring them briefly, one after the other. "Boy, you have some nice paintings here. Did you request for them yourself, or is it that they knew you were a holy man and so allotted you this room?"

"Am I holy? You don't know what holiness is," replied Kojo.

When they got to the room door, Jay asked, "Is the food here very expensive?"

"Why are you asking?"

"If the food is good enough and not too expensive, I think we could do with having a quick bite downstairs and then come back to the room, instead of going to Chinatown; it is a bit rowdy there. We could go another day when Sandra is around."

"The food here is utter rubbish and expensive," said Kojo, "but I am at your service. Whatever pleases you, boy."

"No, man, rather I am the one at your service. Take it that I am the one inviting you for dinner. As far as I am concerned, you are a visitor."

"Don't forget that I am working while you are still a student," said Kojo.

"I am on scholarship, you know," said Jay. "I earn money as a graduate student research assistant. Don't forget that."

"OK, right now you are in my abode, temporary as it may be," said Kojo, "so you are my guest. I have to host you. You will host me when I come to your place."

"All right then, you win," said Jay.

"We do have nice Spanish, Italian and Thai restaurants here—by Queensway," said Kojo. "Do you like their cuisine?"

"How far?" asked Jay.

"Just a Tube station away, on the same Central Line as here. And we can actually walk down," said Kojo.

"I think I prefer oriental dishes to Spanish or any continental dish," replied Jay, "so Thai would be a natural choice for me." So they went to a Thai restaurant about a seven minutes' walk from the hotel, returning to the hotel room after they had finished. They talked late into the night, starting with the whereabouts and progress of some of their undergraduate close friends. Jay talked of when last he had seen them and what they were doing then.

"Lisa completed her master's program, got married to a pastor, and moved to the West Midlands, where she became a lecturer at a university. Radka completed her master's program and moved to Houston, Texas, for her doctoral program. After his master's, Avtar got a job with PricewaterhouseCoopers and, after nine months, was posted to their New York office. You already know that Robinho got a job with Goldman Sachs."

"Yes," affirmed Kojo. "I am still in touch with him. He has been transferred to their Manchester office and is currently doing a part-time MBA program at Manchester Metropolitan. Thank God I did my MBA at Legon; I would have been the only one left out with only a first degree among our close friends."

"Now you've beaten all of us," said Jay. "Wow, what with you heading your company's London office only three years after graduation, the sky is the limit for you, boy."

"Well, I thank God for His grace," said Kojo.

"Any plans for a doctorate?" asked Jay.

"Sure. I am enrolling in our alma mater this fall," replied Kojo. "It is good to make a dash once and for all, and forget about it rather than punctuate it. Academics are tough, and if you don't run through them at once, you will lose your zeal. It is extremely tough when you start raising a family. That is why you are in good stead. Tell me, what of Levy and Matt?"

"As I said earlier, they both enrolled at a law school here in London," said Jay, "for their one-year law practice course. On completion, Levy got placement for a two-year solicitor's apprenticeship. I have not heard of him for over a year now. As for Matt, something happened that changed his life forever."

"What happened?" Kojo asked in eager anticipation.

"He went with some friends for a night out in the East End," said Jay. "On their way back, they entered the East India Dock Link Tunnel from A13 Newham Way. Right inside the tunnel, the driver lost control and they hit the left wall, bounced to the right, bounced back to the left, and on and on until the car became a crumpled metal heap.

"All five occupants were rushed to the Royal London Hospital at Whitechapel, but the driver and the front passenger died shortly after arriving. The other three, including Matt, spent weeks in hospital. I went to visit him in the hospital when Levy told me about the accident. Boy, he was lucky just to be alive."

"When was this?" asked Kojo.

"In the very year of his LPC course, toward the end," replied Jay.

"Were they drunk?" asked Kojo.

"I have no idea, but what do you expect when people go on a night out?" asked Jay.

"Did Matt complete the course eventually?" asked Kojo.

"Oh yes, but that was the end of his legal career," said Jay.

"What happened? Did he link the accident to his studies?" asked Kojo.

"No," replied Jay. "It was what he said had happened when he passed out. He said he saw himself falling and spinning around rapidly into what seemed like a bottomless pit. He said despite the speed of his fall, the pit seemed endless, and he was very afraid and was shouting with all his strength. But the whole place was quiet except for the echoes of his shout. Then, all of a sudden, he stopped falling and was lying horizontal in the massive cylindrical pit, face downward. It was as if he were suspended by an invisible force.

"He still could not see the bottom of the pit. He was frozen with fear but had stopped shouting. Then he started hearing what seemed like echoes of wicked laughter coming in ripples from deep down in the pit and then reverberating all around and getting louder and louder. Then he saw a group of entities—like human skeletons—rising up from the lower part of the pit, bellowing hideous laughter. Smoke was gradually rising from the lower part, but he could still see the skeletal entities through the smoke, engaged in what looked like Brazilian Macumba voodoo dance.

"As they got closer, they increased in number and their laughter became louder and more demonic. Matt felt he was being choked by the smoke as well. Then suddenly the entities became a great multitude from below him and were present all around the walls of the pit. He could see them clearly, the smoke slowly fading away. They were human skeletons with red blazing eyes in their dry skull sockets and vampire fang-like teeth. They were very dry and looked very hungry. They seemed to be in a frenzy as they stretched their tiny bony hands out, trying to grab him. Their laughter suddenly changed to loud screams of excruciating pain.

"Then Matt closed his eyes and screamed as loud as he could. But he could still see the skeletons despite having closed his eyes. He said he was choked with fear and sick to the pit of his stomach. And just as they closed in on him and were about to grab him, an invisible force pulled him up and away from them. Then he screamed himself awake to find he was on a hospital bed. Having concluded it was God who saved him, he made up his mind there and then to serve Him for the rest of his life."

"That was a divine encounter," said Kojo.

"What divine encounter?" asked Jay. "The man was probably hallucinating under the influence of anesthetics, and you are here telling me of a divine encounter."

"Jay, why don't you believe these things?" asked Kojo. "Experience is the best teacher and wise people learn from other people's mistakes and experiences."

"I am not saying there are no divine encounters," said Jay, "but this was clearly not one of them—no, not with that bizarre twist to the story. Sedation or even painkillers in large doses can cause a measure of such weird experiences."

"Jay, you are an incurable doubter," said Kojo. "Supposing all I have been telling you about life and Christianity is true. In the face of the wickedness on this earth, are you prepared to spend eternity in an unending sorrow? I mean a life that has no end with sorrows that have no end. It is simply unimaginable what that sort of life is like and how it feels to be in that state of hopelessness. I pray you don't die in your ignorance."

"I am not a doubter," said Jay. "I believe in God, but I don't like people attributing everything to God."

"So who told Matt he could not serve God as a lawyer?" asked Kojo.

"No one, not even he, said that," said Jay. "He felt it was God or nothing, and opted to be a pastor. So, as soon as he completed his LPC course, he enrolled in a Bible college—an intensive nine-month course. Since then I haven't seen or heard from him. But I was told that at the end of his training, he went back to his native town of Nuneaton, where he set up a church about a year ago. I understand the church is growing rapidly in membership."

"That is absolutely marvelous," said Kojo, savoring what he had just heard. "Thank God for those who hear and obey. Lisa gave her life before I left for Ghana. Matt has given his life. Who knows how many more of our close friends we lost contact with who have changed? I knew you before any of them and have done all I could to make you understand, but nothing will change you. Well, I can only pray." He shrugged his shoulders in helplessness as he spoke.

"Maybe you are not praying enough." Jay laughed mockingly.

"Even Grant is now a pastor," said Kojo.

"Who is Grant?" asked Jay.

Kojo laughed. "You've forgotten Grant, whom you almost came to blows with over the closing and opening of windows during that human rights lecture in our final year?"

"Good for him," said Jay. "I am facing something more important now, and that is getting my doctorate."

"God, I can't believe what you just said," said Kojo. "What is more important than your salvation? Supposing you die tomorrow, what becomes of your doctorate?"

"Leave that to me," said Jay.

"No, I can't leave it to you," protested Kojo, "because life is not about swagger or intelligence. Intelligence is not academic prowess; an intelligent man is one who lives for God and allows God to guide him—his thoughts, his words and his actions. That is intelligence because God gets it right all the time."

"Thanks for the lecture," said Jay.

"What is the gain of your knowledge without Christ?" asked Kojo. "What comfort and hope did the achievements of academicians, intellectuals and the rich and famous gain for them as they lay on their deathbeds? They brought nothing and took away nothing."

"Well," said Jay, "there are those who believe that heaven is a fairy tale and don't care about the afterlife. Maybe that is where they derive their comfort."

"What about you?" asked Kojo.

"What about me?" repeated Jay. "I have never challenged God's existence or His works. So I am different."

"So you think," said Kojo.

"It is not about what I think," said Jay. "The truth is that we must live before we die, and living entails striving to make one's mark, living a better life and profiting society."

"Yes," said Kojo, "and living for God enhances your drive for a better life rather than limits it; it profits society much better. London is host to international peace conferences, but it has no peace of its own because of its godlessness."

"That is your view, not theirs," said Jay. "And even if it is their view, it is their problem, not mine."

"Listen to this," said Kojo. "There was a man who had what could be likened to a doctorate in law. He had dual nationality and was a citizen of the most powerful nation on earth at the time. He was a legislator of the highest order, was blameless in the law of the land and was an excellent orator who commanded the greatest respect of his people and enjoyed the trappings and glamour of high office.

"When he met Christ, he said he counted all his achievements and glories as dung, absolutely nothing, as compared to the excellence of the knowledge of Jesus Christ. That is how important and precious salvation is. Nothing in life or in all Creation compares to it. That man was a very wise man, a very intelligent man. His name is Paul the apostle."

"Well, he was an apostle; I am not," said Jay.

"He was not always an apostle," replied Kojo. "It was his zeal for God that earned him his apostleship."

"But according to the Bible, he initially persecuted Christians, so he is not really a good example," said Jay.

"It is true that he persecuted Christians," affirmed Kojo, "but what many people, including some Christians, don't know is that Paul had always had great zeal for God. Before his conversion, he served God according to Jewish custom. He was a great Pharisee, the separate God loyalists who loved God according to the Jewish tradition. But they were blind to the gospel.

"And it was that zeal for God that pitted him against Christians until the scales fell from his eyes and he knew his zeal for God was the wrong zeal. But the truth he had just discovered not only set him free but also set him on fire for God. And he was able to proclaim the truth that a man is not justified by the works of the law but by faith in Jesus Christ. Meditate on that simple truth."

"Can we talk of something else, please?" requested Jay. "I will change like Matt and Paul did when, under some mysterious circumstances, they met God."

"OK, it is entirely up to you," said Kojo.

"You don't know how to give up, huh?" said Jay.

"If you knew what I know about life, about life without Christ, then you would know why I don't give up so easily," said Kojo.

"But, come, how did you know that Grant is now a pastor?" asked Jay.

"Because, according to Robinho, Grant is the assistant pastor of the Manchester branch of their church," said Kojo. "He left all he had read in school to be a pastor, not just a lay Christian. That tells you there is something special about living for God."

"OK, enough of church matters," said Jay. "Tell me your plans for Afua. When are you bringing her?"

"I don't know if I will bring her," said Kojo.

"What!" exclaimed Jay, surprised. "How can you live here and leave your wife in another country? What sort of marriage is that? How long can you cope with that and with all the problems it will generate?"

"Boy, I am yet to make up my mind," said Kojo. "I've been praying about it."

"Everything is not prayer, Kojo," said Jay. "This is a simple matter of taking a decision. It is about you knowing what you want and going about it."

"Taking a decision is not that simple, Jay," said Kojo. "Everything is about prayer because even in your smallest decisions, you need the wisdom of God to decide correctly. No one knows what the next second holds except He who made that second before it arrives. So we need to consult Him to receive proper guidance to that second. Anyway, I told you how much I hated this place. I don't want my children to grow up here."

"But you don't have any child at present," said Jay.

"I intend to have children," replied Kojo, "and I must include them in all my plans from now on."

"If you hate this place that much, why did you accept the transfer?" asked Jay.

"I prayed and pleaded with the Lord for weeks, but He told me to go," said Kojo. "So I am here at His command, not by my will, and I believe there is a purpose if He said I should go."

"You talk as if you speak with Him face-to-face," said Jay. "If He says you should go, He is sending you and your wife. Or what do you think? After all, He knows you are married."

"That may be true, but I tailor my prayers to specific issues," said Kojo. "I am yet to hear God clearly on the issue of raising my children in this place. At any rate, I have just arrived and need to settle down properly before I bring my wife if I need to bring her. This will be clear by the time I am properly settled."

"Now you are making sense when you talk of settling down," said Jay. "It is not about prayer. A London-domiciled husband who does not want his wife to live in London is seeking the quickest route to the divorce courts. Every woman wants a taste of London life."

"Yes, because, one, they don't know what London is," replied Kojo, "and two, they don't know what marriage is. Marriage is not a platform for experimentation. In my country, marriage is a contract, not a convenience—a loving, holy and pious contract. And much more so for the Christian. It is an everlasting contract of love—unconditional love. It is not a pick-and-choose thing. It is waiting on God, hearing and obeying Him and raising children who are the pride of the community and of the nation. Marriage is mutual understanding based on godly principles. Bible-based marriage has clear instructions on marital ethics and relationships. Those who follow them have no regrets."

"Boy, I love your faith," said Jay.

"Thank you. Don't just love it. Live it and you will have no regrets," said Kojo.

"I will try when the right time comes," replied Jay.

"OK, if there is any right time," said Kojo. "Lest I forget, I am looking for accommodation, so please let me know when you see a good one."

"So soon?" asked Jay. "You've just arrived."

"The earlier, the better," replied Kojo.

"How long have you got in the hotel?" asked Jay.

"Three months, but it could be extended to four," replied Kojo.

"That's a long time, man. Plenty of time to get a good one," said Jay.

"It is not that they are not there," said Kojo. "But affordable ones are very rare."

"It is the Olympics and overpopulation," said Jay. "Do you have any specific area in mind?"

"Do I have any choice?" replied Kojo. "Anywhere I can get a two-bedroom flat for no more than twelve hundred pounds a month."

"You are joking, right?" said Jay. "Big executive like you? Can you get a bedsit for that amount? Wasn't it more than that before you left? You will be lucky to get something like that in London's surrounding towns. You must understand that London is one of the hottest property markets in the world."

"I know, but it wasn't as bad as this when I left," said Kojo. "OK, what of fifteen hundred pounds for two bedrooms?" he suggested.

"That looks a bit more reasonable, but only in Outer London," said Jay.

"I understand the new buildings are like matchboxes," said Kojo.

"Are the old ones better? Are they not the same?" asked Jay. "This is England, my friend. Anyway, let's not become paranoid about accommodation now. We will start a month before you are due to leave the hotel. For now, start looking for a GP to register."

"OK, but it is difficult to register until one has gotten accommodation, so one can register in the local area," said Kojo.

"You'd better register somewhere now and transfer later," advised Jay.

"I understand registering in a local surgery is now an uphill task," said Kojo, "and getting a dentist is like the proverbial camel going through the needle's eye."

"That's correct," said Jay. "So much has changed; that is why I am telling you to register now, though that does not guarantee automatic transfer to a local surgery or dentist. Everything is about the availability of space. London's population is exploding exponentially."

Chapter 15
London Tidbits

"Tell me what's been happening in London since I left," Kojo requested.

"What's been happening that you don't already know?" said Jay. "With global news networks, there is nothing we know here that is not known elsewhere."

"That is with major events," said Kojo. "The local events remain local. Tell me about politics in the country, about the London Olympics, about everyday happenings. You know what I mean—crime, economy, healthcare and all the usual tidbits. I understand that the government has greatly pegged social benefits."

"That is true," said Jay, "but it doesn't go far enough."

"At least it is better than when local councils used to pay millions in rent alone," said Kojo.

"Remember the case of the asylum seeker given an £8,000-per-month accommodation?"

"Nothing near a quarter of that anymore," said Jay. "I think the government is moving in the right direction, but it needs to go further, to force people back to work."

"Yes!" said Kojo. "But there must be a starting point. Democracy is such that if you rush your programs too hastily, you will be voted out of office sooner rather than later. That some politicians are beginning to reason with the working class is something to cheer about."

"You are right there," said Jay.

"All those women who turned themselves into baby factories will now be gnashing their teeth," said Kojo.

"Good for them," said Jay. "Child benefit has also been pegged to two children per family."

"Fantastic," said Kojo. "Exactly what we suggested the day we were discussing solutions to the social problems in the country. Remember?"

"Of course. How can I forget?" replied Jay.

"Tell me something about the London Olympics," said Kojo.

"But you already know that through the papers," said Jay.

"You know I wasn't here when it took place," said Kojo. "And local papers can't report everything. Tell me about the local news about the Olympics, from preparation to the actual events."

"OK, about the London Olympics," said Jay. "There were so many problems, but security was by far the greatest challenge. There was such panic that the government had to draft a large number of soldiers and many police officers to attend to security issues. The government's political opponents made a mincemeat of it."

"I can imagine," said Kojo. "It must have been like an invasion, like a war zone."

"Oh yes!" said Jay. "The soldiers were spread all over the Olympic Park and all the venues, and many areas. There were those in specialist roles as well."

"Soldiers in the streets at peacetime can create fear," said Kojo.

"We live in dangerous times, boy," said Jay.

"How true," said Kojo. "Today's sporting events have become real conventional warfare."

"Yes, because no place is safe any longer from the menace of those who derive joy in the destruction of lives," said Jay. "Not even prayer houses provide sanctuary for those who seek refuge in them, as was traditionally the case. The government wasn't taking any chances. Short-range missile launchers were placed on top of some high-rise buildings to shoot down anything. That is how serious it was. It shows how dangerous the world has become. Even the journey of the Olympic torch around the country was disrupted by hooligans. And for transport and safety reasons, the scheduled duration of the opening ceremony was cut short and some events were canceled."

"They really deserve kudos for ensuring the safety of the games," said Kojo.

"Increase in security concerns is going to be a dominant factor in international engagements," said Jay, "because it is no longer about terrorism alone. There are various groups hell-bent on disrupting events for no other reason than that the world has turned upside down."

"You are right," said Kojo. "Animal rights, friends of the Earth, anti-capitalist movement and many anti-establishment groups."

Jay and Kojo spent a lot of time chatting about world events and happenings both in London and other parts of the country. Then they went to bed very late, about three o'clock in the morning. Jay did not wake up until nine in the morning when Kojo woke him to get ready for breakfast. After breakfast, he went back to his hostel.

Chapter 16
A Divine Encounter

At the completion of his doctorate, Jay was employed as a lecturer by the university. He had wanted to go back to his country, but his father advised him to accept the employment as a starting point. And so he did.

Ever since returning to London, Kojo had been preaching tirelessly to Jay about the need to live an active Christian life, but Jay was not interested. However, all that changed in Jay's first year as a lecturer without anyone persuading him. His dramatic conversion was like a fairy tale from the mystic world.

There was a three-day revival conference one weekend in East London. As usual, Kojo invited Jay, but he declined. During the conference, Kojo bought a number of Christian books and collected materials for evangelism, including tracts. A few days after the conference ended, he visited Jay, telling him how the conference had gone and of the joy and blessings of meeting and fellowshipping with other Christians from various places. He presented him with a gift of one of the books he had bought.

"This is a book I specifically bought for you," said Kojo. "I hope you find it interesting. I also have a tract I am sure will do you some good." He handed him the tract as well.

"Thanks for the book," said Jay. "What is it about?"

"Oh, it is about the dramatic conversion of the author," said Kojo, "a powerful testimony of God's love and care for every one of us, believers and nonbelievers alike." Rather than appreciate the gift, Jay deliberately dropped the book on the floor and tore the tract to shreds.

"You know this sort of book doesn't interest me," he said rather angrily. "And I have told you many times never to give me any tract. I don't know why, but I just hate tracts."

"Is that why you tore it?" Kojo asked gently. "If you don't want it, you should have simply given it back to me instead of tearing it."

"I am sorry," said Jay. "I don't know what came over me." He picked the book from the floor and gave it back to Kojo. "I don't want it," he said.

"Jay, I bought the book in good faith specifically for you," said Kojo. "Keep it and do whatever you wish with it. You can burn it if you like. My prayer as always is for God to open your eyes one day. I wish to take my leave now." And with that, he walked out. Jay ran after him, apologizing.

"See, I have accepted the book," he said, "and I promise to read it. In fact, I thank you for your prayers, and I pray too that God will answer your prayers for me." But Kojo had made up his mind to leave, and so he left.

Jay sat down briefly, wishing he hadn't torn up the tract, but after a short while, he shrugged his shoulders and said to himself, "I made a mistake and I apologized; what else could I have done?" So he left it at that and went about his normal routine.

Four weeks later, on a Saturday morning, Jay arrived at Kojo's place beaming with smiles, looking very upbeat.

"What's up, boy? You look so happy," said Kojo. "Did you win the lottery?" he asked.

"I've found something much more than winning a lottery," replied Jay. "Something more precious than you could ever guess."

"Tell me, boy. You know I am not good at guessing," said Kojo.

"I have found Him, or rather He has found me," said Jay.

"What are you talking about?" Kojo asked, rather surprised. "Who has found you?"

"The Lord," answered Jay.

"The Lord?" queried Kojo, rather unsure if he had heard correctly. "You mean…?"

"Yes! I mean Jesus; Jesus has found me," said Jay.

"Holy Moses!" screamed Kojo, a bit bemused. "How? Where? When? I mean, are you sure this is not one of your usual pranks? Tell me the truth," he demanded, looking at him askance.

"I am telling the truth," said Jay.

"You want me to believe you?" asked Kojo.

"Believe it or not, I am speaking the truth," said Jay.

"How do you know it is Jesus?" asked Kojo.

"By the time I finish telling you, you will judge for yourself whether it is Jesus or not," replied Jay.

"God, this is wonderful news," said Kojo. "So my prayers have not gone unheeded."

"I know you've been praying for me," said Jay, beaming with smiles.

"For years, of course," said Kojo. "Now He has answered my prayers and I am overjoyed. So, tell me, how did it happen?"

"Boy, if someone had told me what I am about to tell you, I would never have believed," said Jay.

"Please, let's go and sit down; this is no story to be told while standing," said Kojo. Hitherto, they'd been standing near the door, where Kojo had let him in. So they moved farther in and sat on two sofas directly opposite each other. "Do I make you a cup of coffee or tea?" asked Kojo.

"No, thanks. At least not yet," said Jay. "I am too eager and excited to tell you my experiences to talk of food. It is a long story, but I will cut it short. It started precisely three Sundays ago, in a dream. A young mixed-race man—judging by his near-magnolia complexion—probably in his upper twenties, visited me in my flat. He said He had been told by a fellow student at the end of my lecture that we were from the same country Jamaica.

"So He decided to come and visit me so we could know each other formally. We then introduced ourselves to each other. He said His name was Mawshakh and that He was one of my students—a freshman. The name sounded strange, being the first time I had heard it. But who am I to start asking people the meaning of their names, especially at first encounter? And who am I to start querying the age of a freshman when there is provision for mature students' enrollment?

"Anyway, you know how dreams are. Somewhere along the line, He, supposedly my student, started teaching me. He started with philosophy—philosophy in general—then zeroed in on western philosophy, taking me through the search for reality, the nature of things, our human perceptions and views of the material world, the principles governing existence, etc.

"He did not touch every aspect of philosophy but covered such areas as epistemology, ethics, logic and metaphysics. He was a bit more extensive in His analysis of metaphysics, particularly ontology. What is particularly interesting is that as we went deeper into these subjects, His teachings became remarkably different from what I had been taught at college in these subject areas. Philosophy was not my main course of study at college, so I didn't go deep into it, but still, I knew in that dream that His teaching was completely different. Asked why the difference, He said what I had been taught was based on human perceptions and human efforts at finding meaning to life, most of which He debunked as largely incorrect.

"Then He moved to astronomy, again brushing through a broad spectrum of subtopics, but He was not as comprehensive here as He had been on philosophy. He taught and spoke with such authority that could only have come from the Creator of such knowledge rather than from one who had merely acquired it. Boy, did my heart burn with an earnest yearning for Him? His Words penetrated my entire being as nothing ever had."

"Boy, I am so ecstatic," Kojo said, interrupting. "I feel on top of the world right now."

"You haven't heard anything yet," said Jay. "That was just the first night and the beginning of many more visits. And to be honest with you, I don't know how long our stay lasted. All I know is that there was no hurry for Him to leave, either from Him or from me. As a matter of fact, if I had had my way, I would never have allowed Him to leave, because there was so much joy in His presence.

"It was so amazing and pleasurable to be in His presence that nothing experienced physically in this world could possibly compare to it. I don't know what level of peace and blissfulness can appropriately describe the feeling I had each time He visited. The warmth was simply electrifying. That first night when I woke up, I was unhappy that what I had experienced was just a dream. I did not want it to end."

"So what happened when you woke up?" asked Kojo.

"I just told you I was rather sad," said Jay. "Neither in real life nor in a dream had I ever experienced anything like that before. Throughout that day I was meditating on the visit and thinking what the dream could possibly mean. I had no inkling that it was a divine visitation. Anyway, nothing happened until the following Sunday when He visited again.

"This time around, He taught on what I perceived was religion. I say perceived because He did not use the word *religion* or refer me to any holy book. Instead, and unlike the lectures on philosophy and astronomy, He asked a series of questions and, to answer them, embarked on an in-depth analysis and exploration of the subject area, including a short brief on eschatology. The knowledge was so deep and rich that it was completely outside the scope of human intelligence."

"Do you remember any of the questions?" asked Kojo.

"Oh yes, vividly," said Jay. "The first question He asked me during the second visit was whether I was happy to see Him again. I said yes. He asked me why. I said because His presence gave me so much joy. He asked why His presence gave me such joy. I said I didn't know why, but what I did know was that there was something about Him that made me very happy when He was around.

"He then said that my happiness was based on my developing an intimate relationship with Him. From there He started explaining the issue of relationships and intimacy, and how human beings were created for relationships—relationships with people, with nature, with other creatures, with our world in general, and with the Creator. He said the relationship was the basis for living.

"What I am saying is just touching the surface, because His teaching on relationship alone couldn't have been less than three hours from my perception—that is if the concept of time wasn't an abstract metaphor in our meetings. The problem is that I can't say precisely when I fell asleep, when I started dreaming, or when the dream ended. All I could remember was when I went to bed and when I woke up; how long I dreamed was simply not within my ability to know.

"The next question He dealt with was 'How shall a young man cleanse his way?' I said by living a righteous life. He smiled, and I was very happy, thinking His smile indicated I had gotten the answer right, but He said it was incorrect. He asked me to think again a number of times, which I did, talking of holiness, humbleness, honesty, trustworthiness, kindness and forgiveness. But He said each answer, although good, was incorrect. Never once did He use the word *wrong* or any degrading phrase to nullify any untruth. Instead, He always used the word *incorrect*.

"Finally, He explained that my answers were good but not correct simply because they were all based on perceptions, and human perceptions differ from place to place. What is perceived as good and acceptable in one place could be offensive in another place. The same with holiness and righteousness. He said the correct answer was that a young man could only cleanse his way by taking heed to God's Word, seeking it and soaking his heart in it."

"That is Psalm 119:9-11," interrupted Kojo.

"He said it was the only thing pure and undiluted in any setting and not given to misconceptions. He then went on an in-depth exposition of that answer."

"Boy, to be taught by the Master Himself is something extraordinary," said Kojo. "You are blessed."

"The irony is that it never occurred to me initially that a being different from anybody else was sitting in front of me and teaching me," said Jay. "From that second Sunday night, it became a nocturnal affair, and all His teachings from that night until last Saturday were based on a human's relationship with God. It was then it dawned on me that this was no ordinary person but the Master Himself. And every day, there was that irresistible craving for His presence, so I eagerly looked forward to nightfall. So last Sunday when He bid me goodbye at the end of the session, I was distraught and very emotional because I suspected He wasn't going to come again."

"Why did you suspect He wouldn't come again?" asked Kojo.

"He had always bade me goodnight all the previous nights," said Jay, "so when He said goodbye to me last Sunday night, I held His hand and pleaded He doesn't go. But He told me He is always with me and that He has always been with me but that I had refused to open my eyes and my heart to see Him and let Him in. But now He has opened my eyes to see and my heart to seek."

"You see what I have been telling you," said Kojo.

"How would I know that you were speaking the truth?"

"Please don't go there, because you know me more than anyone else," said Kojo. "You know when I am serious and when I am joking."

"Yes, I know, but I mean, er, er..." Jay was stammering.

"No excuses; just thank God that He loves you so much," said Kojo. "Now you are convinced. Not everyone is that lucky."

"His last visit, which was last Sunday, was completely different," said Jay. "For the first time since the visits started, He came with a book that I didn't know was a gift for me. The second difference is that He taught nothing throughout that visit. Instead, He sat quietly with the book in His hand, seemingly preoccupied, as if in deep meditation or in silent prayer.

"But all the time He was looking at me with eyes full of love. Despite His silence, the same warmth of His glory was all over the place. I couldn't ask why He was silent, but just sat on my own, relishing the warmth of His presence and even enjoying the silence, because His very presence spoke many silent words. As I enjoyed His presence, an inner voice said to me, 'Be still and know that I am God.' It immediately confirmed my earlier suspicion in the week that this was God Himself.

"When it was time for Him to go, He stood up and said, 'Yours is a busy and fast-paced world. You need time frequently to be with your inner man. Today's lesson was the act of taking out time often to be in silent communion with Me.' I was shocked to realize that it corresponded with what my inner voice had told me. Then He handed the book to me and said it was His gift to me, assuring me that it represented His presence with me wherever I may go.

"I was wondering how He had known that books were my most cherished gifts. You know, nothing gives me as much joy as reading. And He could see how delighted and appreciative I was. But more important is the fact that when I took the book from Him, a small pamphlet fell from it. When I picked it up, I found that it was exactly the tract you had given me which I tore up. This time it was intact. He asked if I'd seen the pamphlet before, and I said yes. He said that, as I could see, it was indestructible because it had pearls of immeasurable value.

"Then He admonished me never to destroy anything I could not recreate, especially something I didn't know much about. I defended myself by saying I thought it was a mere piece of paper. He said knowledge is made up of words, most of which are on paper. He said words can either destroy or create and that this pamphlet carried words that were spirit and life. He said if I knew that the world was spoken into existence, I would've known how important words are and why they are indestructible.

"He repeated that I should never destroy anything, especially something I don't know much about, because I was precious in His eyes. Then He smiled at me. When He said I was precious in His eyes, I felt this sudden osmosis of warm gladness I'd never felt before well up from my inner being. I didn't know that a little tract like that could be so precious, especially in the eyes of God."

"Yes, because man's wisdom is foolishness to God," said Kojo. "A little tract like that could mean the difference between life and death—eternal life and spiritual death. It could be the difference between heaven and hell."

"How would I know?" asked Jay.

"That is why we have to be very careful and avoid hasty reactions," said Kojo. "Tell me, do you remember the title of the book He gave you?"

"Yes, and when I woke up from sleep, I promised myself that I was going to buy the book," replied Jay. "The book was titled *The Book of Life*. There was no author's name on the book; instead, below the title was written *YHWH*. I didn't know what that name or abbreviation meant, but I didn't care. I was going to buy the book whoever the author was."

"You won't see that book to buy," Kojo said, laughing.

"Don't worry, I already have it," said Jay.

"Really? You mean it actually exists?" Kojo asked, surprised.

"Yes," replied Jay. "I will tell you how I got it by the time I finish my story. Now, when I woke up the following morning I was a bit despondent as usual, reflecting on these experiences. I sat for a long time at the edge of my bed asking myself what was happening to me. Was God messing with me, or was this a genuine call of God? Was I actually talking face-to-face with God? Who am I that God should come to me? This was not just a one-night occurrence. So what was all this about? And where was the book He had given me or the tract? Was He telling me to go and buy that book?

"Just as I was meditating, I could feel His presence in the physical. The usual glow of His presence floated into the room with the now familiar warmth and incredible joy. Then something unusual happened. The walls of the room became gradually luminescent and shortly filled with a hazy cloud of very thin fog or light smoke. Suddenly, it was as if I were floating in the clouds with Him. I don't know if my imagination was running riot, but it seemed very real that there was a physical presence of Someone with me in that cloud. Call it an eidetic encounter if you like.

"Ordinarily, I would've been afraid if it was a natural occurrence, but rather than being afraid, I was reveling in it and didn't want it to end. While in that state, I heard an inner voice say, 'This book gifted to you is your daily bread; you must feed on it day and night.' A few moments after that, the cloud disappeared and I was once again sitting on my bed, all alone.

"After the cloud disappeared, for the first time since arriving in London, I knelt down and prayed. Surprisingly, the prayer flowed liberally, seamlessly and effortlessly. The last time I prayed was during my secondary school days, and I never prayed for more than three minutes because I didn't know how to pray. But that morning I was on my knees for more than an hour, and tears of joy flowed freely. Then my thoughts went to the issue of buying that book. All throughout the length of His visits, it hadn't ever occurred to me to read the

Bible. But somehow my mind just went to the Bible. So, for the first time since you gave me that Bible years ago, I picked it up, dusted it off and started reading. I read it voraciously."

"When you said the title was *The Book of Life*," said Kojo, "I immediately knew it was the Bible. But when you said you already had it, I started doubting, thinking you probably had bought a book with that exact title."

"No. It was my reading the first verse that I knew the book was the Bible," said Jay. "But that funny jigsaw of the author's name is what still baffles me. Or is it because it was a dream?"

"Not necessarily. It is a real name," said Kojo. "YHWH is the Hebrew name of God. It is the abbreviation for *Yahweh*, which is one of the many names of God."

"I am going to find out what Mawshakh means," said Jay.

"Mawshakh means the Anointed One," Kojo said, smiling.

"How do you know these things?" asked Jay.

"I know them because I go very deep into anything I do," said Kojo. "For me, Christianity is not just a way of life; it is life itself. And if it is life, I want to know more."

"Do all Christians know these things?" asked Jay.

"I don't know about other Christians," replied Kojo. "Every subject has areas that are of esoteric nature, and only the inquisitive mind dwells on them."

"I hope I will be able to discover things myself," said Jay.

"You will discover more because I know how inquisitive you are," replied Kojo. "But knowing or not knowing these things does not necessarily make you a better or a worse Christian. It does not affect your relationship with God in any way."

"It is good to know that," said Jay. "You know, when I picked the Bible that Monday morning, I didn't know where to start. So I just opened a page randomly and read the first verse that caught my sight. It read, *Your word is a lamp to my feet and a light to my path. I have sworn and confirmed that I will keep your righteous judgments.* After reading that, I said to myself, 'That must be my response to the injunction to feed on the gift book day and night.' That was the first time I had the notion that the book given me in the dream could've been the Bible.

"After reading that passage, I decided to plan my reading and studying the Bible by starting with the first book of the Old Testament and the first book of the New Testament."

"Well, you are a beginner," said Kojo. "I will teach you how to plan studying the Bible as time goes on. You must study it Lectio Divina. Your present approach is only good for a beginner."

"So that morning, I found that the more I read, the more I craved for it," continued Jay. "Now I yearn with a burning desire for His Word every second. Sometimes as I read, it's like the words are leaping off the pages. Boy, I've never experienced this feeling of peace and joy all my life."

"Welcome to our world," said Kojo, "to the club of the happiest people on earth. Christianity is like the rising sun, bringing its radiance to every face and every life. Arise and shine for your light has come. And the glory of the Lord is risen upon you."

"Amen," said Jay.

"But how come you didn't even tell me until now?" asked Kojo. "I spoke to you only two days ago, yet there was not even a hint of anything close to what you've just told me."

"I wanted to savor His teachings without any interruption. If I had told you, you would've been phoning me every day and asking questions I was neither ready to answer nor capable of answering. It was a time to be alone, reflect on life and relish His presence and impartations."

"So you haven't told Sandra?" asked Kojo.

"I haven't even seen Sandra for the past three weeks," replied Jay. "As I said, it was no time for distractions, so after the Lord's second visit, I simply told her that I needed to be alone for some time and that she shouldn't visit until further notice."

"That is frightening for a woman," said Kojo. "She probably thought you were renouncing your engagement to her, or that you were having an affair or some other crazy idea. Surprisingly, she didn't call me, as usually with things like this she would ask me if I knew why you were avoiding her."

"Yes. That's because I made sure I phoned her almost every day to reassure her that there was nothing wrong," said Jay. "But after church tomorrow, I am going to visit her and tell her everything."

"That was very clever of you," said Kojo. "Imagine allowing her to visit during the period. You would have inadvertently stopped the Lord from ministering to you, with all manner of unacceptable talk and actions. You know what I mean."

"The fact that Sandra didn't react with anger when I told her not to visit is enough proof that the Lord has already laid the groundwork," said Jay. "Sandra! Of all people to accept simple instruction without those searching, nail-biting questions? Impossible."

"So you are going to church with me tomorrow; I am so delighted," said Kojo.

"What excuse have I not to go?" said Jay. "I have already been absent long enough. From now on, there is no going back."

"Now that you have enlisted in the Lord's army," said Kojo, "my prayer is that His grace will be enough for you in all situations. May your heart beat to the drum of your Supreme Commander."

"Amen!" answered Jay.

Then they talked excitedly and reflected on a great many things, rejoicing with songs and dancing all through the day. They ate and drank in celebration, and prayed together. Jay eventually left for his flat at about six o'clock in the evening, with a gift of a new Bible from Kojo.

Jay was so excited that night that he could hardly sleep. The following morning, which was Sunday, he went to church with Kojo. It was his first time in church for many years and his very first time at a Pentecostal church service. He sat side by side with Kojo, who had obtained permission to leave his duty post as an usher in order to stay with his friend, and this for a number of Sundays. Jay was just staring like a spectator when Sunday school started.

The same happened initially when praise and worship started. But he lost his cool when the tempo of worship rose higher and higher with songs that touched the soul, backed by heavy instrumentation. He did not know when he started dancing his heart out to the rhythm of the music. He danced and sweated so much that he had to take off his suit jacket to abate the level of heat. But not long after, he sat down. When the preaching started, he actually felt much at ease as the heat eventually left him. He was in rapt attention all through the sermon. He enjoyed the service so much that the idea of time was completely lost to him. When the service ended, he wished it would continue.

"Boy, I saw you got carried away," Kojo said when they got outside and were on the way to the car. "I never knew you could dance that well."

"I never knew that church service could be so enthralling," said Jay. "It is so different from everything I have ever known about church."

"I was laughing within myself when I saw you remove your suit jacket," said Kojo. "It was as if you were oblivious to your surroundings and didn't care who was looking at you. It reminded me of how King David danced before the Ark of the Covenant."

"Why should I care when I am dancing to my God?" replied Jay. "And when the pastor was preaching, it was as if he was talking to me directly. It was as if someone had given him a dossier on my life. There was a kind of burning sensation, a kind of fire if you like, gently permeating every part of my being as he spoke, as if a God-guided laser penetrating my innermost parts.

"I can't quite describe the feeling, but I was both ecstatic and somber at the same time. It was a completely new feeling, very different from the way I felt in my encounter with the Lord in those dreams. This was more of an introspection about my past life. As pure and upright as I may have thought myself to be, I saw there are areas that are not so straightforward and not very palatable. But despite that, I can't wait for next Sunday. Now that the spark has been ignited, the flame can only rise higher and higher."

"See what you've been missing?" said Kojo. "This is life at its best. People often say we Christians are missing out on life. Now tell me who is missing out. Which do you prefer being in a church or being at a nightclub? Which is a better enjoyment? One feeds a life; the other satisfies an impulse. One ends in the joy of living; the other ends in a mess."

"Ignorance is truly a disease," said Jay. "I never knew there were churches like this in town. The music is so different from the usual requiem-like church music, which seems to invoke pity rather than joy. I saw the joy on everyone's faces, and the warm welcome extended to me especially when I stood up as a first-timer here. How I wish all churches were like this."

"You won't know, boy, unless you try them," said Kojo.

"Why all that crap I see on TV? It discourages people from visiting any church," said Jay.

"If you watch Christian channels frequently, you'll find that there are many good ones among them," said Kojo. "But watching TV is not like being there. And if you visit a church a number of times and you don't like what goes on there, you change. You are not chained to any church. It is God's Spirit that guides one to a particular church that becomes home to that person. That should be the prayer of anyone hungry for God."

"What amazes me is how easy it is to be living the wrong life and think one is living good," said Jay, "all because things seem to be going well with the person."

"That is why the Bible says, 'There is a way that seems right to man but the end is destruction,'" said Kojo.

They walked on until they got to the car. Kojo took control of the wheel, both having come in one car. The conversation continued.

"Although God grabbed me directly by Himself," said Jay, "I can't underestimate your role in it. I mean your unrelenting prayers for me. Imagine if you hadn't given me that tract."

"It was neither the tract nor me doing anything as such," said Kojo. "It was God's timing, and we owe Him all the gratitude and the glory for finding mortal men to be useful instruments in His hands to reach the world."

"Every day, my mind searches for the deep things of life," said Jay. "It just dawned on me that this may be the reason God sent you back to London. Because I remember how much you hated life in London, to the point of refusing a good job offer that others could only dream of."

"I am not sure of that. He could have used anyone," said Kojo.

"Yes, but you made yourself available," said Jay.

"It is not a matter of me making myself available," said Kojo, "because so many people are available. If I played any part in it, then it is simply that He chose to use me."

"Stop arguing, Kojo," said Jay. "You have been on my case longer than anyone else would ever have been."

"In that case, I give Him all the glory," said Kojo.

"Now all your preaching over the years is beginning to make sense," said Jay, "and it's all coming back fresh in my memory."

So the conversation went on until they got to Jay's place, where Kojo dropped him off before heading home himself. That afternoon Jay visited Sandra and narrated everything to her. But he did not immediately start coercing her to become a Christian or even to attend church with him. He just told himself that the transformation Sandra would see in him would do the talking.

***

Jay was enjoying his new life and becoming very passionate about God and Christianity. Within three months, he had volunteered as a helping hand in the church. Everything about his life had become centered on church and God. It didn't take long before his fiancée, Sandra, voluntarily started following him to church, despite her previous strong resistance to Kojo's attempts at evangelizing her and Jay.

They were now both very hungry for God. Their newfound faith made it easy for them to develop a new approach to their relationship and to life in general. Since they lived separately, it was easy for them to resolve never to lie in the same bed until they were married. Though only occasionally present at nightclubs previously, they had now stopped going completely.

Their relationship took on a whole new meaning, reflecting the love between Christ and the church, unselfish and total. And all along their new journey in life, Kojo was there to guide and support them. He was very instrumental in their rapid growth in the Christian faith.

Chapter 17
Jay's Thesis

I. The Fire of Desperation

Ever since becoming a committed Christian, Jay had become more and more fervent in church activities and in his relationship with God. He had volunteered as a church worker, lending a helping hand in the media department.

From his first year in his doctoral program, Jay had been contributing articles to some newspapers—local and national—on various issues. But no sooner had he become a Christian than the style of his articles changed. They started reflecting on the Christian viewpoint. And surely, but gradually, he started championing the Christian cause, sensitizing the Christian conscience to the increasing atheism and the increasing incidence of persecution of Christians in society.

It got to a stage where many of the papers stopped publishing his articles because his arguments offended their permissive views. But a few ethnic minority papers were happy to gain the privilege of publishing him. In addition, he started speaking engagements in different churches and began calling for Christian unity in confronting Christian marginalization and persecution. Before long, many church leaders started recognizing him as a true Christian leader, one with no selfish motives.

On his return to London, Kojo had formed an interdenominational prayer group and had tried hard to draw Jay into it, but to no avail. The group had grown to a large membership. Jay eventually joined this group after becoming a Christian and rose to become one of the leaders. They held their meetings every Wednesday evening.

At this particular Wednesday meeting, Jay was to lead. It was usual to start with praise and worship. On this occasion, he had written out his own choice of the first song to be sung on a sheet of paper, which he distributed to everyone present, before the normal congregational singing of other worship songs. He started by saying, "This song is titled *Let the Fire of Your Wrath Rain on Britain*. I want you to sing it to the same tune as *The Rain of Your Presence*. So, let's go, shall we? One, two, go." They started singing:

Let the fire of your wrath rain on Brit'n
Every day in this world—
Unless she repents.
Send the fire of Your presence to work
In all areas of her life.
Lord, let Your fire glow.
Rain on her.

Fire divine sorrow unspeakable,
Overflowing in her soul.
This heart of hers
Is rebellious and unruly.
In Your justice.
In Your justice.

Let the fire of Your wrath rain on her
Every day in this world.
Lord, let Your fire glow.
Rain on her.

At the end of praise and worship, Jay prayed, "Father, anoint my lips that utterance may be given me to boldly declare Your Word to empower Your people for victory. And let Your Word as a fertile seed in the ears of Your people be firmly planted in their hearts to bear good fruits. Father, let Your fire burn this country! Let Your fire burn this country! Let Your fire burn this country! Let it consume everything that denies the knowledge of God. Let—"

He was interrupted by Kojo, who had gently walked up to the rostrum from his seat in the front row, reserved for the leaders, to whisper into Jay's ear.

"Jay, stop! Stop! What are you saying?" Kojo whispered. "What has come over you? Why are you channeling all your energy today into the fire? Fire is violence; fire is destructive." The hall was quiet and watching, not knowing what Kojo was telling Jay.

When Kojo had finished, Jay said aloud, "Sorry, church. My colleague here wants me to stop talking about fire. So I am going to hand this prayer meeting over to him to conduct since I am being denied the freedom to choose my topic."

"No, I don't want to take over," Kojo said loudly. "It is his turn, and he is free to preach on any topic. What I am saying is that he has to be careful what he prays for, because as a child of God, his words are anointed and they carry power—power over life and death. As Christians, we can only pray for good, not for evil."

"Thanks for your warning, Kojo," Jay said gently. "As a long-standing committed Christian, you are the last person I would have expected to say what you are saying now. Today I am preaching on the fire of desperation, which is the fire of God. It is not a physical fire but a prayer fire. I am calling for fire and violence, but not violence as the world knows it. It is spiritual violence manifested in the physical but not of physical origin. And if I call for God's fire on this country, is there no cause for it? And what is evil in calling on God's fire to fall on a country such as this? Is there no cause?

"Answer me, Kojo, because you were a Christian before me. Tell me what country on earth has swum in and drunk from the ocean of sin as this country has? You could as well ask why Elijah in the first chapter of Second Kings called on God's fire to burn the king's two batches of fifty men with their captain. Yet what caused their deaths is less than what is happening in Britain today. And because the prophets of the land have refused to play their role, Britain has been given to the Devil himself to govern.

"Hence, the leaders consult him over every issue. And men who should have called on God to send His fire are reclining in sanctimonious passivity and relishing submarine religiosity. In every age, the saints have been compelled to reprove kings and rulers, reprove erring priests and people of substance, at the risk of their lives. Our generation cannot be different.

"As for violence, should we actually shy away from talking about it when every day it rears its ugly head on our streets? We live in an era of fire and physical violence, so we must not run away from preaching about it."

Putting his persuasive oratory to best use, Jay spoke with excoriating bluntness. "Please know that I am not calling for a riot or for anyone to resort to physical violence. I am calling for the fire of prayers, prayers that are packed with fire that produces results. Not the usual pleading for God's mercy and blessings on a nation. That way of praying is no longer yielding results. It no longer works in this country. It worked when men feared God when society openly abhorred evil and rid itself of evil with immediate retribution for the evildoer when life and issues of life were sacrosanct. But such is no longer the case.

"Today, society is offended by decency and morality. It openly promotes and glorifies evil and all its ramifications. It is so soaked in evil that the gentle prayer for mercy and peace is unable to penetrate its hardened bark. It needs the fire of God to sear the carapace of sin and liberate the soul. So we should now be praying for God's wrath to fall on this country to teach them a lesson. There can be no transformation without a purifying fire. The fire has to come first before the transformation.

"Violence and terrorism are two different things, especially spiritual violence. The result of an earthquake is worse than the result of terrorism, yet it is neither terrorism nor violence in our connotation of violence. The Bible says, 'A fire goes before him and burns up his enemies.' That is the fire I am talking about—the fire of the Spirit of God. Dark forces have taken over Britain and are snuffing out the light of the gospel and robbing the people of their peace. Because peace is not necessarily the absence of conflict; it is the presence of God."

He paused briefly, scanned the entire hall with his eyes and said, "I have news for you, church. This prayer meeting is over. First things first. Many Christians do not quite understand the basic concepts of Christianity, so let us go back to basics. We must address and understand the relevance of God's fire as a deliberate Christian action in a rebellious society. As Christians in this country today, this is not a choice we have to make. It is a compulsory component of the Christian faith if we are to survive as a people within British society. Let me first ask if I have your permission to proceed."

There was a deafening "Yes!"

"OK, let me start by saying that in discussing this, we are likely to exceed our usual prayer meeting time, so if you are bored or tired at any time, feel free to leave." He paused and looked at his watch, his visage darkening noticeably as a mark of his seriousness. He glanced at the audience as if assessing their mood and then fired on, his oratory and mastery of his topic coming on in full force.

"What is the kingdom of God without His fire? How did Jesus empower the New Testament church? By tongues of fire resting on them—and they were filled with the Holy Spirit. Without the Holy Spirit, there can be no true Christianity, and the Holy Spirit does not exist—or appear—without the fire of God. Jesus Himself said He came to send fire on the earth—and wished it were already kindled.

"When the Bible talks of a new creation as a born-again child, it is talking of the presence of God's fire in His Spirit that now dwells in you. Now I am talking of spiritual fire, but even in physical terms, if it will take the fire of God to restore sanity to this country, what is the problem with that? When the guardianship of public morals is taken over from religious authorities by an atheistic political class, who hunt down and eliminate moral virtue and replace it with legalistic political correctness which they cannot define or control but can direct at will, what is there to lean on and what hope is left?

"God's word says, 'We shall all be tested by fire,' our work that is. And your work is your faith. He will pass you through the fire to be refined as silver and tested as gold to be of any use. So shall this country be if it is to be revived? It needs the electric shock of the fire of God, physically or spiritually, or both. And we are the agents of that fire, that awakening.

"Some years ago, western and pro-western megaphones clogged our ears with their own phrase: *Arab Awakening* or *Arab Spring*. Today, we should be sounding the alarm bells to initiate a *British Awakening* because Britain is a country that sees the rags and the deceased state of other societies but does not see her own nakedness and deadness. Britain is a hypocritical country that sings the funeral dirge of other nations but doesn't see her own carcass. And the reason is that the church has long been too reticent; it has been too silent.

"The country's prophets who should speak out have long been hiding under the falsehood of piousness, wearing the cassock of turning the other cheek. They fail to understand that Jesus often spoke in parables and that the society of His day was neither impulsively violent nor overtly given to depravity and injustice. Please know when to turn the other cheek, for everything has its season. Turn the other cheek and you will be roasted alive by an insane society. Why don't you pluck out your eye each time it offends you because the Bible says so?

"You must understand when Jesus is speaking figuratively and when He is not. When He talked of a mountain moving when you order it to do so in faith, He was not talking of a physical mountain. He was talking of the mountains of fear, of sickness and disease, of worries and troubles, and of failures. Please seek the ear of the Spirit when reading the Bible, because turning the other cheek is an admonition on how much we are required to forgive.

"No other religion can tell you to love your enemies. And in obeying this injunction, we are taken as fools and trampled upon. The admonition to turn hatred around and return good for evil requires you to exercise your Christian powers—your faith-packed prayers—for a better society, and not turn the other cheek as a dumb lamb for the slaughter.

"Praying for spiritual reorientation of a society is not the same as praying for forgiveness before I get accused of deviating from the gospel of Christ. Yes, we should pray for God to change the people, but if they refuse to acknowledge God, how will they be changed?

"It is perhaps OK to turn the other cheek or pray for your enemy, but when a mighty nation comes with the legislative power to destroy you, there is no time to turn the other cheek or to pray for your enemy. When your business and your means of livelihood are taken from you by the legislative force, it is no time to turn the other cheek.

"That is the time to call down fire from heaven as Elijah did, a time to speak tongues of fire that rain down a firestorm from heaven, a time for the church to stand its ground and remain relevant to the day's world without compromising its doctrines. Today's church in this country has form but no substance. It is religion without reality, and it is talks and talks without power. Take the flame of the Olympics, for example.

"Some years ago, this city hosted the Olympic Games. The games lasted only seventeen days, but the torch relay went around the UK in seventy days—more than four times the duration of the games. And it covered a whopping distance of 8,000 miles before the actual games commenced. The Olympic flame signifies the values of peace and brotherhood, which are the basis of the Olympics. It was a fire flame, but it was a flame of peace. Ours is a flame of holiness and righteousness, which brings the only peace that truly abides. For such a flame, why are the igniters afraid of the fire of ignition?

"The fire of God is the resting place of the believer. What do you understand by 'The kingdom of God suffers violence, and the violent takes it by force?' Let's put the issue of the fire of God in perspective before I get accused of incitement to violence. Today's Britain is a country that is grossly irrational and intolerant in interpreting issues and people's statements. Forget about the much-vaunted freedom of speech; it doesn't exist here.

"Speech is only acceptable when it falls in line with their preconceptions. Short of that, the press, the entire establishment and even some English Christian clergy would rain tons of bricks in response to it. But I fear no assault, verbal, physical, or spiritual. If God has appointed me, He will ensure I carry the assignment through. I live for God. And if I live for God, I must dissipate the fire of God. Jesus died on the cross, and death on the cross is violence. It is a fire of immensurable proportions—the only justifiable fire that could take away God's wrath on humankind for a holy reconciliation.

"So, putting the fire of God in perspective, let's reflect on the following: Moses saw the burning bush, but the bush was not consumed. The fire that consumed Elijah's sacrifice did not consume the people. The three Hebrew boys were in the fire but were not hurt and didn't smell of fire when they came out. These three examples are just a few of the many incidents of God's fire of transformation of people recorded in the Bible. In each case, the fire prepared His servants for a great victory that led to great national transformation.

"So, when I sing or pray for the fire of God to fall on this country, I am speaking in line with the Word of God. It is not a physical fire, but a spiritual fire that purifies. And if it turns out as physical fire, so what? Let it consume the reprobate and disobedient mind. This country has sunk to a level that requires a sweeping holy fire to physically consume everything for any goodness to return. And those who should call down the fire of God should not be afraid to call it.

"We have to take a stand. We must let the establishment know that we will not stand idly by while they legislate the destruction of this country in the name of rights and freedom. We will be active participants, albeit in the spirit realm. We will use the power of prayer to set this country ablaze. And the good thing is that, unlike physical violence, our own is spiritual violence to pull down strongholds.

"Spiritual violence that no one can be held responsible for its physical manifestation, as people do not believe in anything that cannot be scientifically proven. If ardent militant Christianity is what is needed for us to survive in this country, why are we afraid of it?

"I don't think you people know what we are up against, for if you did know, your blood pressure and body temperature would be as high as Everest. If Jesus says we are in the world but not of it, why are we afraid to confront the issues in the world that are affecting us? We are treated as people of no consequence. We are denied our rights. We are perplexed, persecuted, mistreated and pressed on every side, yet we are quiet, waiting for Muslims and other faith groups to fight our fight for us.

"When such a thing happened to Paul and the early Christians, they refused to be defeated. They refused to despair, refused to be crushed, refused to feel forsaken or destroyed. As long as we remain Christians, we will always be delivered to death for the sake of Jesus.

"But our inward selves should be renewed day by day, by the fire of the indwelling Spirit in us, the fire that makes us more than conquerors in fighting back and claiming what belongs to us. We should carry the war to the enemy camp, not relishing in self-pity and blaming every organ and agency of the establishment for our plight without first putting up any resistance."

Jay smiled, took some steps and shook his body to display his dancing prowess. Then he continued, occasionally pacing up and down the podium, gesticulating and changing his facial expression to engage his audience.

"It is amazing that we have Christian MPs but it is only the Muslim MPs, few as they are, who always speak out each time the establishment lands its crane on our beliefs and principles. We have an all-party group of MPs called Christians in Parliament who are supposed to represent Christian interests but are there doing nothing. Of the 650-member Parliament as of the time the governing party, in the guise of a modernist agenda, launched its offensive against Christianity.

"There were only eight Muslims and at least two hundred and nineteen Christians or pro-Christian members, yet these so-called Christians were silent, and still are silent, in any debate and either vote alongside government or abstain when voting in favor of government legislation that nullifies and rubbishes any Christian principle. They all choose their party lines rather than their Christian principles. It is Muslims who raise issues with the antireligious stance of the establishment. Christians in positions of authority are silent or, at best, post a feeble response.

"At that time, twenty-six Anglican bishops sat in the upper house of Parliament—the House of Lords—as against three Muslims. What difference did their presence make then, and what difference does it make now? How many times have they voiced opposition to the government's onslaught on Christians and on Christianity? Satisfied with their exalted position—unable to put their denominational house in order, afraid to challenge the government's misuse of legislative powers, and unwilling to suffer any criticism or lose any fringe benefits—they sit in pharisaic complacency, quenching the fire of the Spirit and waiting for the end to sing their Nunc Dimittis.

"But there shall be no rest or peace, here or hereafter, not when true believers raise their voices to God for His fire." He paused momentarily and slowly looked from one corner of the hall to the other as if checking the mood of his audience. The hall was dead silent, and all eyes were on him with a look indicating they were yearning for more. Encouraged, he fired on.

"Lame-duck bishops and lame-duck Christianity will result in the peace of the graveyard, as we are witnessing in today's Britain. It is the peace of the graveyard that gave rise to aggressive but lopsided and oppressive political correctness. It gave rise to aggressive atheism. It gave rise to lame-duck bishops defending the call for sharia law to be introduced in Britain. It gave rise to increased foreign aid at a time of severe austerity—the reason why £650 million was given in aid of education to an Asian country only four months after tuition fees were tripled by the government, to rob our children of the opportunity to be educated.

"And this was at a time when the recipient country was spending two and a half billion dollars annually on its nuclear arms, instead of education. But if the easiest way to attract western aid today is through violence, who can seriously argue against it? That is arguing against one's home nation's interests. Such arguments would have worked against the said education aid. The peace of the graveyard is the reason aggressive government cuts, tax burdens and unprecedented job losses were saddled on the citizens—to raise money for foreign aid.

"It is the reason our government continues to pay benefits, despite severe austerity, to foreign citizens of fourteen different countries living in their own countries, through a system of loaded cashpoint cards in what is called the Benazir Income Support Program (BISP), named after a one-time Pakistani Prime Minister, while we are taxed out of breath. And all fourteen countries are mostly of one religion, and it is not Christianity. This is the reason some citizens want to remain jobless, to have enough time to engage in clandestine activities, at home and abroad, and to participate in the uncompromising agitation to free citizens arrested for various crimes at home and abroad. It is the peace of the graveyard.

"It is responsible for silence being the only politically correct language in Britain today. Any honest, reasonable and noble idea or language is termed phobic and offensive. Only persecution of Christians is not phobic and not offensive. The peace of the graveyard stops any use of reason and any discussion or debate on issues affecting any community known for its peaceful disposition. The peace of the graveyard only listens to violence, and spiritual violence is the fire of God.

"The fire of God is what set God's people free from Egyptian slavery; it freed the three Hebrew boys from a Babylonian furnace, and it restored the people's confidence in the power of God on Mount Carmel. Without fire, there is no gospel. The baptism of the Holy Spirit is fire, and without the Holy Spirit, there is no gospel. Fire is violence. We shouldn't allow this country to drift to a level where it loses its conscience or is perceived as the fount of evil in the world.

"A poll on the state of decency in Britain said, 'The culture shows signs of deep moral decay, and the decency decline rate is at 70 percent.' The decline was attributed to the fact that only 4 percent of people attended church on any given Sunday. That was long ago; only God knows what the rate is now.

"This was once the greatest missionary-sending country on earth, but now vast numbers of people know nothing about the gospel and live their lives with false hope or no hope. Yet there are Christians in the land who should have made all the difference.

"Violence in any form, physical or spiritual, is the only language that commands attention. It attracts immediate response. It was Paul's violence against the church that attracted the attention of Jesus and brought Paul to salvation. It was Paul's spiritual violence that brought many souls to Christ and extended salvation to the Gentiles—to you and to me.

"Governments all over the world—including the British government—use violence to make the people submit. Democracy has not changed that. It established the council tax; enforced the tripling of tuition fees; and enforced other antipeople legislation. The power of the state is used through the police to forcefully make the people comply. They talk about the full force of the law as if the law were not man-made, made to suit the powers that be. Protestors are arrested, prosecuted and penalized for opposing any obnoxious law.

"What is that if not violence? Those in power violently use the power of legislation to rob you of your money to give to undeserving people in the name of social inclusion, to give to causes you completely disagree with and to persecute and prosecute you with their obnoxious laws. That is making you as a taxpayer pay for the bullet they use to kill you. They talk and use emergency powers to stem anarchy, which they originated in the first place with their evil policies. Anything emergency is the result of violence, my friends.

"How did Britain become an empire? How did it take the lands of other nations thousands of miles away? How is Britain able to dictate what happens in the Cayman Islands and many other places? What is fueling neocolonialism, which is still a dominant force in the twenty-first century? How do you see a country that destroys your infrastructure and way of life, and kills your people, in the name of freeing you from yourselves? As the custodians of civility, why can't they do these things without violence?

"Because the owners of the land themselves listen only to the language of violence. Violence is the only law they have ever known and is the only law they obey. But when the scales fell from their eyes, the people started fighting back. And they are getting their way by civility? No, by violence. It is the only language their oppressors understand. It is the reason why those who loathe western education are using western technology to make their voices heard. Do you blame them?

"No, blame those who made the technology and used it to impose themselves on the world. Not only that, but also, having used their God-given knowledge to develop those technologies and achieve success in many spheres of life, they now want to oust God and take His place—not to do the work of God, but to rubbish it; Satan's track record. Knowledge without wisdom is dangerous and destructive. And wisdom that does not come from God is no wisdom at all because wisdom is the ability to see and interpret things through God's eyes. And like Satan in Ezekiel 28:14-17, Britain has corrupted its wisdom for the sake of its splendor.

"That is why all its border posts and entry points are very well designed and adorned with so much beauty and splendor: to deceive. They are aesthetically designed and spatially equipped to give a feel of entry into heaven, but that is where it ends. They allure as the last bus stop to heaven, but they are actually the entry points to hell. A country's wealth is not measured by its values but by its values. 'The prosperity of fools destroys them,' so says the Bible, and 'Thou hast broken the yokes of wood, and made yokes of iron.' That is what Britain has done to itself."

II. Church Gone Commercial

"We live in a society that takes offense at every pronouncement that does not favor their self-righteousness. I may be an immigrant, but I am as British as anyone born here could possibly be. The difference is that I am not myopic. Is that to say British people are myopic? Not at all. But they have been conditioned to complacency. To 'Take it or leave it,' and 'Not open to discussion.'

"So, let every British person in this hall and every sane British person anywhere in the world know that I have absolutely nothing against the British in saying what I am saying here. As a Christian, I cannot hate British Christians, who are my true brothers and sisters irrespective of color or race, so I can't speak evil of them. But any true Christian is expected to speak the truth, and that is what I am doing. I am an avid British patriot given to sincerity of purpose. I can never stop emphasizing the fact that only the truth can set one free.

"So I have the freedom to speak the truth as speaking it gives me that freedom. The problem with the world is that running away from the truth makes us afraid, and fear makes us run away from the truth. To be honest, I bless God for the true British Christian. Let me quickly clarify one point here. For every British Christian, you must know that you are, firstly a citizen of heaven—and that citizenship takes precedence over whatever temporary nationality your birth certificate passport or name.

"So, whenever I speak of the ugly side of British attitudes, you are exempted because you are here in transit. Remember, you are in the world but not of the world. You are a new creation—separate from British pollution.

"The case can be argued that religious extremism is the result of political extremism. The problem with British society is that it is a society of mass hysteria that knows not when to stop. Seemingly, it will continue in this vein until it reaches the precipice. This is what is happening to Christianity today. But we must know that those who want peace must prepare for war because the establishment has forgotten that those who make peaceful negotiation impossible also make violent confrontation inevitable. Violence is war and war is violence—conventional or unconventional.

"I hope the government will desist from pushing its persecution of Christians beyond the limit. Today in this country, the kingdom of God suffers violence, and those who should be extremely angry—as to take what belongs to them by force—are playing hide-and-seek in order not to offend. And the unbelievers have violently taken over the church of God and are playing ball with it."

He paused, gazed at the audience intently across the auditorium from left to right and asked, "Can anyone explain to me why the same Jesus who said to turn the other cheek also said the kingdom of God suffers violence and the violent takes it by force? If He tells you to turn the other cheek, why did He say the violent takes the kingdom by force? If Jesus acknowledges that the kingdom of God is being run over by violent people, how can He tell you to turn the other cheek? Is a ban on fox hunting an invitation for foxes to organize a dancing competition in a hunter's kitchen?"

The hall exploded in laughter. Jay continued when the laughter died down. "What do you understand by Jesus' admonition to 'be wise as the serpent and as harmless as the dove?' The serpent, often frightened at the sight of a person, will attack at the slightest sense of danger. And we know how deadly a serpent's venom is. If you know that as a Christian, you are a sheep in the midst of wolves, then you will know when to act as a dove or as a serpent.

"I think a lot of Christians read the Bible upside down. Hence, they don't understand what it teaches. They do not pray for the ears of the Spirit before they start reading. Look at this scenario: the crowd thronged around Jesus, but He could sense that power went out of Him when the woman with the issue of blood touched His hem. Notice that many people touched Him as they milled around Him, but power only went out of Him to heal the woman, because the woman's touch was different.

"It came with spiritual violence, which is faith. There is no doubt that she violently pushed her way through the crowd to get to Jesus. She would have wasted her energy crooning like a dove on the periphery and then would have gone home disappointed if she had turned her chance—her other cheek—over to the source of her ordeal. But today that is what British Christians are doing—having the appearance of godliness but lacking His power.

"Nothing but violence ripped off the roof of a house for the paralytic to get to Jesus. And British Christians will be wasting their time waiting for God to fight their battles. The power of Jesus was available to heal these people, but it never did so, until they forced their way to Him. God has the power to, but He will not fight for you until you invite Him into the battle. He does not force His way into anyone's life but only responds to your invitation, your call. If nations have gone to war over an affront to just one of their citizens, don't you think heaven will go further than those nations over the plight of its own citizens?

"For British Christians, the risk is in not taking any risk at all. Until Christians are ready to storm Parliament and ready to go to prison, they will continue to suffer injustice. If they like, let them keep deceiving themselves under the pretext of quiet resistance. The story was told of an African country where the dictatorship of a military leader got to a head, and the citizens—of different religious faiths and of no religion at all—united in prayer as the only solution to their problem.

"Not in their worship houses or in their private closets alone, but everywhere, including marketplaces, where buying and selling stops automatically at specified times—twelve noon, for instance—and everybody prays, with activity resuming after prayers. At the midnight hour, the dictator collapsed on the staircase of his fortress without anyone firing a shot. Now that is what I call spiritual violence. And we have the privilege of the midnight hour at our disposal, waiting for us to act.

"Because the midnight hour, being a spiritual phenomenon, is only available to Christians. It is a phrase that utterly confuses the enemy. We are the children of light, the light of the world, but there can be no light without fire. Death on the cross is violence, and it took the violence of God to raise Jesus from the dead, casting the man-placed stone away with deadly force. Ever seen a volcano spilling cold lava? If so, then it is no volcano.

"If God so loved the world that He gave His only Son, and this society hates God and His Son, how do you expect it to love you when you belong to God? Society has never loved Christians; it is just that it is getting worse. So let's examine why it is getting worse. If we are honest with ourselves, then we will see that we are partly responsible for what is happening to us.

"British churches have disgraced Christianity and need serious purging. Many churches don't deserve to exist or be designated as churches. Many do not represent God. They are self-serving, causing embarrassment and problems for the church as a unitary entity. Churches are giving unbelievers enough reasons to be scared away, enough reasons to mock and criticize Christians, enough reasons to blaspheme the church, and enough reasons to persecute the church.

"People run to church as a house of refuge to receive compassion love and freedom from various burdens. Instead, they are taken captive and become more burdened as they are used abused and left hopeless by some churches. Many Pentecostal churches, especially some of the ethnic minority ones, have become commercial enterprises as men and women of God seek Hollywood glamour and lifestyles.

"For those who have ears, listen: death ends the glamour here for the glamour seekers and ushers in true glamour for those shunning it here for God's kingdom. And His kingdom is an everlasting one. The commonest Pentecostal phrase today is *my ministry*, with each ministry doing its own thing, building its own empire and preaching the gospel of the trinity of I, me and myself—or me, my spouse and my children. James 1:27 says, 'Pure and undiluted religion before God is to keep oneself unspotted from the world.'

"I am not saying every Pentecostal church is like that, because there are a number of them that stand before the throne of grace preaching the true gospel of Christ, and we thank God for them. But there are many churches with preachers who were never called. They can't express themselves in simple correct English; they simply bulldoze their way and gatecrash into the pulpit for filthy gain. I once went to a church in North London where during the offering you are asked to empty everything you brought to church into the offering basket.

"All your money, including your bus fare, in the days of cash bus fares, should go into the offering basket and then you must pledge any money you have at home or in the bank. You are asked to test God. Who can test God? Yet we are asked to test God by preachers who usurp and adulterate God's mind when it comes to giving. God's house turned into a commercial venture—in Jesus' words, a den of thieves.

"The greatest psychological warfare of all time is in some of London's Pentecostal churches, solely for filthy lucre. Here many churches have become pharisaic, replacing sound doctrine with feel-good theology and preaching grace as a license for foolishness. Many have assumed the role of a social club and have allowed secular humanism to take over Christian ethics, reminiscent of the Nicolaitan church. The widow's mite was voluntary. It was not psychological coercion. Giving should be voluntary, joyful and pleasurable, not compelled to happen through guilt.

"Know this, church: money does not buy salvation. Jesus' gifts are free. Not even a tithe or offering can save anyone. All your giving must go with righteousness. What pleases God is a broken spirit and a contrite heart. The Bible warns church leaders thus: 'The heads thereof judge for reward and the priests thereof teach for hire, and the prophets thereof divine for money; yet will they lean upon the Lord and say, 'Is not the Lord among us? None evil can come upon us.' Let everyone be warned.

"As much as the issue of money is outside the scope of my presentation, let me say this: the metaphor of seed sowing in many Pentecostal churches is systematically and fast replacing the gospel of righteousness—an allegory pushed beyond the limit and started in the United States, where everything is money. It has corrupted a great number of churches in Africa, the Caribbean and South America, and was recently imported into Europe and now is overblown by many copycat money-minded preachers.

"In this country, a church is a registered charity and should act as such. There are crises everywhere and the world has never been in greater need. The church needs money to survive and accomplish its mission, but its money should never be used for one individual's personal aggrandizement. Jesus admonished us to first seek the kingdom of God and His righteousness before anything else. Pastors ought to be more financially accountable to their members, perhaps with an open audited annual financial report.

"In all honesty, preachers deserve to live a good life, but everything should be done in moderation. The lust for money should never be the motivation for setting up a church. Salvation is the foundation and anchor of Christianity and it is free. Anything else is secondary. We thank God for those pastors who act out the true gospel of Christ in a practical demonstration of their compassion for the poor and vulnerable. The Bible says that godliness with contentment is a great gain. We should realize that all our acquisitions, including our most cherished treasures, will one day end up in a refuse dump whether we like it or not.

"Everything came from the earth and to earth shall it all return, including us humans. Gehazi was to be a great prophet but traded his anointing for worldly riches and ended up cursed. But Moses shunned a palatial life of luxury in Pharaoh's Egypt for the sake of the Promised Land.

"Jesus freed captives by casting out tormenting spirits with His commands. Today, some preachers use physical violence and all sorts of gimmicks to simulate freedom from tormenting spirits—all for self-glory. Lives are destroyed in the effort to garner glory for self. Christians evangelize on church premises. Christ said He came for the lost, not for the saved.

"But Christians who are afraid to go and evangelize on London streets in order not to offend go to other churches to steal their members in the name of evangelism. Why go for the already saved? How sorry I am for the church in the United Kingdom. The Bible says, 'The kingdom of God is not meat and drink, but righteousness, and peace and joy in the Holy Spirit'."

Jay paused and dabbed his face with his face towel. His face was stern, his eyes piercing the audience with a blazing fierceness. The hall was dead silent. Then, in continuing, he upped the tempo to heighten the seriousness of his message, mesmerizing the audience with his oratory. There was tension in the air, with a sense of urgency and expectation, as they were held spellbound by his message.

"For the mainstream churches, the fire of God was extinguished long ago. But I want to focus on the Anglican Church—the Church of England—because it has proved itself to be the main scourge of the Christian church of God in the United Kingdom. As the Established Church, it is supposed to lead and give the Christian church direction with a big voice in the affairs of this country. It is so full of discrepancies that it is difficult for it to stand as a force to be reckoned with.

"There are three faults easily identifiable in the establishment of the Church of England.

"The first is that the Prime Minister nominates the Archbishop, who is appointed by the monarch. So the Prime Minister who may not be an Anglican and may not even be a Christian at all chooses someone he or she would be comfortable with. Effectively, the Prime Minister, rather than the monarch, is the Defender of the Faith, yet he or she may know nothing about the Christian faith.

"The second problem is the issue of allegiance. The new Archbishop takes an oath of allegiance to the monarch. So the monarch's personal interests become the Archbishop's guiding principles, rather than the church's Holy

Spirit-inspired principles. Already we can see a conflict of interest in the attempt to please two masters—the monarch and the Prime Minister. God is relegated to the background. Don't tell me the Prime Minister chooses from a list selected by a church commission because that is a mere formality.

"If this were not the case, then the Prime Minister would request the name of only one candidate chosen by the Church. In addition, any major decision taken by the Church of England synod has to be ratified by Parliament—members of which are mostly secular—before becoming law. A house divided against itself cannot stand, and that is true of the Anglican Church. It cannot speak with one voice on any issue. There are always dissenting voices no matter how clear and straightforward an issue is—or how trivial.

"There is no church, not even the Mushroom churches that has its clergy so highly opinionated on every issue as the Church of England. As universal and vast as the Catholic church is, it shows much agreement and consistency. The Church of England has fallen victim to the same unprofitable secular arguments that are full of sound and fury but signify nothing. Psalm 104 says that God makes his ministers a flame of fire, but instead of enkindling that fire, the English clergy have extinguished it through profane and vain babblings and contradictions of what is falsely called knowledge.

"When ministry loses its passion, it becomes an empty profession. There is no doubt that the Church of England has fallen victim to the same indiscipline that has bedeviled British society. I think the entire British realm from every angle is truly jinxed.

"The third defect is the embedded element of politics in the Church's establishment. Making the monarch the Defender of the Faith is to use a misnomer because a faithless or a lay monarch cannot defend the Christian faith. It is perhaps this absurdity that confers on the Prime Minister the right of a de facto Defender of the Faith by appointing the spiritual head of the church. A surrogate Defender of the Faith holds a bad omen for the church. The reason is that the Prime Minister is a politician, and we know what politics is and what politicians are like.

"Let's forget the lies, the deceits, the power and all the trappings: politics is glamour. There can be no politics without glamour. Politicians the world over have their heads stuffed in cloud nine. So when the Defender of the Faith allows worldly glamour to obliterate the defense, the enemy moves in like a flood, because there is no standard against it—no spiritual flood barriers. It is this lack of standard that is destroying the Anglican doctrine and clogging the heads of the Anglican clergy with a myriad of unbiblical philosophies.

"Perhaps their refusal to relinquish the title of Defender of the Faith awarded to them by the Catholic church for the king's defense of the Catholic faith against Martin Luther's Reformation is forever hunting them. Since 1521 to date, they have held on to the title even though they no longer defend the faith by rebelling themselves, so it has become a mere slogan. Hence it has no fire and no relevance.

"The doctrine of the Christian Church is the same the world over, but some Anglican bishops and priests are misrepresenting the doctrine and misinterpreting the Bible, either under the spell of the Devil or for the sheer fun of it. There are so many examples, but given to shortness of our time today, I will give you just two. I was watching BBC's *Question Time* program one Sunday on a high court ruling banning prayer at council meetings.

"An ordained Church of England priest in his full priestly regalia said the ban was good because he does not believe in prayers or in God. Asked why he became a priest if he did not believe in God, he said that he believed Jesus was a good man, but he did not believe that God actually exists. What a paradox!"

A rhythm of hushed puff of disbelief and surprise echoed all around the hall.

"Church, do you see what we are dealing with?" Jay continued. "To believe that Jesus is a good man means He exists, and if He exists, then God exists for Jesus is God. It does not take rocket science for a non-asphyxiated brain to know this. A retired Archbishop of Canterbury once argued for the legalizing of assisted suicide because 'upholding the sanctity of human life without regard to suffering caused in the process could go against the spirit of Christian teaching in promoting anguish and pain, the very opposite of a Christian message of hope.'

"Ha! Britain, who has so bewitched you that even your leaders—secular and spiritual—acutely lack basic reasoning faculty and elementary understanding? Oh, God Himself weeps for you.

"The Bible says, 'Call to me and I will answer you and show you great and mighty things which you do not know.' Apparently, Church of England clergy have paid no heed to this. Let it be known that leadership is not about popularity or glamour. It is about making decisions that put your organization, its mission and the people you lead first. Good leaders know that exceptional times require exceptional decisions—decisions that may be difficult and personally painful, but that nevertheless must be made in the interest of your organization and its people.

"But in the Church of England, the leaders don't know what their organization stands for or what is best for the people they lead. It is all about big titles, big cassocks, elongated gold brocade miters, long chain pectoral crosses and specially designed crosiers. Uneasy lies the head that wears the crown, so says an adage—but this speaks not of Church of England leaders, who either compromise or chicken out at the slightest sign of friction.

"Remember the discord that attended the ordination of women priests and of gay bishops? There is just too much infighting between the Anglican clergy that we are not able to go into it in our short analysis here. But we remember it is the result of these arguments that necessitated the departure of many Anglican priests and bishops to the Catholic church.

"Political crackdown on Christians in this country is a crime against humanity, but who will plead our cause? Christophobia is the greatest phobia in this country today, but no one talks about it. Until something shakes the consciousness of the British people to an extraordinary event that can be remotely or closely associated with Christianity, we will continue to be ignored and trampled upon, as Christians have become the butt of everyone in society.

"I want us to quickly examine two things. One is the advert that says, 'There is probably no God, so be happy,' displayed on buses throughout the UK, on London Underground stations, and on two animated screens in London's Oxford Street. The Bible says, 'People are destroyed for lack of knowledge.' If not, how does the absence of God bring happiness, when we know that most unhappy people are those who don't believe in God?

"Mass unhappiness is the reason for all the problems in this society, and the reason why a former mayor of London and a former Prime Minister wasted public funds in the search for happiness. And using the word *probably* is enough proof that they don't know what they are talking about. In defense of that, they claimed to have been advised by the Advertising Standards Authority to insert the word *probably* in order not to offend. Balderdash!

"I'll tell you what brings unhappiness. It is the absence of God. This is the cause of all the problems and misery in our society today—all the heinous crimes, unimaginable wickedness and disgraceful behaviors in low and high places. The absence of godliness is responsible for government-licensed swinger festivals. It is responsible for the high rate of teenage suicide, teenage pregnancy, family breakdown, domestic violence, street violence, murder of spouses, incest, the orgy of sadomasochism and even the unusual incidence of raping one's own mother.

"There are many other abnormalities in our society that I am not able to go into because of time. Yet our political leaders don't think anything is wrong with Britain. No one can deny having a conscience, and conscience indicates a lawgiver behind each human's sense of right and wrong. But nothing guides the conscience when God is absent, because conscience is God's beacon to guide one's actions.

"In seven short years under just one PM, centuries of tested character-building legislation were revoked by a so-called modernizing agenda. And those subsequently privileged to occupy the exalted office after this PM outdid him and each other to demolish whatever little good was left. Today we are seeing the result of these changes, and if we are honest with ourselves, we know which is better.

"I tell you, leaders have a lot to answer for. Those who legislated God out of our schools and out of our national life will pay not only for their own sins but also for the sins of others, and the collective sins of the society. And make no mistake about it, no one escapes the final judgment, whether we like it or not and whether we believe it or not. Any sane society must detest politics without principles, reputation without character, knowledge without wisdom, pleasure without conscience and without boundaries. These are the bane of godless societies.

"I say woe to any society that has no Christian voice or Christian action. The lack of a Christian voice or action resulted in the offensive memo on Pope Benedict's visit to Britain. The leaked memo for the visit proposed that the Pope open an abortion ward; bless a gay marriage; launch a range of his own brand of condoms called *Benedict condoms*; back a Miss Developing World beauty contest; reverse the church's policy on women bishops; sponsor a network of AIDS clinics; spend a night in a council flat in Bradford; and do forward rolls with children to promote healthy living.

"How else could you embarrass someone? This is purely in line with the government's position on church matters. It is expected that the Foreign Office should have assigned a seasoned Christian diplomat to head a team of experts who would propose ideas for such a visit. Instead, a thirty-one-year-old non-

Christian was assigned to lead three junior members of the department, all in their early twenties, for something as important as the Pope's state visit. That is how much Whitehall regards us. The appointment of this juvenile team to oversee an important issue is a clear indication that they deliberately invited the Pope to insult him and denigrate the church.

"Don't be fooled by the hastened apologies and expression of regret which resulted solely because the memo got leaked. If such were not the case, then why was there no apology when the memo was emailed to Downing Street and three different government departments before it was leaked? And why was no one disciplined? Instead, those involved were said to have been sent on 'urgent diversity training' and later transferred to other sections.

"With this being so, why won't secularists organize to protest against the visit and threaten to arrest the Pope? Six men who had been arrested under terror laws during the visit were set free because, according to the judge, 'They did not intend on killing the Pope.'

"The British press has nicknamed the Catholic Church *the Church of Sinners.* It should be known that God would not have instituted the Church if there were no sinners, but more important is the fact that *the Church of Sinners* only exists in a nation swimming in sin. No matter how much the church tries, it will to some extent always reflect its local domain. Hence, no church denomination is completely free from sin, unless it is a church uninhabited by humans.

"But since the Church in England is mostly inhabited by English people, it cannot be different, because it is difficult for a segment of society to rise above the level of the mentality of the majority.

"At Pope Benedict's resignation, the British press was agog with mockery, indicating he had played a major role in reducing the Catholic church's popularity and its authority. They dubbed him contentious, claiming he left the Vatican more despised and resented throughout the world. I doubt if Catholics share those opinions.

"One newspaper jested, 'He retired at the age of eighty-five due to ill health, but the BBC, Rome and Vatican City correspondent was equally over eighty and had worked there for more than forty years under four popes.' Yet the BBC did not ask the over-eighty correspondent to do the reporting on the resignation. Instead, a BBC *News at 10* anchor and its European editor were sent to cover the story. That is an indication of how effective their Vatican City correspondent was.

"First and foremost, it is a mark of humility to voluntarily leave an exalted office when you know you can no longer function effectively due to age or health problems. Secondly, the BBC correspondent's responsibilities nowhere compare with those of the Pope, who heads a nation of more people than the entire population of Europe—West and East—who are scattered throughout the world. Most presidents and Prime Ministers leave office after eight years, which is almost the number of years Pope Benedict XVI served, except the sit-tight ones who had nothing to offer after those years.

"It takes a very popular and lovable person to attract a crowd of more than two million people in one single meeting as happened in many countries Pope Benedict XVI visited. It is difficult to say for sure if the western press assault on the Vatican, especially with its lewd version of modernism, did not contribute to the Pope's resignation. And to spurn Pope Benedict, the western press welcomed and reached out to his successor, Pope Francis, with superstar accolades.

"They depicted him as a liberal and reforming pope and as the people's Pope, which almost got the new Pope carried away with their antics, yielding to an earthquake of the Church to which Vatican observers referred to mildly as *lifestyle ecumenism.*

"It is very surprising that there was no media hype at the resignation of the then-Archbishop of Canterbury, who said, 'My job is too much for one person.' Yet, he was far younger than the Pope, and his job was nowhere near half the responsibilities of the Pope. The only reason for media silence was because he was always dancing to their tune."

III. Government of the Living Dead

"A British Prime Minister, while in opposition, constantly referred to Britain as a broken society and once labeled the government of the day, *a government of the living dead.* Government policies then, as they are now, had no human face, lacked sensitivity to the people's yearnings and were devoid of reason, logic and common sense. The government was dead in every sense of the word. It was so dead that a TV celebrity made bold to call the then-Prime Minister *a one-eyed idiot* for *fooling the people with his lies.*

"The evils of society were promoted and entrenched as *rights*. The government, then as now, went out for its own gain, feeding the nation with all the negativities of the human experience, using political correctness as a tool. However, experience has shown that political correctness is nothing but a euphemism for indiscipline and waywardness. It is the coat of despotism and the West's equivalent to the East's totalitarianism.

"This accuser politician probably had good intentions and may have tried his best when he became Prime Minister considering the sheer enormity of the problems he inherited. But he made two grievous mistakes. Difficult problems need enough time to incubate ideas that produce lasting solutions. Too much haste results in throwing out the baby with the bathwater. The second and more serious mistake was when confronted with grave problems, he did not consult God first, as the wise do.

"That is what David did when confronting Goliath in the valley of Elah and in confronting the Amalekites after the plunder of Ziklag. It is the same thing King Hezekiah did when threatened by the Assyrian king Sennacherib. And we know the results of these encounters.

"If we lose the Bible, we lose our conscience; and if we lose our conscience, we lose our bearing. And that is what happened, for instead of consulting God through His servants, this Prime Minister consulted a party that is well-known for its stand against godliness and all that it edifies, a party that promises one thing and does the very opposite, as exemplified by the debate over the increase in tuition fee.

"In taking counsel from this party, the Prime Minister applied Rehoboam's wrong concept of governance by the *scourge of scorpions*. But that was what cost Rehoboam ten northern tribes. The PM was lucky to have been resisted by only one northern tribe, although that tribe consists of thirty-two local councils. However, there were other forms of resistance. The nation's youths surprised him with their own brand of resistance in the streets of major cities in the country.

"Even nature shed bitter tears of disapproval through ravaging storms with flooding—the likes of which hadn't been seen for more than two hundred years—and necessitated the greatest emergency the country had seen since World War II. There was also the case of the unusual incidence of many sudden sinkholes opening up in many cities. And strange fires suddenly erupted on rooftops by lightning, and in the streets by way of manhole fires, underground cable sparks, etc. Destructive windstorms and mild earthquakes completed the cycle of almost everyday occurrence in the warning season of nature's revulsion.

"When God hides His face from a nation on the brink of moral bankruptcy, nature reacts with violence; but leaders feign ignorance, hiding behind the shield of *natural disaster* to escape blame. Everything has boundaries that restrict bad and evil behaviors—nature, nations, communities, organizations and families. Even Britain has laws stipulating behavioral boundaries. But when it comes to nature or moral boundaries, Britain has no restrictions.

"Once the beacon of light to the world when its forefathers served God, Britain is now the devil's advocate, thanks to the pleasure-seeking glamour brigade termed leaders. How times have changed? Today's Britain has become the Potter's Field because no one appreciates the role religion plays in shaping and sustaining human existence. Schools used to help mold children's character, but not anymore. As a result, Britain has become a toxic and destructive society. The establishment has become institutionally anti-God, anti-Church and anti-Christian.

"It is said that if you repeat a lie often enough, it becomes the truth. Hence, people now live by the government's lies and deceptions. It is hard to believe that this same country produced the likes of John Wycliffe, whose great zeal for God resulted in his being the first man to translate the Bible into the English language and William Tyndale, who gave the English Bible to the world by being the first to print it."

Jay paused for his audience to digest and absorb all he had been saying, and then he fired on.

"Let's reflect for one moment and think of the environment we live in, not just as Christians but also as human beings. Let's consider the whole brutalizing environment in which we live today. Far from being one of the most civilized centuries of human history as they want us to believe, a strong case could be argued that this has been one of the most destructive, the most bestial and the most violent.

"This society has gotten so used to violence that it's natural intuition and emotional response is dead. Response to violence has become selectively subjective, quite passive in certain contexts and outright reprehensible in others. Is this dichotomy one which can be justified, or it is a simple case of expediency?

"The deadness of any society entangles everyone in that society, including the righteous, and in the end, everyone will be swept away because they have become polluted with the prevailing unrighteousness. It is a paradigm shift of grave consequences. This is why we must fight for our rights. Any Christian wishing for Old Testament times, when evil was immediately visited with punishment, is wasting his time.

"The blood of Jesus has sealed that to allow for repentance. God respects covenants, especially the blood covenant of the New Testament, which has made the world think He is inactive or does not exist. What we must do is to prove that God's power is still very active on earth, for God reigns in the affairs of men. And this power responds only to the faithful prayers of true Christians.

"We must take extreme offense at people playing God, from people acting as individuals, to entire governments and everything in between. In their corrupt hands, power becomes absolute and they spread their evil outside of natural laws, unfettered by any deterrent, any detection, or any sense of higher authority. They have replaced God's laws with human rights. That is why here people would rather die fighting for their rights than live to fight another day because they prefer their rights to their lives. Any right outside of God's commandments is no right.

"And they keep moving the goalposts because we are tolerant. Indeed, we have been far too tolerant to the point of foolishness. Emboldened by our silence, new spurious legislation to nail us jets out of Parliament like water from a burst water main. And this gives impetus to citizens' mockery of our faith. So they made a caricature of Jesus Christ with a mocking message as a Christmas card; we kept quiet.

"They said we should not wear a cross or any Christian symbol; we smiled. They said we should not display any Christian symbol anywhere, not even in our cars or on any of our private property; we agreed. They said we should not say anything relating to Christianity in public; we affirmed it with a nod. They said we should not herald our church service with a bell or any jingle of any sort; we accepted. They said we could send Christmas cards as long as they contained no Christian or godly messages; we clapped our hands.

"They forcefully changed Christmas lights and decorations to winter lights and decorations; we pledged our loyalty. They said renowned Oxford Street superstores should stop playing Christmas carols at Christmas so as not to offend anyone. No one considered that that act in itself is an offense to

Christians, but still, we maintained a calculated, albeit uneasy, equanimity. They denied us the right to foster children because we insisted on telling young foster children the truth about life. Instead of taking offense, we cheered. They nicknamed Cardinal Ratzinger *the Panzer cardinal* and as a Pope called him *Rottweiler*—in plain language, a dog; we laughed.

"They took our church buildings from us and extorted money from us in sold lands as replacements for new buildings, then denied us planning permission in order to extirpate our religion; we maintained philosophical calmness in order not to offend the courts. They warned us in unmistakable terms to pray only in our closets; we gave them the thumbs up. But even at that, and like Daniel, our neighbors eavesdropped on our crooning praise worship or searched out a cross on our meeting doors, then reported us as an offense to them.

"And *bam!* Like a bolt out of the blue, the local council descended on us with a court ASBO demanding that we never utter any Christian word or make any Christian gestures, even within our closets. And like a lamb led to the slaughter, we were not allowed a word in court, as is true in many court cases. We are the only community in Britain today that loses their cases before such cases are brought to court. Going to court is to formalize our guilt—against the legal norm of being innocent until proven guilty.

"It is giving a dog a bad name in order to hang it. As the Bible says, they 'caused men to ride over our heads; we went through fire and through water.' And so we play to their plots by our complacency and cowardice. God will bring us out only if we confront the situation head-on.

"It is quite illogical that in the twenty-first-century freedom country where animal rights will not allow an abusive word against a dog, and where human rights are placed above life itself, Christians are crucified left, right and center for believing in a crucified God. Since God did not resist His crucifixion, Christians are called not to resist their own crucifixion. And the devil's advocates in cassocks are calling on Christian schools to admit only 10 percent of Christians and give 90 percent space to non-churchgoing families—as a gesture of community spirit.

"Yes, the Devil's eagles have now landed in the church. The church now follows the crowd sheepishly in the macabre carnival of the ungodly. What is a faith school with 90 percent unbelieving pupils of atheist and liberal parents in a democratic country? By democratic principles, it is nothing but a den of

God-mockers. And the irony is that all these advocates are not lay Christians but Anglican priests and bishops with a few of their Catholic counterparts—the flame quenchers."

IV. Unabashed Hypocrisy

"A serving Prime Minister embarrassed himself by declaring a long-standing party loyalist a *bigoted woman* on air for no reason whatsoever other than because political leaders as utter bigots see everything as bigotry. This is the same reason the man who appointed a former Archbishop of Canterbury pretended to be an Anglican. He loved politics more than God and deception more than truth. His defection was a stark repudiation of the Anglican Church and its theology.

"Having destabilized the Anglican Church by pretending to be an Anglican, he then pretended to be a Catholic and went as far as to the Vatican, possibly to destabilize the Catholic church, forgetting that it was neither a state church nor under his jurisdiction. Charisma without character knows no boundaries.

"In our days, we have witnessed the coming into office of a black US president; we have witnessed the swearing-in of the Palestinian authority and the subsequent endorsement of non-member observer state status on Palestine by the UN General Assembly. We have witnessed the Arab awakening. All came at a price. The persecution of Christians has become the common ground on which old enemies settle their differences, if only temporarily. The Word of God says Creation is earnestly waiting for the eager manifestation of the sons of God.

"Creation is waiting for you and for me to manifest the kingdom of God on earth. 'Let it be done on earth as it is in heaven' rests on you. The power that said, 'Let it be'—and it was—is in you and is waiting for you. Until you manifest the fire of God, you shall by no means enter heaven. You will be crucified here and hereafter."

The audience laughed, some standing up and punching the air with their fists. Once more Jay mopped his face with the face towel, then took the glass of water from the pulpit and sipped a little.

"Perhaps the way I am presenting these matters on the surface is not making enough impact for you to understand what we are up against. When I spoke of the way we unwittingly encouraged them to mock us, I wasn't telling comic stories as you might think; they are real. Time constraint prevents me from giving examples of specific incidents.

"I want someone to tell me how many times a government official has spoken any positive word about God or Christianity in this country. The only time a British Prime Minister spoke positively about Christianity was in the faraway United States rather than in Britain and that was in the 1980s. Another public figure who said something positive about religion did so long after he had left office. He was a former education secretary and later Home Secretary.

"Earlier, I spoke of a Prime Minister who professed Christianity but waited until he left office before revealing his true denominational identity. Something terrible is definitely wrong with this country. Why do the leaders only speak the truth when they are far away from home or after they leave office? This is one of the major differences between Britain and the USA, but I will come to that later. Leaders running away from the truth is the principal reason we are in chains in this country, all of us, religious and non-religious alike.

"That shows that there is a spirit of darkness in this country holding leaders hostage and preventing them from speaking the truth or acting upon it. That is why they deliberately denigrate religious faith. It is the reason why in Liverpool, the design for a six-hundred-and-fifty-three-foot sixty-seven-story cross tower called King Edward Tower was criticized and vehemently opposed and forced to be altered by Merseyside Civic Society. Its critics said it turned the skyline into a cemetery. The only reason for saying that is because it has a cross shape.

"However, the architect defended his design as a symbol referencing one of the ultimate places in human spirituality. I certainly agree with him. My prayer is that it may be to everyone as he imagines it—a graveyard for some and a spring of life for others. Such was the sin of Pilate—for knowing the truth, yet asking Jesus, 'What is truth?' after telling the Jews he found no fault in Him—and thinking that washing his hands would exonerate him from the willful sin of miscarriage of justice.

"And so are the judges here feigning ignorance of the truth, asking us, 'What is truth?' and condemning us as they condemned Jesus. But our victory is assured for we shall triumph as Jesus triumphed. The government has now displaced God in the affairs of this country. Britain is now leading the world in intolerance of the Christian religion. The war against Christians has taken such a turn that, in the absence of any legal basis to criminalize a Christian, phrases of existing laws are twisted and distorted to confuse and convict.

"Lost cases involving Christians that were lost because of a miscarriage of justice are used as principal references on which judges rely in dismissing further Christian cases. Also, indiscriminate use is made of the Public Order Act to nail Christians—and it does not surprise me that many of the more recent Acts of Parliament from the year 2000 were deliberately meant to criminalize Christians and force them to conform.

"While I do not want to use this platform to list all the discriminations and miscarriages of justice against Christians, to prove that the offenses against Christians know no bounds, I have to refer to this one particular case.

"It was in Horsham, West Sussex, that a school that allows Muslim and Sikh girls to wear headscarves and religious bracelets banned a sixteen-year-old Christian girl from wearing a Bible-verse-engraved *purity ring* denoting no sex outside marriage. When the case got to court, the deputy high court judge in upholding the ban as justified ordered the girl's father to pay twelve thousand pounds as the cost to the school. In this country, children's identities are protected.

"Even their names are not mentioned because of legal reasons. And parents are not supposed to be held accountable for their children's crimes. But all this is thrown overboard when Christians are involved. Hence the girl's father was made to pay twelve thousand pounds for the crime, which he did not commit. This was in a country where a city trader conned investors out of thirty-two million pounds and where a robber who stole one hundred and fourteen thousand pounds from HSBC Bank in Coventry was each asked to pay back just one pound by two separate courts.

"Yet for merely wearing a ring that was not even exposed, if really that was an offense, a teenage girl was fined twelve thousand pounds, which fine was imposed on her father for fathering a child who professes purity of mind and body. Yet a girl who maliciously threw a baby in front of an oncoming bus in Croydon was fined only fifty pounds. Her father was not dragged into the case. That tells you how much they hate us. Church, do we belong here? How else do you want to be told that you are not wanted here? We must stand up for our rights."

V. Travesty of Justice

"While I do not want to go into the history of this country, permit me to nullify the claim of an appeal court judge that Christianity has no special place in this country. This was expressed during a case some years ago about a Christian marriage guidance counselor's having lost his job and his court cases over his sacking for refusing to give sex therapy to a couple.

"The Lord Justice of the appeal court, in snubbing a retired Archbishop of Canterbury who tried to intervene in the case, said, 'Legislation to protect views held purely on religious grounds cannot be justified.' He added, 'It is an irrational idea, divisive, capricious and arbitrary, as preferring the subjective over the objective.'

"There are two ways to interpret his views. The first is that judges are above the law because he was clearly arguing against the legislation and not the substance or validity of the case. Arguing against established legislation is a violation of Acts of Parliament, which is a criminal offense, but nowadays the State takes exception when such is against Christian principles.

"The judge argued vehemently more like a defense lawyer than a judge, embarking on a spurious analysis of precepts of theocracy against that of general law and concluding, 'The state, if its people are to be free, has the burdensome duty of thinking for itself.' Who are the thinkers for the state? The government. And who is the government?

"Individuals, who think according to their own perceptions. Are we then really free when the state thinks for us? I don't think so; conformity is the only thing the state does for its citizens. You can see why there is so much crime and wickedness in this country. People are not allowed to think for themselves. The government's thinking for us makes everyone live on impulse. That is why our capital city has become the world's biggest youth graveyard.

"The state's thinking for us resulted in people who were given state honors being later found to be morally bankrupt and convicted of various crimes, including pedophilia. It is why a man was convicted of the *crime* of attaining orgasm instead of withdrawing while copulating with his legally married wife, who voluntarily agreed to engage in the act.

"Sometimes I wonder why they make laws in the UK when there is always a *rights issue* that will rubbish the law. Life here revolves around rights. Unfortunately, rights here are anything but true rights.

"The second is that his views nullify the Crown because the Crown's stamp of authority and express faith is religious and Christian. The Crown is the

Defender of the Faith, and the faith spoken of here is the Christian faith. So nullifying the Crown denies the existence of the state—the state that is supposed to be thinking for all of us. What a paradox and a nullity of his own thesis.

"This clearly shows his acute ignorance. Contrary to his arguments, Christianity does have a special place in this country, as depicted by every structure of the state. And attributes of the Christian God are reflected prominently in various state events. The English national flag is St George's cross. The British national anthem, *God Save the Queen/King*, speaks of God's love and protection.

"The Houses of Parliament are the seat of the British government. It has St Stephen's Chapel, St Margaret's Church, and a host of other symbols representing its Christian foundation. It also has Moses's Room, with a large fresco of Moses bringing down the tablets of the Law from Mount Sinai. Westminster Abbey, a church, occupies a special place in the history of England and Britain. The power and authority of Parliament are reflected in the lyrics of the song—after which the hourly chime of its famous clock, Big Ben, is patterned,—which states: 'All through this hour, | Lord, be my guide; | And by Thy power, | No foot shall slide.'

"It is the Bible—the Word of God—that inspired Britain's *Magna Carta*. Time does not permit me to elaborate on this. Part of the coronation ceremony of kings and queens of England since 1689 are the words spoken with a gift of the Bible thus: 'Our gracious king/queen, we present you with this book, the most valuable thing that this world affords. Here is wisdom; this is the royal law; these are the lively oracles of God.'

"One of England's greatest jurists acknowledged that the Bible has always been regarded as part of the common law of England. Examples abound, but I have restricted myself to these few only because of lack of time. With learned people's reasoning like this appeal court judge, I would not be surprised if one day someone were to take the government to court seeking the removal of the cross from the English flag.

"The appeal court judge further spoke of his disenchantment with 'the promulgation of law for the protection of a position held purely on religious grounds' and sees it 'as preferring the subjective over the objective.' The problem with the word *objective* or *objectivity* is that its definition is actually subjective. It all depends on individual views, which are neither constant nor universal. It was objective when the law was made and subjective to its opponents, but vice versa when it was abrogated.

"Therefore, if anything is subjective, it is the law itself, because what was objective in the eyes of the law yesterday has become legally subjective today or has the potential of becoming subjective tomorrow. It all depends on the predilection of the authority of the day. We must advance this argument a little further. If religion or the notion of the existence of God is subjective because you don't believe in God, then your thinking is faulty.

"Let me illustrate it this way: Everyone believes in the existence of the mind. Your mind is who you are. It is your mind that determines and controls your actions. If it is possible for your mind to be completely functionless, even if your body is biologically alive, then you are no longer living, or at best you are no longer thinking right.

"That means you've lost your mind. In the same way, if you perceive the existence of God as subjective because you can't see Him physically or can't perceive the experimental manifestation of His presence, just as you can't see your mind physically, then you are not thinking right, so you have lost your mind. It is that simple.

"This is the reason the Bible says only fools say there is no God. And only fools can declare that Christianity has no higher status in this prehistoric Christian civilization where the laws are based on Christian doctrine."

Jay paused briefly, his face dotted with sweat and then continued: "Honestly speaking, but for Christ's injunction that we should not resort to violence, I'd say that these are the types of judges who deserve to be shot on sight, right on their judgment seats, for sitting on their brains and allowing their emotions to take over their sense of reasoning and of judgment. Please pardon my infuriation. This judge is a typical example of Christ's criticism of lawyers in Luke 11:46, the type of people who deliberately choose hell and want to drag everyone along with them.

"The issue of reason is subjective in Britain because what is construed as reasonable is not. That is why we have arguments like these, and it is a travesty of reality in the case of this Lord Justice of Appeal. It is a travesty of reality that makes it possible for highly placed people in society to literally act out their names in practical wickedness—names such as Livingstone, spilling out hot destructive lava everywhere to prove that a stone is a living object; Supper stone, spilling out superfine on juveniles and schoolchildren to prove how super wicked their stone is and how dumb their legal standing is; balls, bulging out their flaming red eyeballs like overinflated balloons to intimidate people and kick their lives out of shape like a deflated football until booted out of office by electoral landslide; and Law, arguing about the subjectivity of a belief in an unseen God to prove that the law as an ass could be trampled upon as the final frontier of legal jurisprudence.

"When pride and ambition are cherished, and men exalt their own theories above the Word of God, then intelligence can accomplish greater harm than ignorance. I tremble for this country because God's justice will not sleep in this land, but must stand. As I said before, I have a comprehensive list of the unjust treatment of Christians in this country, but time does not permit me to list those incidents; however, these few are enough to wake us up and prod us to fight for our rights."

VI. Open War

"In this country, the law is truly an ass, and the judges are making a fool of it. And so are they making a fool of us because we are reluctant to fight back? We are the only community that does not hate any group of people. Our only offense is in speaking the truth and desiring the best for the country, but they are fighting us because they don't want to depart from their evil ways.

"They are enslaved to every contemptible habit—slaves to fear, slaves to doubt, slaves to depression, slaves to sex, slaves to alcohol, slaves to an empty life—all because they deny the truth and the Source of life.

"Giulio Andreotti, one-time Italian Prime Minister, once said, 'Power wears out those who don't have it.' That is what people with power think, but we'll prove them wrong because we know who has the ultimate power. How many of us here have ever heard that name—Andreotti—or know that he ever walked on the face of this earth? Where are the powers of yesteryears? Gone and forgotten.

"The motto of a traditionalist Anglican movement called Forward in Faith says, 'No compromise of truth and no limitation of love'. And practically living out our lives by this injunction does not make us weaklings or limit our ability to fight for our rights.

"At the time of the *purity ring* judgment, the university tuition fee was three thousand pounds. It costs twelve thousand pounds for a four-year degree program. What the judge did was deliberately ruin the child's chances of getting a university education, without which it becomes easy to manipulate her and feed her the wrong concepts of life. Her father was punished for the proper upbringing of his daughter. That is one of the many hidden evil plans the British establishment has for the treatment of Christians in this country. But we will frustrate all their plans.

"Who can honestly tell me that this judge does not deserve to be shot on sight on his judgment seat for such a naked miscarriage of justice?" Jay rolled his eyes from one end of their sockets to the other as he scanned the audience.

Then he offered his apologies: "Once more I am sorry for my exasperation. The sting of death is sin, and the strength of sin is the law. And the law in Britain is no better than dumb picnic donkeys for fools in judges' gowns. Hence, in the zeal to frustrate Christians and kill Christianity, the rule of law is no longer recognized. But no one can kill Christianity.

"In the mid-seventeenth century, Oliver Cromwell banned Christmas celebrations, but today Christmas is still being celebrated. During the French Revolution, the leaders did everything they could to wipe out Christianity forever. But today Christianity still exists in France. Russian communism said, 'Christ's kingdom is invisible; his rule is in the heart of men and therefore cannot be tolerated.'

"Today Christianity still exists in Russia because nobody and nothing can wipe out Christianity. It has thrived despite attacks from the Roman Empire, despite the Viking raids, despite the Boxer Rebellion, despite Nazi oppression, and despite so many other oppressions. Because anything that is genuinely of God cannot die. One of the forefathers of the Reformation said that the Bible is an anvil that has worn out many hammers. In our day, it is a crane that will grind every stubborn heart to powder.

"So don't lose faith. All we have to do is to apply spiritual violence through prayer, since other methods have failed as no one wants to engage with us in any civilized form whatsoever. Jesus said that if your eye offends you, you should pluck it out. That is spiritual violence; that is the fire of God. We must call down the fire of God to consume our enemies. They talk of laser-guided missiles. Ours will be divinely guided bombs landing on their heads and their homes through the power of prayer. We will know which has better pinpoint accuracy and more lethal efficacy.

"It will not be long before Christians are accosted on British streets and possibly murdered for being Christians, and churches torched. The setting on fire of the historic Grade II listed Church of Ascension in Salford on a Sunday, which according to police was deliberate, is still fresh in our minds. You want to be a cool Christian? Scream, rant, rave and cry with all the sentimental sanctimony in you; it will make no difference. No emblem of our faith should be seen on our business premises or we will lose our licenses.

"The plight of Christians in this country is enough to sensitize your minds to the fact that an open war has been declared on us because of our beliefs. There are many people who don't care what happens in society so long as it does not affect them directly. You must know that what happens to one will one day happen to another unless it is nipped in the bud. Some of you don't even read papers or listen to the news.

"Now, the question is: how do we fight for our rights with so much division in the church? In Jeremiah's words, 'Oh that my head were waters and my eyes a fountain of tears, that I might weep day and night.' Apply this to the church in the United Kingdom. Jesus prayed that we would be one because a house divided against itself cannot stand. Three persons in one God is an example of unity in diversity: of relationship, of love and of accord.

"When Christendom was united, no government or power anywhere in the world could withstand it. Please note that this was the case even when the church became many denominations. But they had one inviolate doctrine. Today the doctrine has been violated by many preachers who have either diluted the original doctrine or composed their own to suit their own purposes. They argue over words and manipulate and philosophize scripture to justify their crash individualism. And they take godliness as a means of gain.

"Yes! False preachers are taking over the house of God while the watchmen are busy arguing over semantics and funds, oversize and aesthetics. These are preachers who adore and worship church buildings instead of God, who is the reason for the building. The finest cathedral in the world is only a pile of stones if we do not learn how to find Christ there and if we do not learn lessons in living, which that cathedral will be a guide for our happiness."

Jay's words were punchy and direct to the point. He glanced at his watch, raised his head and looked at the audience, his eyes skirting every corner of the hall. Then he continued with renewed energy.

"What Christian voice is there in this country? None. If any, it is the voice of disagreement. Any nation without a Christian voice is doomed—doomed for the Christian and the non-Christian. The communion of saints is interdenominational and is the only thing that can save the church. No unity, no victory. Some disagree with Catholics because of their use of the crucifix, or because they pray the Hail Mary; others argue over pedophile priests. They will not attend any event held in a Catholic building, as a mark of their hatred.

"Others will have nothing to do with the Anglican Church because of its distorted and compromised doctrine. They will not go to a Seventh-day Adventist church because the Adventists worship on Saturdays. There are too many reasons to avoid the Methodist Church, the Presbyterian Church, the Salvation Army, the Evangelical Church, the Pentecostal Church, or any church.

"Well, my friends, you should know that there is no denomination without a fault. If you want a perfect church, then you will belong to none, because none is complete. Nothing that has to do with humans is perfect. I may not necessarily agree with all that goes on in my particular denomination or the local church I attend, but as a Christian, I can choose to go to any church. The Bible is my ultimate guide.

"Therefore, any church where the words of the Bible come alive and invade my innermost being is where I belong. So, don't let the church be your guide; let the Bible be your guide. Membership of a church is necessary—to learn and grow, and be in fellowship and in communion with believers. Therefore, be less critical of any church except the one that is fronting for the Devil. We should all be one.

"Let's not lose sight of the many good humanitarian services the churches have done, especially the Catholic church and the Anglican Church—healthcare, drinkable water, schools, etc., even in the unreachable parts of the world. The contribution of these two churches to the positive development and social well-being of the world is immeasurable and far outweighs the evils of a few pedophile priests.

"Anybody who grew up in a third world country will understand what I am talking about. Even in this country, the church as a collective noun has helped pull many young people out of drugs, gangs, prostitution and various crimes. Many have been pulled back from the brink of hopelessness. They have been given hope, have been helped to rebuild their lives and have been given a chance to make their marks on society. The developed nations only borrowed the idea of humanitarian aid from the church.

"Whatever moral problems exist in the church, it is still largely the best hope for mankind, and stands as man's best achievement in terms of human character development. We should therefore pray and work toward church unity. We must tear down the walls of religion and denomination. The Book of Life does not record your denomination next to your name. There are no denominational labels in heaven.

"Here we have Catholics, Anglicans, Baptists, Methodists, Evangelicals, Pentecostals—in fact, any denomination you can think of. Our membership covers a broad spectrum of the entire ethnic mix of London's more than two hundred and fifty nationalities. So we are a hybrid of the true Christian church of God. Our common goal is to see the kingdom of God lifted up in our lives and in the United Kingdom.

"United we stand, so also we want the Christian church in the United Kingdom to be united. We must be united in order to be counted. A divided army never wins any war. I know it is difficult for all church denominations to come together because of sharp differences on moral and social issues. But what joins us together is much more than what separates us.

"Even the Anglican Church—I have criticized their highly opinionated clergy—have some of their members still adhering to the true doctrines of the church, especially such orthodox groups as Anglican Mainstream, together with the already mentioned Forward in Faith.

"So don't think the Anglican Church here is a write-off. Many of their clergy have been fighting the Christian cause more than other denominations. In many instances, the Anglican Church has tried matching their words with action, as small as this effort may be. Now imagine what could be achieved if other churches were to join forces with these Anglican clergy.

"The Bible tells us that the thief comes not to steal, to kill and to destroy. And we know that the thief is the Devil, using the establishment as a camouflage. It is our joy he wants to steal; it is our faith in God he wants to kill; and it is our souls he wants to destroy, in order to drag us with him to Hades. That is why we must fight.

"If the Devil-influenced people can protest against the Pope's visit, even threatening to arrest him; if they can openly advertise on London buses that there is no God; if they can stop us from ringing our church bells and stop us from wearing crosses, then what length do you think they will not go to, to destroy the hope we have and the faith we share? When Christian leaders unwittingly join their ranks, do you need reminding that we are not fighting flesh and blood? If they can go for the Pope, who else is safe?

"Oh, you people don't know what it takes to be a Christian. Wake up and open your eyes. Live the Bible—it tells you to fight the good fight. Let me remind you that Christianity is war, and you must fight to win. The moment you give your life to Christ, you automatically declare yourself the Devil's enemy. And that makes you a soldier of Christ. Soldiers don't hide in their closets; they don't take orders from enemy commanders. And anyone, whether in politics, in the judiciary, in the press, or wherever, who has no regard or fear of God is your enemy.

"Any authority or anything that exalts itself against the knowledge of God is your enemy. The problem with today's Christians is that they don't know the power within them and they don't know their weapons. He who says to decree a thing and it shall be established has already established those victories in you. All that is required of you is to step out and declare your ownership of those victories.

"But today's Christians are afraid to declare anything, let alone claim the victories. And the reason is because they have not prepared themselves. We have Christians who cannot fast even for a day. We have Christians who cannot and do not know how to pray. Those who do cannot pray for half an hour a day. Some don't believe in the power of prayer; others' prayers are nothing but gimme, gimme—all for themselves.

"We have Christians who do a five-minute browse through the Bible in noisy congested public transport en route to work. We have Christians who regard a one-pound offering as over the top. They cannot partner with Christian charities financially. An atheist bus campaign in London by the British Humanist Association, aiming to raise fifty-five hundred pounds to advertise the slogan 'There's probably no God,' raised one hundred and thirty-six thousand, one hundred and ninety-seven pounds in just the first week.

"That is a measure of the degree of aggressive atheism in Britain today. It is an indication of the war we face. But we don't seem to be ready yet. Christians would rather subscribe to useless debased TV channels and programs than financially support positive Christian action. Pastors would rather live in mansions and ride the best cars than embark on a robust financial counterattack and aggressive bombardment of secular thoughts through various media outlets.

"It is the fear of the state that refused official jets for the Crown and No. 10 that has foreclosed pastors in Britain owning private jets. Paul spoke of disciplining his body to bring it to subjection, lest when he has preached to others, he himself should be cast away. Pope Francis warned against what he called *existential schizophrenia*. Pastors, be warned: our prayer is that the first does not become the last.

"I am sorry for the Christian who wants to be the salt of the earth and light of the world but doesn't want the seasoning heat of the salt or the heating flame of the light. Jesus said if the salt loses its taste, it will be good for nothing and will be thrown out and trampled underfoot by men. Until your anger achieves furnace heat, you will continue to suffer. Almost all of Christ's miracles were preceded by action as He asked the recipient to do something. That is faith in action.

"The Israelites were not just praying but were also taking action. They complemented their prayers by marking their doorposts with the blood of the Lamb. The Red Sea did not part until they had set foot in it. They did not wait for God to drive out the inhabitants of the Promised Land; they fought for it. Realizing in his hideout that running from one's persecutors is no solution to one's problems, Moses confronted Pharaoh with boldness. Take particular notice that it was only when he acted on the rod in his hand that it became the rod of God. Heaven helps those who help themselves. Until you get mad, the world will not listen to you.

"The State can legislate anything against us, but no one can stop us from praying or acting on our prayers. In fighting the good fight, the Bible tells you to take up the whole armor of God, that you may be able to withstand on an evil day, and having done all, to stand. The evil days are already here, and you must fight. If you didn't need to fight, the Bible would not have admonished you to do so repeatedly.

"Let your faith not be shipwrecked by the ordinances of evil men in power. The Bible lists the following: armor, breastplate, shield, helmet and sword. These are war implements, but it is of no use putting them on if you are not ready to fight. These are faith weapons and must be fully deployed with your prayers. The fervent prayer of a righteous man avails much.

"Unfortunately, Christians in the west don't know how to pray because they have all their needs met. They hardly face life-or-death situations. When you find yourself between the enemy and a brick wall, nobody will teach you how to pray. Peter was shackled hand and foot, but the church kept the intensity of their prayers. Not only did the chains fall off, but also even the gates opened of their own accord—not one gate, not two gates, but three heavy iron gates. That is the power of prayer; we must pray fervently.

"After the 7 July terrorist attack in London, another followed quickly on 21 July, which some said was a coincidence that none of the bombs exploded. It is unbelievable that the makers of the four bombs of 7 July with their devastating deployment were also the makers of the four bombs of 21 July and that all failed to detonate. My friends, the simple truth is that it was not a coincidence that they all failed to detonate.

"It was purely a God incident. It was people's prayer after the 7 July blast that stalled the 21 July attempts. Now imagine such a miraculous answer to a rebellious people's half-hearted and disjointed emergency prayers that attended the 7 July bombings. How do you think God will not answer the genuine cry of His children persecuted in Britain for their beliefs? But prayer without faith and action amounts to nothing.

"The book of James tells us that faith without works is dead. And what is a work? Work is action—a-c-t-i-o-n, man," Jay shouted, his eyes sparkling reddish, showing his seriousness, as his visage darkened. Then he continued: "This is where, despite the wrangling in the Anglican Church, they have taken a step farther than the rest. It is about the only church in which some of the priests, few as they may be, are making official complaints of the persecution of Christians to the authorities.

"But good as this may be, it is not enough. British politicians are above the law and beyond reproach. They have made this country a nation that exalts itself against the knowledge of God. They do not hear the voice of the people. They operate a television type of government, where the people can only see them but can't talk to them. They alone can talk to the people. They can't see or hear the people. They don't know what is happening in the streets because they are in their lofty TV studio-styled offices.

"The people can only see their elected representatives from afar as on TV but can't speak to them. And that reminds me of the reason the government banned fox hunting. The only reason is because politicians are foxes. Jesus Christ is not known to waste His words or say untruths. If He called Herod a fox, He definitely knew what He was talking about. And our politicians have proved Him right.

"Jesus said you should not give what is holy to dogs or the precious gems of your hard labor to pigs because they will trample on them and rip your jugular. We should not allow the establishment to trample on our pearls—our faith. We must force them to stop ignoring or persecuting us. We have to speak the only language they understand. We must shake them awake to reality. Spiritual violence is the resting place of our faith. Maybe I need to define faith here and say why faith without action is dead. Or better still, define it in conjunction with hope since the two are inexplicably linked.

"What is hope? Hope is an expectation or a desire for something not yet revealed. And faith is the substance of things hoped for, the evidence of things not seen. Hope is an eagerness for something not yet manifested, and faith is the substance of something not yet seen, something hoped for.

"Without faith, there can be no hope because faith is the substance, the evidence, of that hope. And it is godliness that brings hope because you cannot base your faith on anything or system outside of God. People who have no faith in God are therefore hopeless. Hopeless people are desperate people because they have nothing to live for; they have no reason to pursue life with vision and determination. That makes them very dangerous. That accounts for the very dangerous nature of our society today.

"Faith is a simple belief. It does not require laborious logical reasoning; it does not require effort or strength—not willpower, but a simple willingness to trust and believe. That is why I find Britain to be the greatest paradox on earth. British people like hard things. To be worth it, simple things in life have to be made hard, very hard. If it is simple, it is not worth the effort or even the attempt.

"This also accounts for why salvation is rejected by the British because it is free. Faith in God is too simple to be real and be believed. British people are too learned and too sophisticated, too evidential and logical, too scientific and factual, to accept things not seen, to accept simple truth and simple childlike faith without which, Christ said, no one can enter the kingdom of God. That is why I thank God for those British people, irrespective of race or color, who have truly accepted childlike faith in Christ.

"I bless God for them. It is very difficult to be British and Christian; the two don't mix. Despite the abundance of material things and comfort, which has robbed people of the quest for God, these people have entrusted themselves to God. May God's light and grace ever shine in their lives."

And his audience shouted, "Amen!"

Then Jay continued, "When a nation sets itself up against God, it is very difficult for individuals to live out their faith because of the systems put in place to frustrate them. And the Devil takes advantage of the systems to confuse the people's minds.

"It is the simplicity of faith that is its undoing. And in a land where people believe only in sweaty, difficult and concrete evidence as proof of a thing, faith becomes a lost cause. The only proof of faith is in practical demonstrations. It is when your prayer is backed by faith and supported by practical action that it becomes the Rhema of God, which produces results.

"So until you take your fight to the British establishment, no one will listen to you. Recently, the Commission on Religious Education in Schools recommended renaming the subject of religious education as *Religion and World Views* to include the study of atheism, agnosticism and secularism. Added to this is a newspaper report that London youths are evangelizing people into Satanism. This is evidence of how far the Devil has taken over this country.

"These incidents should serve as a wake-up call for Christians not to be paralyzed by fear and inaction, but to be bold. How I wish many of us knew what the reformists went through at the hands of the Catholic church during the teething years of the Reformation. We know British society too well for us to remain complacent and fight our battles behind closed doors. If our normal lifestyle is taken as an offense, we must not apologize for it.

"There are occasions when offense becomes an important weapon of defense and warfare, and Christians should not shy away from it. Wearing a cross does not make one a Christian, but the fact is that it remains our symbol, our identity. It is like telling a Briton not to wave the British flag or telling a black man he must not let anyone know he is black or a white man, white. Until a law is passed making it illegal for any person to wear any religious symbol, it becomes a persecution for Christians to be denied that right. And we must fight with everything at our disposal to claim our rights.

"It is ironic that in a country where highly placed people wear the Nazi swastika at fancy dress parties, and where some British soldiers brazenly make Nazi salutes in front of the Union flag without arrest or prosecution, the Christian cross has become an instrument of criminal prosecution at every turn. Living is war, and those who don't want to die had better not live because the earth is a battlefield. Until God becomes your purpose for living, you are not yet a Christian. No country but Britain builds up the weak by pulling down the strong. You cannot be a Christian and not have a vision, and you cannot have a vision and remain complacent.

"If the demands of a community increasingly cut one off from that community or if the demands of involvement put a strain upon alternative patterns of community life, then war is inevitable. No nation can engage in a civil war of multiple factions at the same time and survive. And Christians are not going to stand by as idle onlookers. We must be active participants. If this country wants to destroy itself, we must be a major catalyst in the process. I'm talking of destruction as a refining fire, the aftermath of which is righteousness that makes the people of God.

"Violence transformed the calendrical 9/11 (11 September) to the emergency number 911. It was no accident or coincidence. It reduced the Twin Towers to ground zero, which was almost taken by force to become a mosque, with the blessing of the No. 1 citizen. That is the consequence of the absence of adherence to Psalm 119:9-11 in a society. Do you seriously think it is a mere coincidence that numerals 9 and 11 feature so prominently in this incident? The Bible does not lie, my friends.

"When your actions become the Rhema of God, the enemy will run when no one is pursuing it. A thousand will fall at your side, and ten thousand at your right hand, but you will be standing victorious. More so when we have the backing of chariots of fire in the spirit realm and multitudes of Christians all over the world in the physical realm praying with us." Jay paused and smiled.

"O, I see a river whose streams shall make glad the city of God. Christians are that river; their prayers, the stream; and London that city, representing the United Kingdom. So I call you, my brethren, for action. I want you to think of all I have said here today. I want you to think deeply about all that is wrong with our society, with our government, with our press. I want you to think of all that is wrong with our generation. There is just one thing, only one thing, wrong with our government, with our press, with our society and with our generation. But before that, let's briefly reflect on the keynotes of our generation.

"Ours is the generation that has been robbed of everything the world has to offer—opportunities, hope, morality, godliness, faith: you name it. We have been deprived of every positive thing in life. Instead, we have been told that the negatives are the only way forward. Yes, the fathers have eaten sour grapes, and the children's teeth are set on edge. The sins of evil leaders are visited upon their people. And we now have to live with the consequences of our leaders' bad choices.

"That is our generation—your generation, my generation and our children's generation, a generation that must die for the earth to survive, accused of causing global warming by breathing. Ours and our children are the generations for whom the joy of graduation has become the stress of university debt. So we should not aspire to higher education, because degrees and research don't come cheap, although these things were free for our leaders' generation. With no sound education and no quality jobs, those who naturally don't want to work are better remunerated.

"Thus our productive generation must die for the unproductive to survive. Our generation must lose more than half their earnings for the economy to survive. Ours is the generation that is denied any pension and so must work until we drop dead, yet pay the highest tax. Our generation must not have children, because according to anti-natalist movement, baby nappies and disposables are suffocating the environment and killing the planet. Our generation must die for animals to survive.

"Our generation is the generation of prisoners where the sane lock themselves up in their homes in fear of murderers who have taken over the streets. And the street gangs that make the streets unsafe are prisoners of their own psychosis. Some are prisoners of substance misuse and slaves to unearthly lifestyles. The rest are locked up in state prisons, where their vengeful and destructive escapades may be curtailed to some extent.

"Ours is a generation that cannot own property and cannot afford rent, because we have been taxed out of pocket by the government, with rent hiked out of our reach by foreign buyers. We are told that the economy is bad and we are in it together, but that has not stopped local councils from building multimillion-pound properties with our tax money, free for those who choose not to work because it is their right to be accommodated. Thus the British government has turned laziness and unruliness into a highly rewarding profession.

"Ours is the generation that cannot own a car because we are told it is a luxury, yet public transport has been prized out of our reach. We are the one-parent generation, on behalf of whom schools are forced to act as surrogate parents as we grow up without family values and no cultural or community values. Yet our teachers are made to fear their pupils, with reported classroom violence against teachers from children as young as four reaching epidemic proportions.

"We belong to the generation told that the effect of the atom's big bang on Hiroshima and Nagasaki resulted in destruction and disorder that lasted decades and affected even those unborn then. But our generation is now told that the big bang of another atom—the Higgs boson particle—is what created the earth and all the orderliness in it. Since a bang is a bang, how can it create order and disorder at the same time? My friends, God spoke the world into existence, and the sound of His voice was mistaken as an explosion of immeasurable proportions named *the big bang*.

"Yes, we are the generation that does not know the normative appellation of a man or woman, as it is obsolete in modern times. Ours is the lesser generation: feelings—heartless; relationships—meaningless; marriage—joyless; family life—loveless; attitudes—careless; wives—useless; husbands—hopeless; mothers—worthless; fathers—reckless; babies—fatherless; children—mannerless; youths—jobless; workers—pensionless; leaders—shameless; politicians—tactless; Parliament—clueless; society—directionless; the masses —helpless; our time—godless.

"Despite all these things, our hope in God remains endless because salvation is priceless and our God is timeless."

VII. The Communist Credo

"In our days, we have seen the family unit destroyed and the many problems emanating from this swept under the carpet by governments that pretend to know it all. That is what happens when a controlling spirit takes over a nation. Strike the shepherd and the sheep of the flock will be scattered; control the minds of the leaders and the people will be lost.

"The youths of a nation are the lifeblood of that nation, but here the youths are destroyed by the leaders. It is the communist credo—the wrong concepts of life—used by the Devil to destroy nations. I will just list a few of them for you to know what is happening.

"The communist credo says to corrupt the young; get them away from religion; get them interested in sex; make them superficial; and destroy their ruggedness. It says, by way of specious argument, to cause the breakdown of the old moral virtues: honesty, sobriety, continence and faith. It encourages civil disorder and encourages the fostering of a lenient and soft attitude on the part of the government toward such disorder.

"It suggests dividing the people into hostile groups by constantly harping on controversial matters of no importance. It advises to get people's minds off their government by focusing their attention on athletics, sexy books and plays and other trivialities. It advocates destroying the people's faith in their natural leaders by holding the latter up to contempt, ridicule and obloquy. It supports making the government disdain the people, overburden them and leave them helpless.

"This is what is happening in this country. Unfortunately, the people are ignorant of this. Most of them, having never lived in other climes and not knowing the difference, allow the government to take advantage of them by deceiving them with the wrong concepts of life, which they accept unquestioningly, with everyone being made utterly sheepish. This is a country where holiness is a crime and righteousness is an offense. I have great fears for the future of this country. If the past no longer illuminates the present, the future is in jeopardy.

"Our generation can no longer rely on the dictionary for the meaning of words. We are allowed to roam about in search of the meaning of life as what gave us life and meaning has been shredded in the quest for freedom. We Christians must live as unbelievers for peace to reign. Because society must homogenize, we must all become perverts to assume a national identity.

"Ours is the generation that drinks iniquity like water because we are told that the only way to be happy is to think that there is no God. As if the absence of God brings happiness. A nation that feeds its children with the wrong concepts and values of life should await the wrath and destructive instincts of its youths.

"The August riots of some years ago have not taught our leaders any lessons. There is no failure more disastrous than the success that leaves God out. No people have ever benefited from riches if their prosperity corrupted their virtue. But that is what prosperity has brought upon Britain, just as Deuteronomy 8 warned.

"Now to my question: what do you think is wrong with our generation, our government, our press and our society? Only one thing is wrong. The absence of the Word of God in society is what is wrong with us—the absence of God is wrongly interpreted as rights and freedom, that is freedom from godly principles. Psalm 119:9 says, 'How can a young man cleanse his way; by taking heed according to the Word of God.' But our leaders have legislated God and His Word out of our society and out of our lives.

"Any freedom outside the Word of God is no freedom. But despite this knowledge, the British establishment has rejected the freedom that is in godliness in exchange for things that dehumanize us. And it has imposed this rejection on all of us. This is why we must fight. If it were possible to rewrite the Bible, the British establishment would have done it to serve its own purposes and sway the world into perdition.

"I want us to understand one fundamental point, and that is that we Christians are not against individual choice in terms of how people want to live their lives. We appreciate the fact that people are different and that they have the freedom to choose their own way of life, just as we have the right to choose ours. What we are against is governments and agencies of the government forcing us to abandon our way of life and live other people's choices.

"We respect people for who they are, but we have a fundamental right to choose who we want to be, whom we relate with, and how we relate with them, just as others have. No one should be forced, in the name of inclusiveness or tolerance, to welcome into his home a person who would poison his food, or pollute his water or corrupt his family. People should respect others' beliefs, but no one should be forced to accept those beliefs. This is our contention.

"In life, there are only two guarantees: you are born and you will die. What you do in between is entirely up to you. So don't allow anyone to dictate to you how you should live your life. This is a call to duty, a call to action, a call to be who God called you to be, a call to drop the prayer bomb on this country and on all enemies of righteousness and of holiness in the United Kingdom.

"True freedom comes with godliness. Therefore, we must reject the exaggerated claims of any offer of freedom and new life through political reordering of human affairs. Such reordering polishes sin to make it acceptable. Ignominious living is termed a lifestyle; adultery is euphemized as a fling or having an affair; promiscuity is called being sexually active; abortion is seen as prochoice; prostitution is sex work; and noncommittal cohabitation is a partnership.

"A failed relationship, even if toxic, is polished in a soft tone as one's *ex*. Dictatorship is draped in political correctness. Serial underperformance and insubordination are ADHD (Attention Deficit Hyperactivity Disorder). Rebellious people are activists. Today's youth use the word *wicked* in place of *good*.

"The malaise of the government's bad policy on society is whitewashed as a scourge of modern life to make the government blameless in its policy failures. General laziness and disobedience are excused as a *medical condition*, and a free choice of those who suffer from one or more of the many State-invented diseases so they may remain juvenile and unemployed, etc. They tell you it is the twenty-first century as if the sun does not rise in the east and set in the west or as if the cycle of night and day has ceased. Britons and Islanders still drive on the left side of the road in the twenty-first century, against the convention in the rest of Europe.

"There is absolutely nothing in all of human history to indicate that man has the power to create a utopian society. Just as none of the so-called intelligent machines can be as intelligent as their makers, so can no human be as intelligent as his or her Maker. Refusing to acknowledge this basic truth is the thing that is responsible for most of the problems on earth. Truth is freedom, and the truth is not encountered in the abstract, but in the agonizing decisions of living.

"The finish line is the place of truth translated into action, action under the pressure of decision. The Christian cannot separate his prayers from his decisions, or separate the Word of God from the call of faith—faith backed by action. I speak of an action as the prophetic force of the gospel, challenging the evil powers manifested in the structures of injustice, division, greed and unrestrained power.

"So often lost because of the absence of Christian action from the conflict and from the fiercest part of the battle of everyday community life. This has devastating effects on the church. The Christian church must become the place where the mechanism and policy of good and godly governance of the state are dictated by Christians in the spirit realm before they are revealed to the leaders in the physical. Without that, 'Let it be done on earth as it is in heaven' can never come alive while the church remains concerned with a form of religion where the gospel is associated with conformity to unearthly and unholy political and social manipulations.

"For those who think what is happening is mere discrimination and not persecution, listen carefully. State repression of Christianity in communist countries started slowly like this. The Jewish Holocaust was not a sudden mass hysteria. It started with one democratically elected leader's policy that went beyond the borders of Germany. In the same way, here party policies through one leader have become national policies and are gaining ground like wildfire and extending beyond British borders to Africa and the rest of the world.

"Having tested our patience to the limit without offense and emboldened by our determined silence, our leaders decided to pit us against the society with a series of offensive legislation. We do not have any problems with any community of people in this country. We love every community just as they are, and they are free to choose how they live their lives.

"But they too must allow us to choose how we live our lives. Loving others is no reason we should fold our hands while war is waged against us, our jobs are taken from us, and our businesses are forced to close. We don't want any war, but it has been brought upon us by way of stealth and deceit for no reason other than that we seek the good of society by insisting people depart from evil. But because their work is evil, they want to silence us. They started the conflict on their terms and timing. But it will end on our terms and timing.

"Dare God to arise and watch His enemies scatter. Our God is a consuming fire. The tragedy of religion without power is that it leaves you ignorant of the incredible potential of prayer. Prayer moves God, and when God moves, things happen and situations change. God does not pass judgment upon a country that has incurred his wrath without any warning. He repeatedly issues warnings and calls for repentance, but if the country rejects His calls, then He brings His judgment suddenly upon that country.

"We have reached that point in this country now. And make no mistake about it: whether we like it or not, God's fire is going to burn Britain. Whether physical or spiritual fire, I don't know; what I do know is that God's fire is coming. And any wise person would do well to escape it because there is no preventing it. The Bible talks of men calling on rocks to fall on them. You will see something worse than that. The Bible talks of God doing a thing that tingles the ears that hear it. You don't know what the tingling of the ear is when it is from God. Pray that you don't experience it. There are situations that will make people pray for death to come, but it will elude them. And don't think that because you are a Christian, you will escape; even if you escape, you will feel the shock waves.

"These are no ordinary times. They are extraordinary times, and extraordinary times demand extraordinary prayers, not normal ways of praying. And this is where we step in, with prayers backed by action. But what action am I calling for? To go about destroying things, maiming and killing? No, because that will hurt the innocent. Shrapnel does not know who is a Christian and who is not.

"We must embark on a massive protest. Hardly any week passes by without one protest or another by every segment of society against issues they don't agree with; Christians in this country are the only exception. Nowhere did the Bible say we should not protest over evil ordinances. Jesus never said we should become the weeping children of the world.

"God did not move for the Israelites until they had gone to Pharaoh through Moses. And He will not move for us until we have called Him into our situation. He will not do anything until we have taken the rod of God in our hands as Moses did and go to the authorities, the pharaohs of the land. And the rod of God in our hands is not prayers; it is action—protest. Protest, man, protest."

Jay's forehead furrowed with untainted fury as he spoke, and the audience listened with rapt attention as if they were hearing these truths for the first time and as if what they were hearing was an abstract quotient in the empirical reality of everyday life in the country they lived in and were part of.

He continued, "What is right? There is no such thing as right because right is only a concept with no defined connotation. The world is gradually drifting to a stage where sanity and law will become obsolete because of people who are obsessed with rights and protests, and the speed of information is mobilizing a global force of jobless and wayward people into a formidable force of protestors.

"It is in this country that I came to know that there are professional protestors. Sometimes the protests relate to issues that have absolutely nothing to do with us in the UK but have as their only purpose the aim to disrupt our normal daily lives. Only God knows how much protests are costing the economy. While Christians are wronged all the time, they prefer to remain quiet because, like everyone else, they will find relevant passages in the Bible to justify their calmness.

"So they are daily subjected to red terror and a harvest of sorrows because they will not fight back. Humility is not stupidity. Our leaders are forcing us out of our jobs and closing down our businesses for sticking to our principles, yet we are quite like common criminals being led to the gallows. If all the bishops take to the streets to protest over an issue, who will dare arrest any of them, and who in the government will turn a deaf ear to their complaints?

"What stopped them from marching to No. 10 through London streets after the encounter between a former Archbishop of Canterbury and the Lord Justice over a sacked Christian marriage counselor? Imagine if they were from various denominations, especially if joined by those in the House of Lords; who would dare challenge them? And how can't the government be afraid? But I would not be surprised if compromising Anglican bishops were to sabotage such an attempt; after all, they are the only clergy members of the House of Lords.

"They should be bold enough to confront the government on issues concerning Christians. It is against God's command to be bold, for Christians to make cowards of themselves.

"I like Israel for one thing. Surrounded by hostile nations, Israel has no choice but to defend itself without listening to world opinion. From the creation of the state of Israel in 1948 to the present day, world opinion and international political action have continuously shifted strongly against Israel.

"In the same way, opinion and political action have consistently shifted very strongly against Christians and Christianity in this country, especially since 1997, when the rascals and God-mockers took over the government. Israel would have been uprooted from the face of the earth if it had listened to world opinion. Likewise, Christianity here will be completely uprooted if we don't take action now, and I mean *now*!" Jay shouted this last to give weight to the urgency required for action.

"My reference to Israel has nothing to do with the rights and wrongs of the Middle East conundrum, but I use it for comparison purposes. Now look at this. It was Britain through the Balfour Declaration that resulted in the creation of the state of Israel. Today, Britain treats Israel almost as an enemy. From the style of news reporting to expulsion of Israeli diplomats, to agitation for sanctions, Britain is always at the forefront, always ahead of others.

"It is British MPs who go to Arab lands to protest against Israel. They are the ones who would declare their constituencies an *Israel-free zone* as happened in Bradford. It is the British press that brands high-handed and disproportionate Israel's response to rocket attacks, without saying anything against such attacks. They condemn such a response but refuse to mention the civilians the British gruesomely killed in the Middle East and other parts of the world in their *coalition of the willing*.

"That is why we are daily bombarded with the news of the occupied West Bank, with no mention ever made of the EU's illegal occupation of parts of the West Bank, where they have spent millions of our tax money in building hundreds of homes without our knowledge and against international law in their double-dealing in contravention of the UN's Oslo II Accord. They subvert all conventions and laws with technical jargon as weapons of defense, rather than admit wrongdoing. While the US deports terrorists who set foot on US soil; Britain grants them asylum to terrorize us because 'they will not get a fair trial in their country.'

"Let them call me a rabble-rouser or a terrorist; I don't care, because I will not be the first to be so-called. So they called the PLO and Yasser Arafat; so they called the IRA; so they called Hamas, the Kosovo Liberation Army, and many others. Today many of these organizations are governments recognized by the international community and their erstwhile leaders' government authorities and given the red-carpet treatment by those who called them terrorists.

"The Irgun commando unit in particular, branded a terrorist organization by Britain, had some of its leaders awarded the Nobel Peace Prize. That is how irrelevant and vain British appellations are. A former IRA commander was given a state banquet here and shook hands with the Queen when the Queen was alive."

VIII. In the Limbo of Collective Ignorance

"Now for a nation that is given to seeking evidence, I present you just two pieces of evidence to save time—testimonies of what faith backed by action can do. My first example is the case of a police officer in Barnstaple, Devon, here in England. He was so worried about the poor crime detection rate in the area that he asked Christians there to pray for improvement and arranged quarterly prayer meetings for the purpose.

"Within a few years, the crime detection rate rose from the poorest to one of the highest in the country—from 26 percent to more than 40 percent—and serious road accidents fell from ninety-seven to thirty-two in just one year.

That was a big risk on the part of the officer in a country where a request for prayer immediately ends in a sack, although the public reaped the benefits as Christian actions always do.

"My second example is that of a landscaper who bought a piece of land by Newton Abbot, also in Devon, in 1972 and obtained temporary planning permission for a mobile home. In the year 2000, he started building a church without seeking any planning permission after the temporary permit had expired. A couple of years later, the local Teignbridge council realized they had missed a four-year deadline to issue enforcement notices.

"That omission automatically gained the landscaper-turned-pastor planning permission for the church building. The pastor confirmed that he had been led to do it and never doubted for a moment that he would get permission. In his words: 'The Lord doesn't start something He isn't going to finish.' A council spokesman had this to say: 'Unfortunately, some of the development on this site slipped under our radar, partly because there had been absolutely no complaints about it. This may be because it can't be seen from the nearby roads. With limited resources, there can be rare oversights.'

"Yes, this man prayed and believed God and followed up his prayers with practical action. If he had *prayerfully* waited for the council, he would never have built any church, because there has been a deliberate but undocumented policy to deny planning permission for any church building in England. We have too much commonplace evidence to prove that.

"If he heard from God, then his action wasn't illegal, because our Father owns the land. And when God is in it, it will always slip off the physical radar because our weapons can't be seen from earthly roads, the air, or the sea. Ours is a spiritual warfare. So be encouraged by these two testimonies, each of which asserts divine involvement. Oh, I see victory coming our way.

"But we must not take things for granted. In January 2013, an atheist church called Atheist Sunday Assembly was set up in Islington, London, by two comedians to *celebrate life without God*. It started with three hundred members at their first meeting. The assembly grew so quickly in number and territorial coverage that in less than two years, they had more than seventy branches spread across the UK and most of the western world. That is how fast atheism is spreading around the world. Only God knows the coverage at present. But you must know that atheism does not lead to secular neutrality.

"Western philanthropic and compassionate foreign aid is derived from their forefathers' Christian predilection, but today these humanitarian acts are being tied to sinfulness and an anti-Christian stance. As an ethnic minority, I am grateful, very grateful, for what the west did for the world, its humanitarian efforts and improvements in living standards.

"But I'd rather live in the Dark Ages with godliness in the midst of all the problems of that era, than live in the twenty-first century with its godlessness, despite the countless achievements. Because these achievements were not attained as a consequence of their godlessness.

"Some years ago, while Britain was still in the EU, school diaries popularly called the *Europa Diary*, printed by the European Commission in Brussels, had a comprehensive list of the religious festivals of Sikhs, Hindus and Muslims. It also listed Jewish and Chinese festivals and *Europe Day*, but Christian festivals including Easter and Christmas were completely excluded, despite three hundred and thirty thousand copies being delivered to UK schools—a supposedly Christian country. Guess what Christians' reaction?

"Only one Irish priest complained, prompting an inquiry by the EU. The result was a single statement of *regrettable error*. Case closed. That was the end of it. That is *Christian* Europe. I am sure many Christians didn't know about this, let alone react. This is why I love Muslims. If it were them, you would have seen massive protests all over Europe. The commission would have been forced to make a public apology and reprint the whole diary. Among EU politicians, few reactions came only from Italy, Poland and France. None from the UK.

"A former French government minister who lamented the omission as unacceptable observed that Christianity in Europe has 'fallen into the limbo of collective ignorance.' And there is no worse ignorance than the ignorance of your Maker and His ordinances, which is deadly. But such ignorance is mere pretense; it is deliberate because, during the drafting of the EU Charter, all the leaders flatly rejected a suggestion by one of them to include something about God and godliness. The French still fare better in Western Europe when it comes to Christianity.

"Time does not permit me to list other European offensives against Christians. The UN is not different from Western Europe, not when veto power rests in the hands of five permanent members of the Security Council, three of whom are secular in word but atheistic in action, with the other two being atheistic in both word and action. The UN is united only in ignominy. So don't expect any sympathy from any international organization, because they've aligned themselves against God.

"The church has the power to transform the social-political scene of this landscape, for the spiritual transforms the physical. We must not allow the present decay to continue."

"For a start, I am forming a pressure group called Justice for British Christians—J4BC. It will be a platform for a united Christian voice and Christian action. We will deploy everything at our disposal to make our case. We will grip the government by its jugular until they listen to us. They will not just listen but will also do what we want. We are taking this country back to God. If others are pressure groups, ours will be a fire group. We will heap the fire of God upon this country until it repents.

"We will stand up for any Christian in this country victimized in any way because of his or her faith. We will have a network of prayer warriors all over the country and internationally, bombarding heaven 24/7 with prayers for this country—and not prayer as you know it. This is a fire-action prayer. We will form a formidable army of protestors from all denominations, including non-Christian volunteers, ready at a nudge to storm the streets. This country has not seen anything yet. They will see Christian action in full force and will taste its sting. I will say no more; next week I will distribute information leaflets. And everyone is free to join."

Jay paused, his eyes roving the hall, as he mopped his face with his face towel before continuing. "A country is great not by the size of its land area or by the size of its population, but by how great its leader is. And a leader is great when he leads with the vision of God, because God's Word says, 'Without Me, you can do nothing.' This is the biggest difference between the UK and the US, the belief that it—the US—is a nation under God.

"I am not saying that every American leader is necessarily very godly, but they don't completely turn their backs on God. For any country, acknowledging God in the affairs of the state makes it easy for the leaders to lead by godly principles. It makes it easy for them to consult God's prophets and to ask citizens for prayers. Forgiveness is one of the hallmarks of godliness, but forgiveness in Britain is seen as a sign of weakness.

"Forgiveness makes it easy for a nation to first and foremost seek solutions to problems before seeking whom to blame, rather than seeking a scapegoat before ever thinking of solutions to the problem. That is why here we have so many inquiries that have not solved any problems. And the spirit of vengeance always sees any punishment as *never far enough*. Apportioning blame and seeking vengeance wipes smiles away and blots out any hope for tomorrow.

"The US may not necessarily be a forgiving country, but it is far better than Britain. This accounts for the gulf between the US and the UK in the rate of advancement in many spheres of life. But advancement aside, this difference is typified by the first response to the 11th September and 7th July terrorist attacks. When the 11 September attack happened, one of the first things the president did was to request that all Americans pray for the victims, their families and the nation. He himself went into total isolation at the National Cathedral in Washington, DC, to pray.

"When 7 July happened in London, the Prime Minister, a Christian, addressed the country on the steps of a hotel in Gleneagles and later at No. 10 Downing Street. Not a single word of prayer or of seeking divine guidance was contained either in his speech or that of the London mayor, both of whom avoided St Paul's Cathedral. Another example is when tragedy happens, the official US consolation message to a bereaved family is 'Our prayers are with the family,' while the British consolation is 'Our thoughts are with the family,' a sign of how God-averse they are.

"But with faith and action, we will triumph over the British establishment in our struggles. The signs of our triumph are already on the horizon. We have not yet won our struggles, but the union of the British kingdom is already disintegrating. I am not talking of the empire which disintegrated before many of us were born. Remember the revolting northern tribe?"

IX. Soldiers of Christ

"It is worth noting that since the letter *B* became the confluence between the second part of Great Britain's double-barreled name and the name of two successive Prime Ministers, the spirit of Belial has been at work, unleashed from the spirit realm, to take over Britain. That Belial spirit came and took hold of British leaders to do his will. From the Christian Prime Minister nicknamed Time Bomb, because of the speed of his modernizing agenda—who ousted God from Britain—to the grumpy God Blamer Prime Minister, so named for blaming God for all that is wrong with society, to the Demon Chameleon Prime Minister, there has been no let-up.

"The Time Bomb Prime Minister, or TB for short, and his successor God Blamer Prime Minister, or GB for short, to the lyrical Prime Minister Demon Chameleon, or DC for short, a sobriquet for his Maradonic dribbling fluidity in words and actions—words and actions that were equal and opposite, words that were music to Christian ears, and actions that pierced their hearts like Judas' kiss. He was the composer and songwriter of *Broken Britain*. Angered by his surname's first letter missing the *B* mark by a hair's breadth, he went on a rampage in search of a solution to *Broken Britain*. These were the leaders who broke Britain beyond repair and set a benchmark for subsequent leaders to trample on Christianity with reckless abandon. Until they stop legalizing illegalities, Britain will forever remain broken.

"Added to the above-mentioned British leaders are other enemies operating from the periphery and some later operating from the center. As dry deadwood makes the best firewood, so do mountain stones, trying to prove they are alive, spewing hot volcanic lava. And so do dead stones in London politics act as killer leeches, or KL and Bar-Jesuses, or BJ, against Christianity as if their sole purpose in politics is the destruction of Christianity.

"Before I round up my presentation, I would like to take this opportunity to thank various Christian groups and organizations in this country, including Christian businesses and individuals who in their own little ways have stood against the onslaught of the enemy and the godlessness of the establishment.

"In particular, I want to thank those who have been helping with funding Christian court cases, such as Core Issues Trust, Christian Concern and Christian law organizations such as the Christian Institute. I do not like mentioning names on occasions like this, but I wish to take exception in specifically thanking former Archbishop of Canterbury, George Carey and the former bishop of Rochester, Michael Nazir-Ali, who despite their retirement fought strongly for the Christian cause.

"In war situations, retired soldiers are recalled from their retirement. Also, when the leadership of any group of people, as happened in the Church of England, is weak, those who have left the stage are recalled to restore credibility and confidence. These are the reasons Saul went to the Witch of Endor to disturb Samuel's rest.

"Brethren, if we don't believe in ourselves, no one will believe in us. 'Behold, I give you authority over all the power of the enemy' is a promise that can never fail. So be confident of victory; we have the backing of a higher authority. Let us adopt the mindset of the British SAS, a mindset informed by their motto: *Who Dares Wins*. That is why they are the best in the world.

"Know that God answers the prayers of the faithful and honors those who honor Him. In North Yorkshire, a local doctor maintained the clock at St James Church in Clapham for thirty years. On the day he died, at ninety-two years of age, the clock mysteriously stopped at the exact time of his death, and not until after his funeral was it restarted. The action of the clock was God blocking all the clatter from the earth in order to enjoy the heavenly music of the angelic choirs welcoming His son home.

"Let me quickly give you two signs of assured victory. Amidst the debris of the World Trade Center after the 11th September terrorist attack was a seventeen-foot-tall steel beam in the shape of a Christian cross. That cross was not an ordinary beam and wasn't there by the will of man. It was a divine presence—of faith, of hope and of healing—in a place of loss and grief. It represented resurrection power.

"And nearer home, the architect who designed St Paul's Cathedral, Sir Christopher Wren, in the course of his work, found a single piece of stone bearing the word *resurge*: 'I will arise.' He placed the stone at the heart of his design. I promise you, the church of God in the United Kingdom will rise again."

Jay ended his speech by singing the song *Stand up for Jesus*, and the audience joined in, backed by heavy instrumentation. All began to dance as they sang it.

At the end of the song, he said, "Let that song reassure you of victory, no matter how formidable you think the enemy is. Please, when you get home, try to read the story behind this song, which proves that even as we take our last breath, we will still be standing up for Christ. Nothing can kill the Spirit of Christ in us, and that makes us victors all the time.

"Please don't forget to take my message to your individual churches. Let them know that the British state has declared war on us and that we must be ready to fight."

With that, he said a short closing prayer and packed his things on the pulpit. He picked up his iPad and other items and stepped down to join the crowd.

There was thunderous applause as he ended. For almost three hours, exceeding their normal prayer meeting time, Jay had held the audience spellbound with his speech. They were so enthralled that they didn't care how long it lasted. As he concluded, there was a predictable tension in the air. It was as if what they had just heard was dawning on them for the very first time. Everyone in the auditorium was fired up, their blood literally aflame. He'd whipped up their emotions, and they were now filled with holy anger, giving utterance to their desire for action as they milled out of the auditorium. Many went to shake hands with him, congratulating him and thanking him for sensitizing their minds.

Friends and groups were amazed at the depth of his knowledge, the ease of his recollections, the speed of his thought and articulation and his grim comportment reflecting the seriousness of his message. It was as if the revelation had hit them like a thunderbolt. It was a classic testimony of his scholarship and his academic prowess in obtaining first-class and distinction in his degrees. The speech was the talk of everybody as they went home. Outside, the air was thick and surreal.

On the way home, Kojo was driving, full of admiration for his friend. He said, "Jay, that was simply marvelous. I was looking at you as if I were looking at a complete stranger rather than the Jay I know. I know you are naturally brilliant, but this night you were exceptional. I sense the finger of God in your presentation. I thank God for your life. You are my hero."

"Thank you," replied Jay. "And you are my mentor. Whatever I am today in Christianity is due to your patience and mentorship, for which I am immensely grateful to you and proud of you."

"We give God the glory," said Kojo. "You were brutal, blunt and unrelenting; not even the church was spared."

"Righteousness demands honesty," replied Jay. "And if the judgment is to start in the church, one cannot but be honest and say it as it is."

"I remember that day in your shared school accommodation with Matt," said Kojo, "how both Robinho and I jokingly predicted that you would be a captain of God's army. I think that prophecy is about to be fulfilled."

"I don't have any choice in what the Lord chooses to do with me," said Jay. "I'd rather praise those of you who believed without any divine encounter." And so they talked cheerfully until Kojo dropped Jay off. And then he went home.

Chapter 18
The Call of Faith

Barely a week after Jay's address, the text of it was leaked to several newspapers, which published it in its entirety. It was usual for congregants to audiotape or videotape sermons at church services, prayer meetings, crusades and conferences. Some such tapes were usually given to friends to play. But somehow this one got leaked to the press. And once it had been published by one paper, others joined in, and it spread like wildfire.

Various print and broadcast media houses presented different editorials regarding the address. While some were very hostile and confrontational, there were those that took a softer view, acknowledging that there had been instances of injustice but frowning at *incitement to violence* as portrayed in the address. Some openly called for the revocation of Jay's citizenship under the 2006 Immigration and Nationality Act. An MP from a third, main party actually went as far as tabling a motion in Parliament in support of such a call. But it was not considered for debate for lack of merit.

It is amazing how God works. The media blitz to demonize Jay suddenly had him shot into the limelight. Someone only seldom heard of in the pages of a few newspapers through his occasional voluntary articles had suddenly become the face of the British media, as his photograph was printed on front-page banners, and as his physical appearance in a series of interviews on radio and television reached every home. These interviews helped the public understand what he stood for, but opinion was divided depending on individual attitudes toward such issues. But on the whole, his message struck a chord with a great section of the public.

Despite the uproar about his activities, Jay was undaunted in his crusade. Refusing to engage in combative dialogue with his media enemies, he repeatedly used them to his advantage and kept his focus on his mission. It was as if there were an invisible force compelling him in all he did.

A few days after the address, Jay established a number of Christian pressure groups—Justice for British Christians (J4BC), Britain for God (B4G) and United Christian Joint Action Front (UCJAF), among others. Justice for British Christians was principally responsible for fighting Christian causes in the UK; Britain for God was a worldwide network of Christians interceding with prayer for both Britain and British Christians; United Christian Joint Action Front was responsible for principally networking with all denominations to achieve Christian unity within the UK.

Of all the groups, Justice for British Christians was the strongest and was always in the headlines because of its activities. It became a strong platform for Christian action. No issue was too big or too small to evade their quick and sharp reaction. And membership was growing in quantum leaps. Jay used it to mobilize Christians in their fight back.

The group organized a series of sit-ins and numerous signature petitions. Having been much exposed by the popular press after his address had been leaked, Jay found it easy to stamp Justice for British Christians on the society as a force to be reckoned with. Ever since becoming a Christian, his articles had increasingly taken on the Christian view, until he became a full-blown Christian advocate. In addition, members of the group who were Christian intellectuals were dishing out strings of articles and write-ups strongly challenging the government's stance on Christian issues.

Member solicitors became too eager to go to court, freely representing Christians and Christian views at the slightest affront. There were instances when the group preempted the perceived government attitudes toward particular issues and acted premeditatedly to ward off any perceived affront or offense. They had permeated government offices at all levels, acting as spies and leaking government secrets deemed to be against the interest of Christians. And once these were leaked to the group, the members made a big issue of it.

Oftentimes there were concerted and simultaneous attacks on any such policy or program through posters, billboards and a series of demonstrations, even when the issue had not been made public by the government. Other Christian pressure groups suddenly found their voices through the activities of Jay's group.

There were several frequent protests, and Justice for British Christians was never short of people ready to protest at a wink. As predicted, many professional protestors who were neither Christians nor religionists, some of whom may have accidentally bumped into the protests, simply joined without even knowing what the protest was about.

Normally, Jay would have been sacked from his job, but there seemed to be an invisible force that hedged him against the plots of the enemy. The university he had attended and later became a lecturer for was under intense pressure to sack him. It was under secret but serious scrutiny, having been home to the Christmas Day bomber. The university senate had a number of meetings to reconsider Jay's position, but they could find no sufficient grounds for relieving him of his post.

In fact, there was insufficient evidence to discipline him. His actions and write-ups were within the bounds of freedom of speech. Secret cameras were planted in many parts of the university, and even in Jay's house the church he attended and the places where he held his prayer meetings. To his detractors, he became an untouchable public nuisance. All the official traps set to catch him failed. He fought many court cases, both for himself and for various Christian groups and Christian causes.

Despite many Christian lawyers representing him free of charge, he enrolled part-time for a law degree at his university. He wanted to know the law and be both authoritative and knowledgeable in the use of legal loopholes so as to avoid entrapment. He grew very fast in his relationship with God. Prayer and fasting had become second nature to him. And he practiced righteousness to a fault.

The zeal for God was so much in him that metaphorically he constituted himself a one-man riot squad, bashing and banging anything that came against the Christian cause. He set up a trust fund to help Christians who had lost their jobs or businesses through court action because of their Christian beliefs. Individuals, Christian philanthropists and Christian businesses and churches voluntarily contributed generously to the fund. He also organized many fundraising-sponsored charity walks for the same cause.

Additionally, he set up a number of Christian advocacies where Christians with any issues whatsoever could channel their complaints. Such complaints were investigated to ensure they were authentic before issues were raised with the appropriate authorities and agencies. One particular advocacy group was the Committee on Public Information for Christians (CPIC), which was responsible for liaising with various churches, collating information from Christians and churches on any affront against Christians and churches, and disseminating this information to other churches.

CPIC was also charged with organizing and informing churches and distributing literature on protests and possible protest dates, venues and assembling points. The church's voice was getting louder and louder. And things were beginning to happen. Court premises were now stormed by a large number of protestors when Christian cases were being heard.

A number of incidents happened that were difficult to explain. A judge who left the court at the end of his working day got swallowed up upon stepping into a manhole. But nothing was found inside the manhole when it was opened and scavenged. Another judge was blown to pieces by a sudden manhole explosion while walking along the street. Another judge had a heart attack on the judgment seat soon after passing judgment.

Another died in hospital from the injuries he had sustained when non-Christians hijacked a Christian protest, storming the courtroom in large numbers and beating up the judge. All four had individually passed judgment against Christians. These, with other similar, but less dramatic, incidents gave a semblance of divine intervention. But to the general public, they were chance occurrences that had no spiritual dimension.

However, one was so spectacular that it struck fear into the hearts of many discerning people. It was the case of the sudden fire at a new university college in London. The college had started with facilities at Jay's alma mater with the first enrollment in the third year of Jay's doctoral program.

After many years, it was ready to move to its permanent site in an Outer London suburb. Prior to that move was a meeting of the founding members and senior academics of the college. The meeting was held in the designated senate building at the new site. It was late morning on a sunny summer day when the meeting started, with twenty out of the twenty-two expected members.

The meeting had hardly started when fire broke out in the building where the meeting was being held. It was quite strange how the fire started because it was a bright sunny day with clear skies and no sign of rain. But there was a sudden roar of thunder and flashes of lightning, which ended in a split second—still with no rain—but somehow ignited a fire in the building, which lasted less than five minutes. The duration was so short that the fire crew had just arrived as the last flames were dying out. But within that short duration, the building was completely burned. All that was left were charred brick walls and supporting metal struts in parts of the building.

No flame had touched any of the surrounding buildings. All twenty attendees were burned to death, and it was difficult to ascertain the identity of the charred remains. It was a stroke of luck that the two surviving academics, both Americans who were absent, had been late in arriving as they were actually on their way to the venue. Investigations carried out to ascertain the cause of the fire were inconclusive. The main investigation concluded: it was an accidental spark occasioned by an act of nature.

The establishment of the college was the subject of much criticism: its tuition fee was the highest in the country. Despite initially touting itself as a university college, it had no degree-awarding powers and had no research students. Its undergraduates, on successful completion of their studies, were awarded the college diploma and the supporting university's International Programs degree, which was a distance-learning degree. The founders of the college were well-known God-mockers who saw everything in life as an opportunity to further their agenda.

Especially because the college's subject areas were mainly in the humanities, the establishment of the college was seen by many as a means to propagate its anti-God offensive with vengeance. Because of all the criticisms surrounding its establishment right from inception, the college had been nicknamed *New College of Calamities* long before the fire incident. After the fire incident, with the founding fathers dead, the college died a natural death. It had been one of the institutions in the prayer list of Justice for British Christians and many other Christian pressure groups.

Although the society took little notice of what was happening, the British establishment was beginning to get jittery about Christian cases in general and Jay's activities in particular. They had failed to silence him, failed to buy him over and failed to restrict him in any way, but could not entirely ignore him. He was becoming a dilemma for the government to handle. Many people who were outspoken critics of Christian principles were becoming wary and maintaining some measured caution, but that did not stop the persecution of Christians.

Despite bold and sustained Christian efforts at stemming the tide of persecution of Christians and the church, such persecution continued with increasing intensity. One particular group—the Jericho Wall Marchers, an offshoot of Justice for British Christians—took the unusual prophetic step of marching around the seats of government, praying, worshipping and praising God. It was not marching in the real sense of marching, but more of a long line of people walking along specified routes.

Between three o'clock in the afternoon and five in the evening every first Sunday of the month, they would march around the Houses of Parliament and City Hall, the latter of which housed the London Assembly. It was not possible to completely march around the Houses of Parliament because of its close proximity to the River Thames on one side. So they marched around it by walking a rectangular route through Westminster Bridge, part of Parliament Square and Milbank, then through Lambeth Bridge to Lambeth Palace Road and back onto Westminster Bridge.

That made parts of the route far from the building, but it was enclosed together with parts of the River Thames within the marching area. In the case of City Hall, they simply walked on the ground around it. Because of the long distance, they had to walk around the Houses of Parliament, the group there marched around it only once, while those at City Hall marched around that building seven times.

Each group normally gathered together for a short talk and prayers before the marching started. The Houses of Parliament group gathered at Emmanuel Evangelical Church on Marsham Street. As they marched or walked along their designated route, they would be singing and praising God. Then at the end of the march, they would shout a very loud "Hallelujah!" They had instructions to stop at specific predetermined places—seven in all within their long route—to pray and then maintain perfect silence for a brief moment before continuing their walk. For effective coordination, the group was usually segmented, with each segment under a leader.

On the other hand, the City Hall group was only a single unit. City Hall was surrounded all around by a large area of pedestrian pavement made of granite surfacing, and on the right side, it featured a beautiful lawn close to Tower Bridge. The River Thames was at the rear, while other buildings were at the front and on the left side. Members of the City Hall group usually waited in one of the coffee bars within the premises during winter months, then came out when it was time to start their march. They then would assemble on the right-hand side floor area of the building under the canopy of the extended upper floors, and sometimes on the open lawn during summer months.

They were usually led by one person at any particular meeting. Both groups followed the same process, with their leaders detailing the prayer points for the day. Then they would start by praying for the day's events before the actual marching commenced. Whereas they sang various songs; their starting and ending song was always *Let the Strongholds of Britain Fall Down Flat,* which they sang in the present tense instead of past tense, but to the tune of *The Walls of Jericho Fell Down Flat.* They sang it as follows:

Let the strongholds of Britain fall down flat.
Let the strongholds of Britain fall down flat.
As the children of God are praising the Lord,
Let the strongholds of Britain fall down flat.

Over time, many Christians from different churches joined the march to greatly swell their number. The City Hall group never really isolated themselves from the throngs of tourists and sightseers within City Hall premises, but they ensured they were not distracted by their presence. They would march or walk along the periphery of the entire premises, singing and praising God all the way around once, then gather on the porch or lawn for a short while to pray and keep a period of perfect silence. They would do this seven times.

At the end of the seventh time, they would shout a very loud "Hallelujah!" It was only at the end of the seventh round that they would shout "Hallelujah!" before dispersing to their various homes and other places. Despite their being mocked by members of the public, they continued this practice every first Sunday of the month for years.

Chapter 19
The Puzzle of Chequers

I.

Meanwhile, the persecution of Christians continued with the loss of several court cases by a number of churches and individual Christians. Preachers were summoned to court for talking about miracles and healings on the pulpit or for saying anything perceived to be politically incorrect. It was so bad that Christians were beginning to be arbitrarily arrested for things that constituted no offense, even for giving out leaflets and flyers in the street. The grounds for some arrests were so flippant that the cases ended up in non-prosecution.

One Sunday afternoon, two young men were giving out Christian tracts along Bishopsgate, by Liverpool Street station, in London. Both were arrested by police and taken to the station, where they were interviewed and charged with conspiring to cause public nuisance contrary to common law. One of them was additionally charged with possessing an offensive weapon in a public place, namely a cross, contrary to section 1(1) of the Prevention of Crime Act 1953.

Christian leaders vehemently protested the arrests and charges, arguing that no offense had been committed and that the Acts of Parliament under which the men were charged did not apply because giving out leaflets in the street was not a crime, and possessing a cross did not amount to carrying an offensive weapon. They made strong representations to the government about the charges, but that did not stop the court case from proceeding. The case attracted much publicity, and for once, the press took issue with the police and the justice system over the arrest and charges.

A series of editorials analyzed the relevant Acts of Parliament vis-à-vis the offenses said to have been committed and called for the quashing of the charges, but the government refused to intervene. As a result of the publicity generated, the court was always packed full with many people, including non-Christians, on trial dates. And on the day of judgment, the courtroom was fuller than ever. On pronouncing the men guilty on all charges, the judge was attacked and the courtroom was thrown upside down. The judge was beaten up and many people, including some Christians, were injured, some seriously. Some Christian leaders, including Jay and a host of people were arrested.

Church leaders refused to appeal the judgment and instead called out Christians to a massive daily protest at Whitehall and Parliament Square. More Christians were subsequently arrested almost on a daily basis. Many bishops of various denominations not only joined but also actually led, the protests. Four Anglican bishops, including a retired Archbishop, two Catholic Archbishops and a TV celebrity who was a Christian, went on hunger strike.

Christian leaders refused to call off their daily protest, demanding that everyone arrested be freed. The protests spilled over from London to other cities, and for the first time in the history of the Christian church in Britain, bishops and church leaders carried a protest march to No. 10. There were fears that hooligans would hijack the protest and that a repeat of the summer riots would ensue. Highly placed well-meaning people were appealing for calm on both sides, but the bishops were already on the warpath and refused to yield any ground.

As a result of the bishops' protest at No. 10, the Prime Minister, Tim Lane, decided to invite the Archbishop of Canterbury, the Catholic Archbishop of Westminster and the director general of the Evangelical Alliance to a meeting at Chequers. The purpose of the meeting was to set the agenda for a proper meeting of church leaders representing most of the denominations in England and Wales with the PM and senior government officials, to address pressing issues affecting Christians in the UK.

It was arranged for the Archbishop of Canterbury from Lambeth Palace and the Catholic Archbishop of Westminster to meet the Prime Minister at No. 10 and travel together with the PM to Chequers. The director general of the Evangelical Alliance had an official assignment in Oxford on the day and was to travel separately from there to Chequers later that evening, as the meeting was scheduled for the next day.

Chequers is located approximately forty-one miles from Downing Street and is a country house near Ellesborough, to the south of Aylesbury in Buckinghamshire. It is the country residence of the Prime Minister of the

United Kingdom and could be used by the PM to hold a private conference of some of his or her ministers, receive foreign visitors, or entertain guests as a special privilege.

The Archbishop of Canterbury was the first of the two bishops to arrive at No. 10 for the journey to Chequers. It was a late spring afternoon with a clear sky after a light rainfall. The car screeched to a halt in front of No. 10 Downing Street. The Archbishop of Canterbury alighted and walked to the door. Just when he was about to grab the big brass handle, the door was opened from the inside, with someone ushering him in. He walked straight through an entrance hall, being conducted by a police officer, to a small reception room and to a large red sofa.

But instead of sitting down, he chose to stand, gazing at a spot as if lost in thought. There was no time for sightseeing or being enraptured by the material opulence of the place—the distinctive black and white checkered marble floor of the entrance hall, the specially designed one-of-a-kind guard chair sitting in one corner, or the stone triple staircase with no visible support and its wrought-iron balustrade adorned with a scroll design and mahogany handrail.

This specially designed masterpiece of a staircase was the first thing that immediately caught a visitor's fancy. The Archbishop had seen it a couple of times he had been privileged to show up there. This was no ordinary visit and certainly no time for frivolities. A short while later, a waitress passed him by carrying a coffee tray to a large meeting room where a refreshment table was being set up.

The Archbishop was still standing by the red sofa when the PM walked briskly down the staircase to meet him. As they met, they shook hands and exchanged pleasantries. With the Prime Minister leading, both men walked away from the reception room and toward the large meeting room where the waitress had carefully laid the tray on a coffee table. The tray contained a big mug of coffee, a big mug of tea, a bottle of fresh milk, sachets of sugar, a small container of sweeteners, four empty tea/coffee cups with their saucers and a tray of unopened packs of assorted biscuits.

The table also had three bowls of assorted fruits, one at the center and two toward each end of the table, and decorative flowers in five vases strategically placed at different points on the table. The coffee table stood between two large antique-looking satin-covered sofas resting majestically at the center of the large ornate room. Besides these items, the room was spaciously empty.

As soon as both men entered the room, the waitress left. The PM pointed the Archbishop to the coffee table, but the latter showed no interest. Instead, he asked the Prime Minister when the Catholic Archbishop was expected to arrive. Receiving "Any moment now" in response, he looked clearly restive and his demeanor tense. To ease the tension, the Prime Minister started sharing some jokes with him, and from there, they started chatting about things completely unrelated to the issues at hand while awaiting the arrival of the Catholic Archbishop.

Despite the jokes and chitchats, the Archbishop still felt quite uneasy. It had started at the time he left home for the PM's residence and along the way, he had tried to figure out the cause but could not lay hold of any concrete reason. He could not convince himself it had anything to do with the present crisis, but at the same time, he could not discount that idea outright. He tried as best he could to drown out the feeling by focusing on their conversation, but it had little or no effect.

Soon, the Catholic Archbishop arrived and was likewise ushered into the small reception room and to the large red sofa by the same officer. Almost immediately, the same waitress resurfaced by the red sofa and conducted him to the large meeting room. Once they got close to the door, the waitress went back to attend to some other duties, while the Archbishop walked inside.

On arriving inside, he found no one there. He waited a couple of minutes and then walked back to the security by the entrance hall to ask after the PM and the Archbishop. He was told that they were in the large meeting room or some other room. It was easy to get lost in a house with about one hundred rooms inside it. No one had gone out since the arrival of the Archbishop of Canterbury, so security was sure that he and the PM must be somewhere in the building.

They called the waitress and asked about the two men, and she confirmed having left them in the large meeting room. The police security officers, together with the waitress, went to the meeting room and saw no one there. Then they started going from room to room, still with no sight of them. The Prime Minister's wife had been in their third-floor private residence when the Prime Minister went down to meet the Archbishop.

The waitress went there to inquire if the PM had gone back up, but such wasn't the case. There were many civil servants, about one hundred and fifty-two of them, in various offices; he could have walked into any of the offices with the Archbishop. It would be quite embarrassing to announce through the in-house intercom address system seeking the whereabouts of the Prime Minister, so they decided to allow some time to elapse before raising the alarm, while rather silently and slowly conducting their search. Even the third-floor apartment wardrobes, the loft and the manhole in the garden were not spared.

The waitress and a number of domestic staff, together with police officers on guard duty, were detained and questioned. More than an hour down the line and still with no clue as to where they were, security decided that it was time to alert everyone in the building. So the fire alarm was activated and everyone rushed to the designated assembling point, but the two men were the only people missing. The fire alarm simulated a test trigger and therefore failed to attract the response of the fire service crew.

That was the first time it dawned on the officers that the two men had really gone missing. Police reinforcement was requested and a thorough search was conducted within and outside the building, including hidden areas under shrubs and trees in the garden and all surrounding areas, without success. Attempts at contact through their mobile phones yielded no result as the phones were dead, possibly having been switched off.

When strange things happen, the mind sometimes resorts to the absurd in a search for clues. The small reception room at No. 10 had a stack of small pigeonhole-type boxes on the left side, each with a numbered ticket. The tickets were normally taken by visitors after depositing their personal items such as mobile phones, iPods and iPads, which they retrieved on their way out. Even these small boxes were not spared in the search for two full-grown adults. Abnormal situations do necessitate abnormal approaches.

There was a link between No. 10 and the Cabinet Office in Whitehall; this was also thoroughly searched, even with the use of police sniffer dogs, but to no avail. The footage from many CCTVs was examined, but yielded no fruit. The alarm was then officially raised, along with informing the Metropolitan Police commissioner, the Home Secretary, the Chancellor of the Exchequer, the Defense Secretary and senior cabinet members. The Prime Minister's wife was immediately taken away to a secret location for her safety, even though No. 10 was full of security personnel.

The Archbishop's wife was similarly taken away from her Lambeth Palace residence. The Prime Minister's and the Archbishop's phone network providers were contacted to provide detailed information on the last contact made and the last-known location of the phone. The Prime Minister had an app similar to *Find My Friends* on one of his mobile phones which included in his contacts the members of his immediate family and a similar app on another of his phones which included contact information for his senior cabinet ministers. His wife was on the list of the first group, while the Home Secretary was on the list of the second group. The two phones were used to try to trace his whereabouts, but the search returned nothing but error messages on the screens.

The Government Cars Agency of the Department for Transport operated and maintained ministerial cars stored at No. 10. They were driven by specially trained United Kingdom Special Forces (UKSF) close protection drivers and escorted by Protection Command officers in unmarked Range Rovers. UKSF was under the Ministry of Defense. A search of the pool of cars in the parking lot showed that one of the cars was missing. It was the very car that had been assigned to take the Prime Minister to Chequers that day.

The protection officer assigned to drive him that evening was immediately contacted and found to be still in the office awaiting the signal to move, as were Protection Command officers, who were to drive the escort Range Rovers. This was a big puzzle. Who had moved the car from its parked spot? Who had authorized such a movement? Where had the car been driven through that no one had noticed it? Where had the car been driven to? There were these and many other questions.

The vehicle movement logbook was checked and found to list no details of any movement or show any signature of authorization for the particular car. There were always protection officers guarding the pool of cars 24/7, in addition to numerous CCTVs, yet none of the officers had seen the car being driven away, and none of the CCTVs had captured any movement of the car. Contact with Lambeth Palace returned the negative presence of the two men. Contact with staff at Chequers confirmed the Prime Minister had not arrived there.

All roads around Downing Street—from Trafalgar Square through Whitehall to Parliament Square, and from the St James Park area to Victoria Street—and all adjoining roads within a half-mile radius of Downing Street were on lockdown, closed by a police cordon. Southwark Bridge, Westminster Bridge and Lambeth Bridge were also closed. Roadblocks were immediately mounted on strategic roads leading to all London airports and at various points on the North Circular Road and South Circular Road and major London entry/exit junctions on the M25 motorway.

A police major incident room was set up close to the intersection point between Downing Street and Whitehall, by the Berry Wing section of the Cabinet Office building. An assistant commissioner of police headed the investigation team. A quick closed-door ad hoc meeting was held by senior government officials to decide when and how to break the news to the world.

The disappearance occurred around half past four in the afternoon but was only made public through the BBC *Breaking News* slot at half past seven. But before then, office workers in Central London going home had witnessed severe traffic jams, and those around Trafalgar Square, Piccadilly Circus and Victoria Street up to Victoria Rail Station had seen increased police activity but were not sure what was happening.

There were hushed mutterings of terrorist alerts, which were clearly false. The St James Park, Westminster, Embankment and Charing Cross Tube stations were closed. A lot of plain clothes UK Special Forces personnel joined the police in their search, including Special Air Services and Special Boat Services.

A Dauphin II helicopter from the elite Blue Thunder unit was suddenly stationed permanently at Parliament Square, and its seventy-man strong crack squad was spread out all around. At the same time, a Wildcat AH1 helicopter of the Joint Special Forces Aviation Wing (JSFAW) and a specially equipped police helicopter—Airbus Eurocopter EC-135T—of the National Police Air Service were hovering around the EC1, EC2 and the SW1, and from the NW2 down to the HA4, postcode areas of London.

The influx of convoys of antiriot police vehicles from outside London constabularies and the presence of the firearms units, clearly indicated that something very serious had happened. With heavy traffic jams and road and Tube closures, many people had to walk long distances before getting means of transport home. Friday rush hour traffic for weekenders became a nightmare.

Breaking the news was extremely difficult and embarrassing for the government. This was Britain, a world leader and more invincible than invincible in its security intelligence operation, it had been outwitted, embarrassed and shaken to its very foundation. What was to be told the world? But there was no running away from it.

Once the news came out into the open, many BBC programs were suspended and replaced with frequent live scenes of police and special forces activities. The police on their part could now openly seek information with regard to any possible sightings by members of the public. An emergency phone line was set up and the number beamed to the public on TV and radio channels. As soon as the news was broken by the government, it was all over the world's TV channels and radio stations.

"Breaking news: British Prime Minister disappears, feared kidnapped. Information is sketchy, but it is reported that he disappeared with the Archbishop of Canterbury on the grounds of No. 10 Downing Street at about 16.30 local time. The nation is on high alert and soldiers are being drafted in to help the police in their search. The authorities are piecing together a timeline of events and are urging the public to come forward with any information they may have. So far no group has claimed responsibility, but some sections of communities in cities around the world, including Britain, are already celebrating the disappearance, purporting it to be a kidnapping."

TV and news media throughout the world suspended their normal programs to focus on the hottest news ever, filtering out of London. For the British print media, by the time the news broke, it was too late to print late editions, so it became the front-page headline the following morning. And so it was in some other countries, while in yet others, depending on the time zone, it was stop press, with the same screaming headlines in their late and special editions. Social media was agog with conspiracy theories and spurious information. It was quite dramatic and mysterious—rather unthinkable and unbelievable for a country like Britain.

The national security threat level was raised to critical, the highest level. Although the risk of terrorist threat to the UK was part of daily life, no prior warning of a specific threat had been reported before the incident. But despite this, what had just happened necessitated the Joint Terrorism Analysis Center (JTAC) of the MI5 to raise the threat level to maximum.

They urged the public to be on the alert and report any suspicious movement or activity to the police. Israel's intelligence service Mossad and its elite special forces unit, the Sayeret Matkal, offered to assist but was politely turned down, as were the French, German and US intelligence and antiterrorism units.

After the news broke, police received a number of phone calls of possible sightings from motorists along the A40/Western Avenue London-Oxford trunk road. The phone calls, indicating the car was heading away from Central London in the direction of Oxford, had come from different places, but all along the same stretch of road. From after the Egware Road flyover through Park Royal, Perivale and Greenford and all along the stretch of road up to Northolt, all gave the exact description of the car and the direction it was heading.

None could say precisely if it was the Prime Minister's official car, but all the descriptions exactly fitted the car's make, model and color—although none could say who was in the car or how many occupants there were. The windows were tinted and it was difficult to see the interior of the car. None saw the vehicle registration mark. The only suspicion people had was the unusual presence of four motorcycle security outriders, two in front and two behind. Surprisingly, there were no escort Range Rovers.

Sighting times were progressively up from a quarter after five in the evening to about six o'clock. Roadblocks were immediately mounted at several points along the road to Oxford. However, beyond Northolt, there was no report of any further sightings. But that did not stop police activity from going beyond, though it was heavily stepped up around that particular location. Roadblocks were also mounted at frequent intervals on all the connecting roads from A40/M40 leading to Chequers—A355, A404, A413, A4128, etc.

Specialized robotic electronic tracking devices with long-range coverage were deployed at New Scotland Yard, from where they picked up signals from the car's tracking sensors along the reported A40 route, but could not pinpoint the car's exact location. Then specialized radar equipment that looked like lawnmowers was moved to Northolt Airfield to help scan the entire area for possible signals. Another Blue Thunder unit helicopter with its troop was subsequently stationed at the airfield to comb the entire area.

A freshly burned car was eventually found at the airport in the bush about a quarter of a mile from the tail end of the runway. It was not certain whether the burned car was the one being hunted or was another car, as only the metal frame of the vehicle was left, everything else having completely burned to ashes. There were no charred bodies, indicating that no one had been burned up in the car. The PM's missing car had several special safety features, though classified.

These safety features ruled out the possibility of its having burned because it was fireproof. It was a Jaguar XJ X351, silver-colored, with a five-liter, supercharged V-8 gasoline engine producing five hundred and three horsepower with a top speed of one hundred and sixty-five miles per hour. It had bombproof security armor, bulletproof triple-glazed polycarbonate-toughened glass and a titanium- and Kevlar-lined interior.

The front driver's door was equipped with an oxygen supply in the event of a chemical or biological attack. It could also release tear gas to subdue angry crowds. The tires were specially designed to resist the effects of punctures, thereby allowing the vehicle to continue driving smoothly when any of the tires were punctured.

Underneath the body of the car were explosive-proofed linings with thirteen-millimeter steel plates to ameliorate the effects of a grenade attack. The car also had gun ports for security staff to return fire should the car be attacked. It also had a tracking device that reported exact movement and location at any time to Scotland Yard's control room. This device seemed to have failed, deepening the mystery.

Northolt Airfield, sixteen miles away from Central London, was a military airport but was also used for a few civilian flights. It was already past its operating hours for the day, and the last flight had departed almost two hours before the disappearance occurred. It was therefore assumed that whoever was holding the PM and the Archbishop were not far from the local area.

The airport was cordoned off as a crime scene; everyone on duty or present at the time was questioned. Only a few people, mainly military security staff, had been at the airport at the time, so it was easy to interview all of them. The airport commandant, a group captain who had finished work before the incident, was recalled and also questioned. But no one seemed to have spotted anything or seen the car driven to the airfield, including the burned car.

Nobody saw any smoke or flames or smelled any burning metal. And none of the CCTVs at the airport, upon examination, had recorded the car's movement around the airfield. Specially trained tracking dogs were deployed, and aerial surveillance by the helicopters already in the air was becoming more focused in the area, combing every nook and cranny for the two men. Antiterrorist squads worked flat out all through the night.

The remains of the burned car were taken back to New Scotland Yard and a thorough forensic examination was conducted. The forensic examination yielded no result. No fingerprint or any mark indicating any contact with any object was found on the car's exterior or interior. But the examination clearly indicated it was not the PM's car.

Two small civilian planes and three military planes that had been left overnight at the airport were thoroughly searched, to no avail. The questions on everyone's lips were: who had driven the car, who the security outriders were and where the motorcycles had been taken from. No police or security motorcycle was missing. The whole thing was a complete mystery. Time was running out fast, tensions were rising high.

The disappearance baffled everyone. It was as if the two men had just vanished into thin air. Had they been kidnapped? If so, who would have taken them? Rumors on the street had led to fingers being pointed at a number of groups, but so far no terrorist group had claimed responsibility. There was an embarrassment in the air, as thick as a dense cloud, worsened by TV live transmissions and a lack of clues.

As expected, calls were coming in from every corner of the British press for the Metropolitan Police commissioner to resign. A small group of placard-carrying protestors had quickly gathered around the police cordon at Trafalgar Square, also demanding the resignation of the commissioner.

II.

The PM and the Archbishop were oblivious to the mayhem they had caused. In their minds, everything was going on as normal. They had entered the car in accordance with official protocol and were conscious of being driven to the military airfield, but were completely unaware that the Catholic Archbishop was supposed to be with them. They were also unaware of the presence of the security outriders escorting them all the way to the airfield.

On their arrival at the airfield, the rear doors were opened, one after the other, by a security agent who had quickly come out from the front seat. The two backseat occupants disembarked and walked briskly to two waiting immaculately white horses. Intuitively the men mounted the horses and raced away from the airfield onto a dry, rough and untarred dusty road.

Military personnel in the airfield did not see when they arrived or when they left on horses. In fact, they did not see the car they had come in or the waiting horses, or the outriders, who simply vanished on arrival. The PM and the Archbishop had no control of the horses. The horses were acting on their own free will but were acting in complete unison. It was as if they had been programmed with specific instructions on what to do at specific points on the route throughout the journey. The rough dusty road stretched for miles on end, and the horses were running at breakneck speed. The road was lonely through a stretch of dry scrubland that expanded on all sides as far as the eye could see.

The two men were conscious of the fact that they were each riding a horse and traveling somewhere, but they did not know where they were, where they were going, or how long it would be before they reached their destination. They could not even talk to each other and did not know that anything unusual was happening to them. So they were not afraid, although they had lost track of time. The weather was bright and sunny all through the journey even though night had fallen in London.

They thought they must have crossed many countries when they arrived at the edge of what looked like an ocean. The horses stopped running and walked into the water. The men thought the horses wanted to drink after such a long journey, but no, the horses were walking deeper and deeper. And just when the two men thought they were about to be swallowed by the water, they suddenly found themselves in a very wide dry tunnel beneath the water.

Neither the horses nor the men were wet, even though their legs and parts of the horses' legs had dipped into the water. What surprised them most was that the entrance to the tunnel originated from within the water, with the water flowing across the mouth without entering into the tunnel. And there was no swirling of water around the mouth of the tunnel, no splashing of waves and no whooshing sound of water.

The whole tunnel topography was exactly as it was on the land they had been traveling. Once inside the tunnel, the horses picked up speed again. As the men journeyed, the tunnel became wider and wider, until it became an open environment with a vast mass of shrubbery and other vegetation as far as the eye could see, and with a rough dusty road that was exactly like the one they had been traveling before they reached the water.

Eventually, they reached an area of thick forest, but the road remained as dusty as it had been. They journeyed another very long stretch before they sighted what looked like the roof of a house appearing on the horizon far ahead of them. The roof became more visible and got bigger and bigger as they got closer.

III.

Back in London, the major London airports—Heathrow, Gatwick, Luton and Stansted—were put on high alert as security was beefed up. All smaller airports in other counties closer to London were also placed on high-security alert—Southend, Biggin Hill, Redhill, Hatfield, et al. London City Airport, which was the closest airport to Central London and located nine miles away on the eastern side of town, was immediately closed, even though there had been no information of any unusual activity there.

The airport was a civilian airport operating flights mainly for local and European destinations and a few international ones. Daily flight operations usually closed by 22:00 hours, but on this day the airport closed at the same time Northolt Airfield had. The only commercial heliport in London, located in Battersea, was also closed. And most European airports were immediately alerted to the security situation in Britain and the need for extra vigilance. All staff at the City Airport were subjected to serious scrutiny before being allowed to return home.

North Woolwich Police Station was home to the Special Operations Branch (SO18) of the Metropolitan Police Service, providing security at the City Airport. More armed officers were deployed to support those officers. Also closed were West London's White Waltham Airfield Aero Club and Booker Airfield in High Wycombe, both of which were used more as recreational airfields for flying club members, and for such crafts as gliders, rotary-wing aircraft and vintage aircraft, among others. They operated mainly in the daytime but were closed all the days the search lasted.

Meanwhile, the Met Police Service Marine Policing Unit (MPU) had increased the number of its fast-response vessels monitoring everything on the River Thames for any unusual activity on the waterways. The MPU was joined by a detachment of the SBS, the navy's crack Special Boat Service unit. British Transport Police maintained a very heavy presence at rail stations in London, especially at the St Pancras Eurostar terminal.

The morning following the disappearance, a crisis committee meeting of senior cabinet ministers became something akin to a war cabinet. It was called COBRA. The Cabinet Office headquarters, 70 Whitehall, was where the Crisis Response Committee was located, in Room A, which was the Cabinet Office Briefing Room, hence the acronym COBRA. The meeting was chaired by the first Secretary of State, Jo Baker, and she was expected to report back to MPs later in the day in an emergency session of Parliament. The COBRA meeting was brief and yielded nothing.

It was mass hysteria that morning. The world press had descended on London, and all sorts of rumors were flying about, both in the streets and in the press. Thankfully enough it was Saturday, a work-free day, which made the traffic situation less of a problem in the morning period with all the road closures in the affected areas. In addition, many offices, including some business premises within the police cordon, were officially closed.

Meanwhile, the military had been placed on high alert and was on standby, while heavy police reinforcements had been drafted from all outside London forces, with more than half of these ransacking all the bushes within the entire Northolt area and the surrounding towns. The airwaves were abuzz with police and military intelligence messages. Air control around the world was on high alert. The large meeting room at No. 10 became a paint shop of police forensic activity, supported by military intelligence.

From the counterterrorism team of the MI5, officers were assessing intelligence, studying briefs and analyzing intercepted communications and surveillance video clips, especially in relation to known individuals and groups of particular concern. They ran several checks on irregular data, hoping to spot connections and identify patterns that would help generate ideas on how to progress with the investigation. They liaised with agent runners and mobile surveillance officers for new leads in an effort to bring senior security officers up to speed on their activities.

The major incident room, on its part, was a beehive of activity, and the atmosphere there was electric. There was a lot of shifting of papers and documents. Data entry on computers was racing away as every detail of information received was scrutinized, recorded and computerized. Every bit of time was noted and checked against information received to account for progress made or for any lapses. Orders were commanded and instructions given and acted upon to the letter. Details of specific instructions, conversations or messages between officers, or phone conversations between officers and members of the public, were noted.

By the evening of that day, the call for the police commissioner, Sir Paul Collins, to resign was getting louder. Early that night a candlelight vigil was held by a small group of sympathizers camped by the police perimeter cordon near Trafalgar Square, where they prayed earnestly for the two men and for the nation. Twenty-four hours had gone past, and the police had not gotten any nearer to the answer than when they first started.

IV.

Still on their journey, when they got close enough, the Prime Minister and the Archbishop saw a house in full view directly in front of the road, though still far from them. They found that it was the roof of the house they had seen from far off. Soon the road ended where the house was. The house was in a large compound demarcated in front by a short western red cedar hedgerow that had recently been pruned.

Lining the inner side of the hedgerow was a brick fence of the same height as the hedgerow, about three feet, and stretching about fourteen feet on either side of an iron-gated entrance, itself about twelve feet wide. From the end of the brick wall on either side, the cedar shrubs grew very dense and tall, more than thirty feet in height and ran as far as the eye could see. The area from the front gate to the house was about forty feet long.

The house itself was an average-sized bungalow that could have gone for a four-bedroom flat by British standards. The whole ground in front and about six feet on the left, right and rear edges of the house was paved with assorted-color interlocking bricks exquisitely arranged in a symmetric pattern to form a beautiful tapestry. Aside from that, there was nothing extraordinary, as everywhere else was a green field. It looked as if the house had just recently been built or refurbished. It still had the smell of new oil paint, Ginger Glow Dulux, gold in color.

As the horses approached, the gate opened of its own accord and then closed after the horses had gone through. The horses galloped into the compound and stopped abruptly in front of the house. The whole atmosphere in the compound felt festive even though there were no decorations. Smoke was seen rising from the chimney at the rear of the house, lazily wending its way into the beautiful sky.

A flight of three stairs led up to a small veranda, about twelve feet long from the extreme right wall toward the left. A stainless steel balustrade with a handrail ran from either side of the first stair of the open staircase, from the left side to the left end of the veranda, while the right was straight, buried in the wall. The entrance door was directly in front of the staircase by the right wall.

All three front windows were to the left of the door—single-glazed, untinted and equidistant from each other.

When the two men dismounted, they instinctively walked toward the door of the house, looking all around the front compound. As they looked, they discovered that the horses had disappeared. The Prime Minister was in front, and he gently tapped on the door. A male voice within invited them in. The Prime Minister took hold of the aluminum-clad door handle, turned it downward and pushed the door gently open, then went in, followed by the Archbishop.

The interior turned out to be a near-square open plan. Directly opposite the entrance door was another door that opened into a corridor. The right wall between that door and the entrance door had three windows similar to those in the front wall, whereas there was none on the opposite wall. The rear wall too had no windows. The left wall had one door at about the middle of the wall, equidistant from both ends. The entire interior was painted the same color as the outside. The walls were completely bare of any hangings or decorations.

There were no light bulbs or any electrical appliances, but the room glowed in ethereal luminescence, completely different from normal daylight. It was also the optimum room temperature. The ceiling was of varnished plywood, and the flooring was of high-gloss brown pecan laminate wood. Two large single-seater executive leather chairs with hand rests on either side sat side by side, backing the entrance wall and facing the rear wall. There were no other furnishings.

When they entered the house, there was nobody, so they began wondering who had asked them in. But there was an indescribable peace and tranquility that surpassed comprehension. As they stood scanning the interior with their eyes and taking in all they could see, the rear door opened and a young man entered the room. He was about twenty-seven years of age, tall and lanky, with a longish face, a long pointed nose, blue eyes and defined cheekbones. His hair was cut short and very light brown. His face was so smooth that He may never have grown any beard.

He wore a plain white T-shirt on top of dark blue denim jeans, with striped white Adidas trainers on His feet. Despite the simplicity of His attire, it had a sartorial elegance to it. There was something about Him that defied description, a radiance that was celestial. It was as if He floated in the air as He walked. As soon as He entered the room, the whole atmosphere changed.

It was as if His physical presence emitted an incredibly bright shining light with a warm, lovely soothing brilliance that suddenly filled the room and seemed to have been sprinkled with a heavenly fragrance. He walked straight toward the men, smiling as He shook their hands and embraced them, one after the other, welcoming them with exceeding joy and excitement.

"Welcome, gentlemen," He said in a pure English Midlands accent. "It is My pleasure to have you around. Please take your seats and feel at home. I will be with you shortly." His voice was like a song to their ears, but it also had authority to it. He walked right back through the same door. They sat down, the PM on the right and the Archbishop on the left. For no apparent reason, they just felt exceedingly elated.

Then, to their amazement, shortly after they had sat down, they saw a table emerge from the rear wall, directly in front of them, and gradually roll toward them and stop in close proximity to them. For the first time since leaving No. 10, they were frightened.

They instinctively stood up and shifted as if to run, but the kind and gentle voice came to reassure them: "Please sit down and don't be afraid; nothing can touch or harm you, no, not while you are here. Take your choice from the table while dinner is being made ready. Once more, you are welcome."

Just then, two round stools slid out from under the table, which was held in place each by an attaching strut for them to sit within easy reach of the tabletop.

As soon as the young man had finished speaking, gentle background music started playing as if filtering in from everywhere—walls, roof and floor. It was cool and uplifting. The two men sat there silently, listening and gazing all around the hall, from the table to the walls, to the ceiling, to everywhere else and back again. They wondered where the music was coming from. They wondered how the table had rolled steadily into place in front of them without tracks on the floor, and how the stool had slid out.

They looked at the large tray on the table; it contained a mug of steaming coffee, a mug of tea, a small jug of milk, a small container of sugar, a saucer of sweeteners, a plate of assorted biscuits, a plate with three small bread rolls, a bowl of steaming mushroom soup and one of vegetable soup, a bottle of orange juice, a bottle of tropical fruit juice, a bowl of seedless grapes and a pack of serviettes. A slip of paper on one edge of the tray had *With compliments—HS* written on it.

"Gentlemen, feel at home and enjoy what is set before you," the gentle voice said above the music. "I'll soon be with you," He assured them.

They sat on the stools and started to eat. The PM only sipped a little orange juice and ate a few grapes, while the Archbishop delighted himself with the mushroom soup and two bread rolls. They could smell the beautiful aroma of the food being prepared and did not want to spoil their appetites by overindulging in the snacks. The aroma was strong, but they couldn't make out where it was coming from. There was no sign of a kitchen or any room in the house. When they finished, they sat back down on the leather chairs, and the stools slid right back underneath the table, which steadily rolled back, unaided, into the wall and disappeared.

While they were eating in silence, they were thinking of so many things. This was an unusual place. They had never been here before and were complete strangers to it. Yet the voice that spoke to them completely dispelled whatever fears they might have harbored. The place was very simple yet very profound, alluring, soothing and overwhelming; they felt completely at home. Nevertheless, there was something not quite normal about the place which they could not explain.

The voice speaking to them simply wafted in from every part of the room rather than from a particular direction. Also, they could not muster the boldness to ask Him who He was or why He had brought them there. On top of this, they couldn't even speak to each other. It was as if their minds had been taken captive to do His will, and they obeyed every instruction rather than compulsion. Additionally, the music was absorbingly therapeutic and celestial—like nothing ever heard on Earth.

As soon as the table disappeared into the wall, a large electronic screen rolled in from the exact spot on the wall as the table had. It was standing on a tripod, which also had no rollers. The screen stopped where the table had stopped and was at optimum eye level and distance.

The voice came again: "Gentlemen, the restroom facilities are to your left for your convenience. Through the door, you'll find a corridor, from where you'll find doors to different rooms clearly marked according to their functions. The electronic screen in front of you is for your entertainment."

The screen was displaying nature in all its beauty and glory—exhilarating scenes of grandeur and tranquility. The scenes were shifting continuously, showing different segments of the natural world and often alternating with various scenes of wildlife. The electronic screen had no sound of its own, but the music that was already playing blended like background music with the scenes on the screen. And the music now seemed to be coming out from the screen's speakers.

"Please relax and enjoy yourselves. I will be with you in a bit. Kindly bear with Me," the young man added.

Both men were transfixed as they initially gazed at each other and remained silent. They focused on the screen but occasionally shifted their gaze all around the room.

A few minutes later, the young man re-entered the room. "Thanks for your patience; please, let's go to the table," He said and then turned and started walking to the same rear door He had come out of. They followed Him. They passed through the door into a small corridor that ended in a door that led outside to the back of the house.

But before getting to that door, they turned left through another door into a large room that doubled as a kitchen and dining area, the two sections were separated by a long table laid widthways at the middle, leaving enough space for passage at both ends of the table. The dining area was immediate to the door, while the kitchen was behind. Both featured oak chevron flooring and the kitchen had custom concrete worktops.

The dining area had a single set of average-sized Georgian mahogany tables with two chairs on either side and one at each end, making a total of six dinners. Each chair was spaciously separated from the adjacent chair. The table was positioned lengthwise in the dining room and vertically to the separation table between the dining room and the kitchen. The table was covered with a spotless white tablecloth.

At the center was a hand-painted ceramic vase containing a bouquet of silk roses surrounding a single stalk of silk lotus at the inner core of the vase, jutting out higher than the roses. Its luminiferous petals emitted different colors in a sequence that produced a very beautiful spectrum. Also placed at the center of the table near the flower vase was a single handwoven basket containing some fresh fruits—apples, oranges, bananas, clementines and a small cluster of grapes.

The separation table, on the other hand, a relatively narrow long table, had a blue Formica top. At each end was a single tall glass jar with an assortment of nuts—hazelnuts at the bottom, followed by cashews, then almonds and finally pine nuts. All around the inner periphery of each jar, and held in place by the almonds and pine nuts, were arranged spaghetti-like strands, rooting from one end and slanting to rest on the mouth of the jar at the opposite end, thus forming a funnel, which towered above the jar. The strands were incandescent and emitted an effervescent sweet fragrance that was difficult to describe and which percolated around the whole kitchen and dining area.

Laid between these two glass jars was a display of various dishes, but mainly English cuisine, set for buffet service. Various food serving utensils—stainless steel ladles, tongues and forks—were properly matched to the right dishes. Eating plates and bowls were stacked on two tall stand-alone metal racks to the right in front of the separation table on the dining side.

On the dining table itself were drinking glasses, cutlery and crown-folded table napkins, all properly laid out in three seating positions. Packets of plain white serviettes also lay at the sitting positions. The luscious aroma from the combination of the various dishes added to the delightful freshness of the room to invigorate one's appetite.

The young man went to one end wall and pulled out a drawer from a set of cabinets. In them were newly dry-cleaned folded white aprons. He asked if either of them needed one, but they both declined the offer. He then pushed the drawer back in without taking one Himself. He had earlier taken off the one He used while preparing the food. He asked that everyone serve themselves.

The PM served himself a few slices of roast beef, some steamed broccoli, some roast potatoes, a portion of shepherd's pie and gravy. The Archbishop served himself a roast lamb, spinach, Yorkshire pudding, mashed potato, gravy and wholewheat muffin. The young man served Himself steamed carrots, green peas, parboiled corn on the cob and a few slices of smoked salmon garnished with parsley.

After serving themselves, the PM and the Archbishop sat close to each other on one side of the table, while the young man sat on the other side of the table directly opposite them as prearranged by the position of the cutlery and drinking glasses. He had shifted the bouquet of flowers and the basket of fruits from the center of the table to one side while they were taking their seats. Before sitting down to eat, He offered thanksgiving for the meal as the volume of the background music lowered of its own accord. It was a sumptuous feast with a lot to eat, including assorted hors d'oeuvres, desserts and drinks.

"You are so quiet," the young man said. "Please feel free and be yourself; talk if you want to. I am at your service. How was your journey?"

"It was smooth but very long, sir," the PM answered, finding his voice for the first time since leaving No. 10 and not knowing why he was reverencing the young man by calling Him 'sir.'

"Those stallions were fantastic, sir," added the Archbishop. "They know the route so well and were faster than anything I have ever traveled with."

"I thought they were going to refill when we got to the big river, but they didn't," said the PM. "Yet they were not tired. They are quite different from other stallions."

"The difference is that they wait on Him," said the young man. "And because they wait on Him, their strength is always renewed. They mount up with wings like eagles; they run and are never weary and never faint." As He said that, He poured orange juice into a glass. After sipping a little, He put the glass back down on the table. There was a little silence, and none of them could ask Him who it was whom the stallions waited on.

The Prime Minister eventually broke the silence, saying, "It was an experience of a lifetime, sir. I mean riding on those stallions. I can't wait for another ride."

The young man smiled and said, "You haven't seen anything yet; wait until you ride on eagle's wings. You are in for a treat."

"Do you have eagles here too?" asked the Archbishop.

"Yes, We have everything," He answered.

"I can't wait to ride on the eagle," said the PM, chuckling like a child. "I wish it was as soon as we finish eating."

"I expect you to have some rest after that long journey," said the young man.

"No, sir," the Archbishop said quickly. "We are not tired. The journey was long but very exciting and so refreshing that we don't feel we have actually undertaken any journey."

"That is true, sir," said the PM. "We were not even hungry. In my own case, it is only the presence of this food that aroused my appetite and I suddenly became a little hungry."

"I don't intend keeping you long here," the young man said, "so you won't be waiting long for a taste of riding on the eagle. But first things first: we will be taking a walk in the fields after dinner. That in itself is an experience on a different level."

"Where are the horses and eagles kept, sir?" asked the PM.

"Yes, sir. When we arrived and alighted," said the Archbishop, "we were looking at this house, and by the time we turned round, the horses were gone—gone so quickly it was as if they simply vanished into thin air. But is there a stable nearby?"

He waited to finish the food in His mouth and then said, "Everything you see here is only here for your sake. The moment you are gone, this place will fly away, including this house."

"Are we going to fly with it?" asked the PM.

"How can you fly with it when you don't know where it is flying to?" He asked in response.

"I am sorry, sir," the PM apologized.

"You don't need to be sorry; you haven't done anything wrong," He said, smiling at him.

"When you say you have everything here, using *We* instead of *I*, I wonder if anyone else lives here with you?" asked the Archbishop.

"We are never separable," replied the young man. "Don't worry, I will explain later. For now, relax and enjoy your meal. We have plenty to talk about later." After a short silence, He added as an afterthought, "Actually, let's talk about London. I never cease to be fascinated with London. Great city."

"It is, sir. It is," said the PM. "It is about the most cosmopolitan city in the world. Its cultural mix is so diverse, it's unbeatable.

"Indeed," he affirmed. "There have been several new landmarks, especially since the turn of the century—Millennium Dome, Millennium Wheel, Millennium Bridge. I can see the millennium spirit has taken over your nation, London in particular."

"Oh, sure, sir," said the Prime Minister joyously. "It is a very nice feeling. It is the spirit of the time. We have added a lot since then: new skyscrapers, cable transport, airport expansion, etc., etc. It has been a fantastic period of development and achievements."

"Splendid," said the young man, looking at the Prime Minister in the eyes. "I hope that includes improved standard of living for the people and enhanced security of life and property." He waited a few moments before adding, "Something happened that was a bit unprecedented very early in the new millennium. Four Metropolitan Police commissioners in five years. Was that also in the spirit of the time?" There was no response and after a short silence, He added, "London! London! London! A city rich and poor at the same time. What a great contrast."

"Very true, sir," said the Prime Minister. "Every city is like that, rich in some areas and poor in others."

"Pity you don't understand my statement," said the young man. "I think after eating you should rest a bit, probably have a small nap. Then we can talk when we go for a walk."

"No, sir," objected the PM, "we are perfectly fine. Aren't we, Archbishop?"

"Of course we are," said the Archbishop. And so they chatted and laughed as they ate until they finished. They ate less than a tenth of what was on the table. The young man carefully covered the leftovers and left them on the table. He asked the men to rest for a while, explaining that the food needed to be digested before taking a walk. And so they rested for what seemed like thirty minutes. Eventually, they went outside through the back door to acres of land stretching all the way from left to right, as far as the eye could see. It was like a massive grazing field, recently mowed.

Various fruit and flower trees abounded in the field, but because of the size of the field, they seemed sparsely dotted. They were in rows far apart but all over the field. The atmosphere was stunning. Rays of light sailed through a vista of beautiful clouds, resting on the fields and transforming the entire landscape into a mass of brilliant scenery. For sitting and relaxing, there were highly polished wooden benches with slanting backrests located at various intervals.

"Sir, while we were eating, I asked if anyone else lives here with you," said the Archbishop.

"That's true," replied the young man. "As I said, We are inseparable, but no one lives here, not even Me. I am on an errand. As I said, this place is here only for your sake and so am I. The moment you are gone, I am gone."

"Then why are we here? Where is this place? Are we still in London?" asked the PM.

"You are definitely not in London, not after that long journey," He replied.

"But are we still on earth?" asked the PM. "Because we never saw anybody on our way here, and it's so far away."

"It's like an uninhabited island," added the Archbishop. "The first time I spoke here, it was as if I had just awakened from a dream. But it looks so real—very real—and yet a bit unsettling."

"Nothing can be unsettling when I am here with you," He said. "Whether or not you are on Planet Earth shouldn't worry you. Although you are very far from Britain, you have absolutely no need to fret. We are here to dialogue, to reason together. I could have come to you in London, but the purpose of this dialogue is so important that a completely secluded place far from any noise is absolutely essential. This place was specifically chosen and created for this purpose. As the Archbishop said, we are on an uninhabited island, at what to you seems to be one end of the earth."

"So it is earth then," said the PM.

"The truth is that this island never existed before," said the young man. "It was created in an ocean for your sakes and must therefore reflect earthly conditions since man's habitat is the earth. The water you saw on your way here is an ocean, and not a river as you thought. We are actually under that ocean."

"That is mysterious," said the PM. "This place is so beautiful and so vast, and with clouds in the sky, that to think we are under an ocean is simply incomprehensible. It is mysterious, to say the least."

"There is nothing mysterious about our being under an ocean," said the young man. "If you are able to create traffic tunnels underwater in your country, then why do you think it impossible or mysterious to create an island under an ocean?" They kept walking, and despite walking quite leisurely, they covered great distances in a very short time. Soon the house was out of sight.

"This place is very quiet and serene. It is like Eden," said the PM. "I could spend eternity here."

"Don't worry, there is a better place than this," said the young man. "This is still earth as it were, not different from any other part of the earth except that it has not been invaded and polluted by humans. There is a place of indescribable splendor and glory that will take your breath away. No eyes on earth have seen it, nor ears heard of it—nor has it entered the heart of man what things await them there that love Him."

"I am sorry, sir," said the Archbishop. "Please don't be offended; I have been meaning to ask this question and have not been able to."

"Oh, sure, feel free to ask any question," said the young man. "You don't have to be apologetic for anything."

"Who are You, and who is *Him*?" asked the Archbishop.

"Oh, I am so, so sorry," said the young man, "for taking things for granted. Parents are not supposed to introduce themselves to their children, and likewise, children to their parents, unless the latter are runaway rebellious children who disown their parents, which I suppose you are not. I am not an absentee parent who does not know His children.

"Hence, I was so excited about your coming that I had to prepare the food and set the table myself—that is how happy I am. I know you very well, even though you say you don't know Me. It speaks a lot about your relationship with Me. But you are not here to receive blame. So for a formal introduction then, let Me say for now I am a Messenger. *Him* is My Master as it were, the Ancient of Days. But He is present here, as indeed in all the earth as HS." His words were almost lyrical. He spoke with such authority that it baffled them.

"Yes, the coffee tray had a complimentary slip endorsed by HS," said the Archbishop. "I don't think we know the meaning of HS; I personally don't know, to be honest."

"I don't know, myself," said the PM.

"I am flabbergasted," said the young man, laughing. "You are pulling my leg, innit, as you say in London. Right?"

"No, we are serious; we don't know," said the Archbishop.

Then He stopped walking and stood still, looking at them in the eye as they, too, stood still.

"I can excuse the Prime Minister," said the young man, "but not you, Archbishop. Just think; think! You are composed of three things—body, soul and spirit."

"Ah, I know," the Archbishop said excitedly. "How could I ever forget? It is the Spirit, His Spirit."

"Good boy," said the young man, smiling and patting the Archbishop on the back. And they started walking again. "By the way, do you still remember your secondary school English grammar?" He asked. "If you do, He authorized me to use the first-person singular noun in speaking to you. He lives in Me, so I speak to you directly in Him. So We are one—inseparably one. That is why I use *Us*. Therefore I have the freedom to use *I* or *We* at any time."

"Sir, that is very confusing," said the PM. "First You said You are a messenger. Then You said You live in Him and He in You. And now You say You have the choice of using the first-person singular or plural. How can we make sense out of all this?"

"Simple—v-e-r-y simple," said He. "So simple that I will leave the Archbishop to explain it to you. Or don't you understand either, Archbishop? Please, let's sit down so the PM can take in what is being explained." They drew near to one of the long wooden garden benches and sat down.

"Within the limits of human perception, I think what You are saying is what Christians call the Godhead," replied the Archbishop. "But recognizing that Your statements may have a deeper meaning than I could understand, I would prefer You to explain. It will enhance my own understanding."

"That is very good; you answered correctly," said the young man. "But that doesn't mean anything to the Prime Minister. Now listen and look at it this way. If three of us here are equal in every respect, and if you send Me to represent you in a meeting or in any situation, and I accept and actually represent you, then at that instance, you are greater than Me, because at that meeting or in that situation, I am carrying your authority, not necessarily Mine.

"Even if My message is a unanimous agreement between the three of us, but I am the one carrying the message, then both of you are greater than Me at that time. Therefore, to that extent, I am right to say I am a Messenger. Now if the three of us here have identical characteristics and are so united that we always agree on all things and in all situations.

"If we see and perceive and interpret and act exactly the same way and at exactly the same time, no one-trillionth variation in any form whatsoever, then I am right to say that We are one—absolutely one. However, this oneness exists within a framework of recognizable attributes, attributes that will make anyone able to easily and immediately distinguish between the Archbishop, the Prime Minister and Me."

"That is precisely what I mean by the Godhead, sir," affirmed the Archbishop, "the combination of three separate, distinct and recognizable personalities and qualities as one perfectly united entity."

"Stop!" the PM almost screamed. "You are confusing me more. This is very hard to comprehend. How can different, separate, distinct personalities be one? Just how?"

"Prime Minister," said the young man, "why is it easy for you to understand that Britain is a composite of four different countries but still one, yet you are unable to understand the Trinity of the Godhead?"

"Look, PM," said the Archbishop, "for lack of a better example, take it like water, which can take the form of liquid, solid, or gas. Another example is the sun, which manifests itself in the three creative energies of heat, light and radiation, a trinity relationship that together makes the sun. You understand now?"

"Not in the least," replied the Prime Minister. "Both examples you gave are easy to understand, but when it comes to personalities, it is entirely a different matter."

"That is not surprising," said the young man, "considering that man by nature tends to relate with the physical. The things of the spirit are spiritual and not easy to understand by the natural man."

"They are not at all, sir," said the Archbishop. "Understanding comes only by faith. Unfortunately, faith is the rarest jewel on earth."

"I know," said the young man. "Ask and it shall be given to you. Now I would like us to take a walk to mainland Britain." They stood up to start walking again. As He was standing up, He saw a bit of grass that had escaped the mower's blade. He hit His right foot against its base in an attempt to uproot it, but the grass was stubborn. So He bent down and uprooted it with His left hand, then nipped off one of its blades with His right hand and dropped the clump of grass. Then He started squeezing the leaf blade with His right hand as they walked along.

"Walk to mainland Britain? Is that a joke, sir?" the PM asked as the young man squeezed the blade. "Do you know how long it took us to get here?" asked the PM.

"I told you not to worry about anything when you are with Me," said the young man. "Only trust Me. It wouldn't take us a minute to walk to mainland Britain if I wanted, but I am bringing Britain to the edge of this island, so we don't have to walk too far. And I will make it far shorter when you are going back to London."

"How is that possible?" asked the Archbishop.

"Don't you believe that I could easily call Britain onto this island?" asked the young man. "Have you so easily forgotten how I told you this island was created just for your sake? Nothing shall be impossible to those who believe.

My friends, if only you can learn to trust Me, you will see exceptional power and glory in action."

"Ah yes! I remember, sir," said the Archbishop. He paused meditatively. "His Word cannot return without accomplishing its purpose," the Archbishop added.

"Now you are learning fast," the young man said, commending the Archbishop. "So let's walk to Britain; it is over there." He dropped the leaf He was squeezing as He pointed toward their front to indicate *over there.* Then He plucked a leaf from a strawberry tree on their path and started squeezing again.

"Look, there is a sea in front, sir," said the PM when they came to the brow of a small hill. "Are we crossing that sea?" he asked.

"Of course. Yes," He replied. "There is no way you can get to Britain without crossing any water."

"What are we going to do when we get there, sir?" asked the PM. "I mean, how are we going to cross the sea?"

"We will cross the sea by whatever means available there," He replied.

"OK, what are we going to do when we get to Britain, sir?" asked the PM.

"What are we doing now?" He asked in turn.

"Walking and enjoying the scenery, sir," replied the PM.

"Good, we'll do the same there," He said. "We'll stop and see what is happening in certain specific places."

"Are you sending us back from there, sir?" asked the PM.

"You cannot go back until we have finished what we are here for, and walking through Britain is just part of it," He replied. He flung the strawberry leaf down in front of Himself and rubbed His hands together.

They were quiet for a while before the Archbishop broke the silence. "How come the weather is the same, sir? It's as if there is no morning, no evening," he said.

"That is the way We love it," said the young man. "Night exists for man to rest after toiling in the day. But here there is no toiling and no tiredness. See how long we've walked through this field, yet we are not tired? Or are you tired?"

"Not at all, sir," they replied in unison.

"What is the magic, sir?" asked the PM.

"Remember what I told you about the stallions," He said. "This place has no comparison to a trillionth of His presence, the very tiniest reflection of which can renew your strength always. It can bring you peace and serenity in greater measure than you could ever ask."

"Does this mean that there is no night here?" asked the PM.

"No, there is no darkness in His presence," He said. "His very presence is the light of men that overcomes all darkness."

"But You said this place is like earth," said the PM. "You seem to speak in parables."

"Where do you think I am talking about His presence being?" He asked. "Earth, of course," He replied. "That is man's domain, where His presence dazzles out darkness from any area of life. Now it is night in Britain and some parts of the earth, but man has not invaded and polluted here. If I were not here with you, your very presence would have caused a lot of darkness—incomprehensible darkness of tectonic proportions."

They walked quietly and slowly, passing several trees, covering a long distance before they came to the beach. When they got there, He sat down on the sand and started to draw sketches on the ground. The PM sat down beside Him and started throwing pebbles, one after the other, into the water, causing ripples. The Archbishop walked a little farther away, admiring the little birds dancing and chirruping on the shrubs around parts of the beach.

"This is certainly a good place to meditate," said the PM. "It is so wonderfully peaceful. I wish the world were as peaceful as this."

"You mean this beach or this island?" the young man asked.

"I mean this island," replied the PM, as he flicked a pebble at a group of ants cramming around an object.

"It could be and was meant to be so," the young man said, "but it can never be as long as there are humans throwing all manner of pebbles at His wonderful works."

"Throwing small pebbles in the sea doesn't disturb anyone, I suppose," the PM said defensively.

"No, here it doesn't," He said. "But in the human sea of the world, pebbles and bigger ones at that, are constantly and unnecessarily being thrown with all recklessness."

"I think You are right," said the PM.

"Of course I am right," said the young man.

Just then, the PM saw a crab wash ashore. He quickly stood up, ran over to it, picked it up and threw it back into the water. Then he muttered to himself,

"At least I have saved the life of this crab." At that moment, a sea snail was flung to the beach by the wave, and he ran and picked it up and threw it back again. Then he started running like a little boy along the beach, picking up and throwing back whatever little creature he caught.

After a while, the young man called them back. They came, the Archbishop with a ladybird beetle in his hand, and the PM with empty hands as he had thrown everything in his hands away when they were called. The young man told them it was time to cross and asked the Archbishop to set the beetle free, which he did.

Just then, they saw a small wooden canoe floating far off and moving toward them. They all stood waiting and looking, with no one saying anything. As the canoe edged closer, the PM and the Archbishop realized it was empty and freewheeling, not paddled by anyone. Then it came as if by some invisible force directly toward them.

When it got close enough, it stopped. The young man entered first, followed by His two guests. Then the boat moved away of its own accord, moving slowly at first, but soon picking up speed. In no time, the beautiful island was completely out of sight. Although they traveled at what seemed to be average speed, they soon covered a great distance, pushing back hundreds of miles. Then they got to the opposite end of the sea, where they anchored and disembarked.

V.

On the third day, being Sunday morning both in London and in many parts of the country, all churches at their Sunday services prayed for the two men's safety and for an end to the quagmire. And so did many churches all over the world. The police were still busy trying to piece together any information that might provide a lead in their investigation.

A senior officer suggested crime scene reconstruction on TV to jog people's minds, but it was considered not feasible. It was reasoned that nobody had seen what happened and that people's memories could not be awakened by memories that did not exist previously. And those who claimed to have seen the car did not know when or how the car left its base or where it was going. They were in no position to add anything to the little information they'd already provided. It was an impossible challenge. Several other investigation methods were considered, but none seemed able to lead to anything useful.

And despite three COBRA meetings within twenty-four hours, nothing tangible had been achieved and no outcome of the meetings was made public.

VI.

Back across the sea, when the young man, the Prime Minister and the Archbishop left the boat, the young man took them across to a small piece of land no more than ten feet by ten feet that had the exact shape of the map of mainland Britain. The weather and atmosphere of the place completely changed from what the weather was on the beautiful island. It turned into normal British weather at that time of year.

They started walking, and the more they walked in it, the larger the land became, soon becoming as big as the true measure of the British Isles. They walked across from south to north and from east to west. They saw many places and many things as they walked across, stopping only at a few places. The first place they stopped was where a herd of sheep were grazing, all alone without a shepherd.

As soon as they approached, the herd panicked and the sheep ran in different directions. The young man called them back, and they all came running toward Him. He gently stroked a couple of them on their heads and their backs in a caring, affectionate way before leaving them.

They moved on and stopped where a group of about five hundred children seemed to have been abandoned. They were of various ages, six months to about four years and were amassed together in a derelict open hall. They were naked, dirty, unkempt, and uncared for and were very hungry. Flies and insects feasted on them. They were crying as much as their strength allowed them. There was no adult to care for them.

The Archbishop asked, "What are they doing here, and where are their parents?"

"They are undergoing experimentation," said the young man. "And these are just a tiny proportion of them. I will show you their parents when we get to where they are."

"What sort of experiment?" asked the Archbishop.

"It is a freedom experiment," replied the young man. "Since Creation, man has been continuously engaged in various freedom experiments, from Eden to the present. The failure of Eden hasn't taught him anything."

"But, sir, I thought Eden was pure temptation," said the Archbishop.

"There could never be any temptation if there were no freedom, and there could never be sin without freedom," said the young man.

"I honestly don't understand the connection between what you call freedom to experiment and these abandoned children," said the Archbishop.

"They are given the freedom to choose what they think is best for them," said the young man, "to choose how they want to grow up, what they think they want to be, etc."

"At their age, that is utterly wicked," said the PM. "It is extremely uncivilized and reminds me of the Stone Age."

"Precisely the opposite," said the young man. "Freedom is the whole essence of today's modernist philosophy. And there is nothing wrong with that if it were freedom as We ordained it. You can only talk of their age if the freedom we are talking about is applicable only to the children if the parents' interests have no part to play in it."

"How?" asked the Prime Minister.

"Don't worry, you will understand when we meet their parents," said the young man.

"So, what is the purpose of this particular experiment?" asked the Archbishop.

"It is to modernize childcare," said the young man. "It is a government pilot scheme that is to become the standard practice."

"Is that in Africa?" asked the PM. "Wherever it is, I will not allow it the light of day."

"Ahem! This is what I was talking about," said the young man. "Man is too keen to impose darkness where there should be none. Why do you need to take the light out? The problem with politicians is that they think they alone have the solution to all problems."

"But we have good intentions to try to make the world a better place," said the Prime Minister.

"Understandably, but you politicians prefer to approach it your own way rather than the Master's way," said the young man. "Well, I think we will talk about this later as I have work to do now. Let Me attend to these children first."

He then flicked two of his fingers, and the house suddenly changed into a beautiful large house with the children inside. The house was well equipped and well-furnished with more beds than there were children. Adjacent to each bed was a set of drawers containing assorted baby and infant needs. On top of the drawers and on the beds were numerous toys. He picked up the children one by one, washed them, dressed them and fed them. He laid all the children on their individual beds and put them to sleep. He flicked the same fingers again and a large perimeter fence appeared, completely enclosing the house and providing a large compound with children's indoor and outdoor play facilities.

As they left the compound, the Archbishop asked, "Who will look after the children now that we are going?"

He ignored the question, instead saying, "The government says social services do better parenting than natural parents."

"Are you saying they will come and look after them?" asked the Archbishop.

"That is their policy," replied the young man.

"They are doing a great job," said the Archbishop, "but that shouldn't take away parents' responsibility, should it?"

"Does the PM agree with your opinion?" He asked.

"Social services does not require using children as guinea pigs for an outrageous experiment or as policy," said the PM. "I will find out the country where this is taking place when I return to Number 10."

"Ah, I love that phrase—*guinea pig*," said the young man, gently poking His lower lip with His right forefinger. "What do you say to many other uses of children for guinea pig experiments?"

"I can't think of any," said the Prime Minister.

"I just mentioned social services," said the young man. "Think of child services, or education services at least."

"Not any that easily comes to mind now," said the Prime Minister.

"Archbishop, can you remember any?" the young man asked.

"No. I can't think of any," said the Archbishop.

"OK, think in terms of the church's stand on child issues," said the young man. "Anyone that has caused a lot of furor."

"Mm, maybe the church's opposition to certain treatment of children in the area of their adoption," said the Archbishop.

"Is that all you can remember?" the young man asked. "In considering that, don't you think it amounted to a guinea pig experiment as well?"

"What do you mean, sir?" the PM said, interrupting. "Children have suffered so much, and we have a duty to defend their rights."

"What rights are you talking about?" asked the young man. "I am talking of children's treatment in various areas as used in guinea pig experiments, but you seem to be more concerned about their rights. Do they have any rights at all?"

"Yes, they have equal rights as adults," said the PM, "but because they can't speak for themselves, they are treated anyhow. That is why the government has to defend their rights. We are used to defending people's rights and freedom of choice."

"Hmm, rights and freedom of choice," He said. "Remember, that was our starting point, the right of the parents of those abandoned children to leave them to fend for themselves and grow up the way they like. And you were grossly offended by the freedom experiment. Where was the government when those children were abandoned?"

"Sir, the government can't do everything," replied the PM. "The parents have their rights too, although we know that children have been on the firing line for too long, but ultimately we have an obligation to defend everyone's rights and freedom. Ours happens to be a free society."

"Obligation. Obli-ga-tion, rights, freedom. Hmm," said the young man, as He gently stroked His lips again meditatively with His right forefinger. "PM, you talk of rights, of freedom and of obligation. We have a lot of probing to do in these areas, but first on the issue of children's rights. I asked a question which you answered partially. Do you think children have any rights at all or any freedom—I mean as humans?"

"They certainly do, sir," said the PM.

"What choice do you think they have in anything concerning them?" He asked.

"They don't seem to have any, sir," said the PM, "which is why we decide what we think is best for them."

"Do you know that everybody has different contributions to make in a child's life—fathers, mothers, siblings, society and so forth?" He asked.

"Of course, I do, sir," replied the PM, "but life is so complex and society so evil that we approach any issue with regard to the best possible interest of those affected. What we have as a society is largely a single-parent family unit—and children have grown up either with their father alone or their mother alone. So I think growing up in different family settings shouldn't really matter."

"Good argument," said the young man. "There are practical psychological implications that matter greatly. A family setting that does not fit into Our scheme can never achieve the purpose of a family for the good of the child, the family, or the society. Your experiment is still in its early stage; by the time it is full-blown and these children are grown up, you will realize you are creating a much bigger problem than you set out to solve."

"But, sir, I think what is more important is their growing up in a loving environment," said the PM.

"What loving environment?" He asked. "Can you even define love—I mean true love? Nothing can be more important than a godly environment because that is where true love is. If you know what love is, you won't subject any child to such an experiment. For God is love, and any true love must be within the context of God's love, which is fully reflected in His ordinances. Just think of it. Do you suppose We simply created things for the fun of it? There is a reason for everything; the definition and role of a family man or woman is different from that of a single person—especially one without a child."

"But the people of the world have accepted the various family settings and different family life," said the Archbishop. "The Bible says what we agree on earth is agreed in heaven."

"Only within our set boundaries by those within the will of the Creator," He replied. "Or else many people and even the world would have been destroyed by evil people who agree on doing so."

"Since we are talking of family matters," said the PM, "would it be right to say sex was meant only for the purpose of giving birth to children?"

"Why do you ask when we are talking of obligation, rights and freedom, as concerns the treatment of children?" asked the young man in response.

"I ask because the world is changing fast," said the PM, "and with different family settings and people with different lifestyles. We now have cohabiting families, partnership families, etc., and some of these family settings can't give birth or produce life on their own."

"We put everything good in Us into every one of Our creations, to be good and fruitful," said the young man. "So if by choice they can't give birth or reproduce life, then something is wrong. They need to go back to the Source of life to produce life."

"But many of them don't believe in anything," replied the Archbishop, "least of all a creative Source of life."

"Then there is a problem because nothing exists that does not originate from a source," said the young man. "It is not recognizing your Source that leads to the loss of your purpose and generates several questions without answers."

"What of the humanist dogma that everything is relative, that there are no absolutes?" asked the PM.

"What do you think?" asked the young man. "If reality is the basis and essence, then there must be absolutes and an original source of those absolutes. Those controlled by relativism or by a truth based not on reality but on their interpretation of reality will live out the consequences of their beliefs."

"So sex is only meant for reproduction?" persisted the PM in his inquiry.

"No, sex is not limited to reproduction only," said the young man, "but it must have an edifying purpose and must only be within marriage. It is a holy thing and should be treated as such. Even within marriage, it should include the appropriate conduct. Anything outside that is disobedience and a sin."

"We look up to the church for guidance, but it has failed us," said the PM.

"It is a government that makes laws and compels everyone to obey," said the Archbishop. "But with that being said, the whole world is going the same way, and the church mustn't be different."

"That is the way of the world, not Our way," said the young man. "Check Our instruction manual for Our definition of a true family unit and of sexual relationship within it. I have something to show you inside that house in front of us."

"Is it about marital relationships?" asked the PM. "And are the wayward, too, your children?"

"No. Why are you obsessed with marital issues?" He asked. "Everyone on earth is My child, and they are free if only they can come to Me. That is why I want to show you what is in the next house, and that is why I am taking you around Britain." By now they had gone a very long distance from where they met the children.

"Sir, you have not answered my question," said the Archbishop.

"Which is…?" asked He.

"You have not told us who will look after those children," said the Archbishop.

"You don't think I am capable of looking after them?" He asked. "Suffer not the little children to come to Me, for of such is the kingdom of heaven."

"But you are not there now," said the Archbishop.

"What is your article of faith, Archbishop?" the young man asked, as He suddenly stood still and looked at the Archbishop intently in the face. "Remember it and your question is answered."

"You seem to know the answer to every question, sir," said the PM.

"Have you been with Me all this time, Prime Minister, and still don't know Me?" He asked as He started walking again. "Despite all that you've seen Me do? Blessed are those who have not seen and yet believe."

"Forgive him, sir; he has doubted from his mother's womb," said the Archbishop.

"Archbishop, by that you have shown more ignorance than the Prime Minister," He said. "Do you remember John 3:17?"

"Yes," said the Archbishop. "For God did not send His Son into the world to condemn the world, but that the world through Him might be saved."

"How then can you ask Me to forgive when you know I neither condemn nor hold a grudge against anyone?" asked the young man.

"If you don't bear a grudge, that means you don't judge," said the PM. "Why do religious people talk of judgment?"

"We are at the house now," He said. "I will answer your question when we leave." It was a pub filled to capacity, so full that some people were sitting or standing outside. Many were completely drunk, and the whole place was very rowdy. There were those throwing up or urinating by the walls outside. The three of them didn't stay long there but soon moved on.

As they left, the young man said, "Many of those are the parents of those abandoned children. Some others are those entrusted to care for them. Still, others are the natural parents of some babies given for adoption because they don't want any responsibility. They all want the freedom to do as they please. In the process, they denied these children the right and freedom to grow up with the people to whom We entrusted them. And it is all because of the government's avowed obligation for freedom, innit, Prime Minister?" He winked at the PM and smiled.

Then He added, "When you said government is obligated to defend people's rights and freedom, you forgot that freedom is unattainable and cannot operate where obligation rules."

Soon they reached a small pond, where a huge fearsome man was standing and throwing stones and all types of missiles into the pond, killing whatever he could see from the surface—frogs, tadpoles, millipedes, centipedes, small fish and so forth—just for the fun of it. They did not stop, and the stone-throwing man did not look at them.

After they had passed the place, the young man said, "That is the shepherd of the herd of sheep we saw, those sheep that scattered when we reached them. He left his duty post to come and kill little creatures because he has power over them. Those who throw stones shall die by them, for whatever a man sows is what he shall reap. And this brings us to the question of judgment."

"Sir, I just remembered something," said the Archbishop.

"What is it?" He asked.

"You said no one lives on this island and that you don't even live here," said the Archbishop. "What of the children and all the people we've seen?"

"We have since left the island," He said. "We are in Britain. Remember when we crossed the sea?"

"But you said this was, er, er, a sort of prototype British Isle," said the Archbishop.

"You don't believe I have the power to take you wherever I like or to recreate anything I like?" He asked. "Do you know the Spirit that lives in you? Don't worry, you will understand when you return to the place you are used to."

"Sir, before we forget, let's talk about judgment," said the PM.

"I am not a man who forgets things," He said. "If I choose to ignore it, it is not because I have forgotten. Tell Me, what do you want to know about judgment?"

"I have always believed there is no judgment," said the PM. "And You seem to have confirmed it by alluding to the fact that You judge no one."

"It is true that I judge no one," said the young man, "no, not in the way of the world."

"So there is judgment," said the PM.

"Of course there is judgment," He replied.

"You said not in the way of the world," said the PM. "I am not talking of judgment here on earth. I am talking of judgment after death. Actually the first question, sir; is there life after death?"

"What do you think?" He asked. "When a seed falls to the ground and dies, it springs into life and then buds. How come the seed is dead but gives out a shoot? There is life hidden in the seed that is interminable which shoots out of its encasement. Similarly, the human body is nothing but earth, where it returns when the person dies, but that is where the similarity ends and things take a different turn because, unlike the seed that sprouts into physical life here on earth, the dead person sprouts into a spirit and returns to his or her Creator.

"The difference is that a person has a spirit, whereas the seed has none. Remember when God molded clay into a man? There was no life in him until God breathed the breath of life into him and he became a living being. The human body is only to give the spirit form while on earth. It does not need any form in the spirit world, to which it returns after physical death. So, like the seed, it springs into another life, but in another world, the spirit world. And unlike the seed, reproduction by the body on earth does not necessarily result in its mortality."

"What of those diseased seeds that rot on earth and never sprout?" asked the PM.

"You already qualified their state," said the young man. "You said they are diseased, so their life has been eaten away by disease. But humans are different. The breath in a human is different from that in animals and plants. The human breath consists of two lives, the physical life, which can be diseased like the seed and can be terminated on earth, and the spiritual life, which is the spirit that nothing, including diseases, can kill. The only disease the spirit suffers is separation from God, which is sin."

"If plants can die and sprout again, then there is reincarnation," said the PM.

"You are asking too many questions without waiting for answers," said He. "Follow a question through to its conclusive end before asking another, so you don't get confused. As for reincarnation, I want you to stop thinking like a child and be not deceived. I used plants only as an illustration; they do not equate to humans. Reproduction in plants does not in any way equate to reincarnation. For humans, there is only one life given, to be lived only once.

"That is why We offer enough chance for anyone who has gone astray to return to the right path because once your spirit leaves the body, there is no chance for reconciliation. So there is life after death, but there is no reincarnation. And this brings us to the issue of judgment. Let us reflect on the human level." He plucked a leaf from a mulberry tree and said, "What leaf is this?" And they answered that it was a mulberry leaf. "Because you saw Me pluck it?" He asked.

"No, we know what a mulberry leaf is and recognize it when we see it," the Archbishop answered for both of them.

"So you judged rightly that it is a mulberry leaf," He said. "That is a form of judgment. Now let us think in terms of a human being. From the first breath to the last breath, a person is judged. The moment a child is born, people start judging whom he resembles—the mom the dad, or other relatives. As he grows, people monitor his voice, his cry, his laughter and his behavior, using these things to judge him and stereotype him.

"At school and at any level of study, his performance is judged. At work, his performance is judged. In social circles, he is judged. In society, he is judged. The government makes laws and sets up courts to judge people's behavior and prescribe punishments. Even at death, people make comments about the look of the corpse's face and make reference to the deceased's character and deeds while alive. That is still a form of judgment. Now if there is judgment all through one's life, why do you think there won't be judgment at death?"

"But the person is dead," said the PM. "Is the carcass going to be judged?"

"The death of a person is not the end of life," He said. "As I said before, life is indestructible. It continues after the person departs this earth, and it is forever. Even God is judged; in fact, He is more judged than anyone else."

"I don't understand," said the PM.

"God is severely blamed for many things on earth, including people's mistakes and foolishness. You can't blame somebody without first judging the person."

"That is not what I am talking about," said the PM. "What I don't understand is Your saying that life continues after the person departs this earth. How can life continue when the person is already dead?"

"The body is not the person," He said. "The body is the sheath encasing the real person. The real person is the spirit within that person. When the person dies, the body decays, but the spirit goes back to the Creator, who gave it to the body. It is the spirit that is judged."

"What of someone who has served a sentence for an offense committed on earth?" asked the PM. "Has he judged again for the same offense?"

"Judgment on earth is fleshly; it is physical," said the young man. "The judgment after death is spiritual. It is the Spirit judging the Spirit, and the judgment is true and perfect because man's spirit does not lie to God's Spirit. It gives an accurate account. So while earthly judgment is based on earthly laws, spiritual judgment is based on Our ordinances, which are to some extent different from man-made or earthly laws.

"A sentence served on earth does not account for anything after death. The only thing that counts is true repentance, only made while alive, because there is no repentance after death. I am sure the Archbishop knows these things and will be a good companion in enlightening you."

"There are many things I don't know myself," said the Archbishop. "I also have many unanswered questions about life."

"That is why we provided the manual to help," said the young man. "Life is very simple if you seek help from the manual, which is deliberately made very simple for everyone to understand. Besides, I am always around to help. So what I suggest, Archbishop and PM, is that you spend quality time feeding on the manual of life on a daily basis. And in doing so, call on Me to assist your understanding, without neglecting the companionship of My other children who dwell in My presence. The essence of community is growing together through interdependence."

"How do I call on You, when after You send us back and I won't see You again?" said the PM.

"By now you should know My abilities," said the young man. "Because you can see Me here, you think I am not where those abandoned children are right now? I am there and looking after them. Listen and take My promise; call on Me always, and I will be with you."

"But how can I call on You when I don't know Your name?" the Prime Minister asked. "You said you are a Messenger."

"Call Me whatever you like; it doesn't change My nature, for I am who I am," said the young man. "Messenger or no messenger, I told you that We are inseparable. He who sees Me sees Him. You've been calling Me 'sir'; continue if you prefer that."

"Simply call him Holy Spirit," said the Archbishop. "Remember the snacks presented to us were signed by HS. I think He is the Holy Spirit."

"'Him' is what I am confused by," confessed the Prime Minister. "Who is Him whom He constantly refers to?"

"There is no doubt He is referring to God the Father," said the Archbishop.

"That's all right then," said the Prime Minister.

As he said that, they came to a giant building. The young man said, "This is a multipurpose worship center, and it represents most of the worship houses in Britain today. It is used by Muslims, Christians, Hindus, Sikhs, Buddhists, Jews and others. You can see a cross on the parapet of one of the heptagons and a minaret on top of another heptagon. You would see other symbols if we were to go around, but we won't go around. We will only peep inside, so you can see what goes on in it."

They peeped through a window and saw crowds of people with much noise. Some were selling goods, some exchanging money and jewelry. The three of them walked away to another window and peeped in, seeing people who seemed to be on a fashion parade. They were gaily dressed like people taking part in the Royal Ascot Fashion Show.

The trio then walked to another window and peeped in and saw some people playing bingo, some playing comedy, and still others dealing drugs. Then they walked to another window and saw many who, instead of worshipping, were sleeping or dozing away. The young man said, "Enough. Let's go," and they walked away. As they did so, He said, "You see what they are doing in God's house, how they are desecrating it and pretending to be worshipping Him?"

"You said there are Muslims, Hindus and other faith groups," said the PM. "Do they also belong to Your fold? I mean, are they Your children as Christians are?"

"What do you think?" asked the young man. "Who created them?"

"God," answered the Archbishop, edging out the PM.

"Good. Every created being is My child, and I love them all dearly, including those who don't believe in Me," said the young man.

They came to what was once a beautiful garden with all manner of fruit plants. A giant Union Jack was hoisted on a very tall metal pole at the center of the garden. They saw noisy protestors tearing down everything in the garden, cutting and uprooting the trees, trampling on the fruits, and killing the birds sheltering in the trees and the insects feeding on the fruits. As the three of them approached, the protestors brought down the flag post, set the flag ablaze and threw it aflame, into the garden. The PM, unable to hide his displeasure, especially at the sight of the blazing Union Jack, shouted, "What are you doing?"

One of them answered, "I saw others doing it, and I joined them."

Another said, "We have nothing to do and are bored, so we decided to keep ourselves busy."

A third said, "This is a free society. We have the right to do what we like."

A fourth said, "We are British and this is what we do."

"No," said the PM. "We build; we don't destroy. That is what we are known for."

After he said that, a huge muscular man wearing a T-shirt and jeans shorts, with scorpion tattoos all over his chest, hands and shoulders, stepped forward menacingly and said, "We are professional protestors. Who are you, and what is your problem?"

"I am the Prime Minister, and my problem is that you are destroying what we spent years building," said the PM.

The man laughed sardonically, revealing two gold-plated canine teeth on the right side of his mouth. He cast a piercing, devilish look at the PM from his head to his toes and back again, laughing like a possessed man. He suddenly stopped laughing and blew a whistle, cupping his mouth between his hands, and three hefty men stepped forward.

The man said, "Teach the PM the lesson of his life; let him learn to respect our territory."

Immediately, one of the men lifted the PM up with only one hand jacked between the PM's legs. The three men started taunting the PM and shouting obscenities at him, but the young man waved His hand at them to stop. And suddenly everything went quiet, and the man who had lifted the PM brought him down gently. Nobody asked any questions or attempted any disobedience.

The young man did not ask them to leave or to stop what they were doing. He simply signaled with His head to the PM and the Archbishop, and they walked away.

As they walked away, He said, "That is what happens when you pay people to stay idle. The confluence between man-made rights and freedom is destruction. Freedom is the mother of sin."

"How can freedom be the mother of sin?" asked the PM.

"Remember Eden?" asked the young man. "It was freedom, freedom of choice, that alienated man from Eden, from God. Yet it was God's love that produced the power of choice."

Not long after leaving the garden and the protesting crowd, they sighted what looked like the Houses of Parliament. As they got closer, the building appeared to be distorted in part and suddenly became like Buckingham Palace. The PM said delightedly, "It seems we are back in London. That place looks like Buckingham Palace."

"You stole the words from my mouth," said the Archbishop. "I was just about to say that."

"That is no Buckingham Palace at all, and you are nowhere near London," said the young man. "That is the palace of the governing council of the United Kingdom, which is camouflaged to look like Buckingham Palace. It is to deceive. If you noticed, it first appeared like the Houses of Parliament before changing to Buckingham Palace. It is where No. 10 and Whitehall take their orders. When we get closer, I will show you that it is no Buckingham Palace."

Even when they drew close enough, it still looked very much like Buckingham Palace to the PM and the Archbishop. All the telltale features of Buckingham Palace and its environs—Trafalgar Square, St James Park, and all the surrounding areas and the peculiar red-tinged asphalt road around the palace—were present. Then He started to show them the few differences between the real and the fake.

At the intersection point of the red cross of the giant Union Jack flying on top of the building was a star with a black outline. The star consisted of two equilateral triangles, one superimposed on the other to form a six-point star. Inside the star was the numeral 666 written in black. At the apex of the vertical arm of the red cross was a crown with the same marked star and the same black outline.

At the extreme end of each of the other three arms of the cross was a tiny black skull. The star and its numeral 666, and the skull, were sufficiently veiled so as to be unrecognizable, and obviously, they were not featured on a normal Union Jack. And the palace was far bigger than Buckingham Palace.

Then the trio walked on away from the palace and, after a long walk, saw what looked like a wall of fire far in the distance. They talked as they went along until they got close. They could hear beautiful songs coming from the direction of the fire. To the utter amazement of the Prime Minister and the

Archbishop, when they got to the wall, they saw that it was actually a massive wall of fire, burning intensely but consuming nothing. It ringed a fence around a massive space, within which was an equally massive wall. The wall was extraordinarily large, and the songs they were hearing were coming from behind it.

When they got closer, the Archbishop said, "This is amazing. I have never seen anything like this before."

The PM asked, "Why fire in a beautiful place like this?"

"Their worship generated the fire," replied the young man. "The fire is a protective hedge around them, and nothing, I say, absolutely nothing, can penetrate that fire to harm them."

"How did they get in, as there seems to be no gate?" asked the Archbishop.

"I just told you that their worship generated the fire," replied the young man, "and that nothing can touch them. They can go through the fire without being hurt, and each of them is surrounded by their own protective fire as they go about their daily business."

"So we will not be hurt if we go in?" asked the Archbishop.

"You will not, only because of My presence," said the young man. "You were purified the moment those horses crossed the gate when you arrived at the house. Minus that you could get burned."

"Why? But he is an Archbishop," said the PM.

"Archbishop?" exclaimed the young man. "Bishop, pope, prophet, pastor, reverend, Christian—they are all names. Our power rests only on those who fervently seek Us, not on names." He stayed in front held the PM's right hand, and asked the PM to hold the Archbishop's right hand with his left, thus forming a line, the two of them behind Him. Then He led them as they entered through the fire unhurt. The singing and praising went on undisturbed.

When they entered the fire compound, they found that the brick wall was only in front of a stand-alone wall that housed no building. It spanned a very long distance to the left and right but was within the fire-hedged compound. The wall was draped with giant Union Jacks, except at the entrance door, which was at the center.

Attached to the middle and to the extreme left and right ends of the wall were three big wooden poles carrying three large Union Jacks. There were small wooden poles attached all along the edge of the wall, each carrying a small flag of a nation—every nation on earth. When they entered, they beheld a sea of people as far as the eye could see in an open-air assembly—people of all nationalities and ethnic backgrounds, men, women, children, teenagers and youths, all singing and praising God in one accord.

The people did not pay heed to their presence when they entered. They were so lost in their praises, relishing every moment, that nothing distracted them the slightest. To the worshippers, the three of them were just other members of their unique kingdom who had come to worship. The trio stayed for a while before leaving, going out the same way they had entered.

When they first entered, the fire was smooth, steady and noiseless, but as they were coming out, the fire whooshed into a huge wild flame, waving and swaying, and crackling and popping. They kept walking and talking as they moved away from the area.

"Why did the fire suddenly get violent and noisy as we were coming out?" asked the PM.

"If we had stayed a little longer, you would have known why," said the young man. "You would have heard unbelievable testimonies of many miracles because so many things happen that are hidden from human eyes. I lifted all their burdens, which the fire consumed as we were coming out. That is the reason for the twisting and sizzling."

"But You said nothing can touch them as they are surrounded by that fire?" asked the PM.

"That is true while they are in there," replied the young man. "But not everyone there came in whole. Some limped in; some went in hunched with unwanted baggage; others ran in out of breath as they blasted away from their pursuers; and yet others were whole but bruised just before getting in. But they have all been made whole and unburdened."

"What happens when they come out?" asked the Archbishop.

"I told you, they are each surrounded by their own fire," replied the young man. "Since they live on earth, they will be affected by the things of the earth. But they will not lose the battle because of their protective fire—if they remain focused as they are there. They will sometimes fall, but they will stand again as long as they beseech Me. But these reasons are not why we came here."

VII.

"I know we are sightseeing," said the PM.

"We are not sightseeing," said the young man rather tersely. "Why are you slow to understand? You are here on a mission. I deliberately chose for us to visit this worship center last because it is for the sake of these people that you are here. They are the reason you have been invited. They represent every tongue and tribe on all the earth, interceding on behalf of the United Kingdom, because your sins have passed forgiveness and you don't know it.

"That building is not in the UK or anywhere on earth. It is not even a spiritual gathering of all true worshippers of God but is made up of those specifically interceding for the United Kingdom right in their various countries and abodes. Only a small fraction of those people are British worshippers. The large Union Jacks symbolize the nation and people they are interceding for. The small flags represent the intercessors' nations all over the earth."

By now they had reached the water, which they crossed on their outward journey to enter mainland Britain. But the small boat was not there.

"I didn't realize we've come back to our starting point," said the Archbishop. "I thought we would go back the way we came, seeing all those things we saw on our way."

"We could have done that if I wanted," said the young man. "But don't forget this is Britain, where the designs and markings of roads hardly allow one the privilege of returning on the same route or even getting one's bearing in any direction. But these are no problems for Me, especially as we did not go by any road or by vehicle. I chose the most effective route for our purpose, which is primarily to see all that we saw."

"So we have gone through north and south, and east and west, of Britain?" asked the PM.

"Yes," said the young man. "Don't you know Britain? Or were the places you saw not familiar? We've covered the whole mainland without necessarily touching every inch of soil. I didn't want to distract you with which part we were in, because I wanted you to focus and ask questions about the things we saw. Tourism is not part of your mission here."

He stretched His right hand to the sea and bent the fingers inward as if gesturing someone to come. Soon they saw the small boat far off sailing unaided toward them. Gradually, gradually, it got to the bank and anchored unaided. They entered the boat, and after it had sailed about ten yards away, it stopped. He told them to turn and look back to the British mainland they had just left, to see what was going to happen. They did so and saw the land they had just left gradually rolling inward until it completely folded like a wrapped paper, leaving them in the middle of a massive sea.

They stood gazing in silence as the rolled land lifted up to the sky, ascending higher and higher until it became a dot and eventually disappeared into the clouds. Then they turned around and the boat resumed its journey, heading toward the beautiful island. They were all quiet throughout the rest of the journey, which was comparatively short, for soon, without two of them realizing it, they suddenly reached the beautiful island.

"Sir, tell us the plain truth," said the Archbishop. "Is this the island of Patmos? Because I can't comprehend what I am seeing. It is like the spirit world is being revealed right here."

"I already told you that this place was purposely created because of you," said the young man, "so you are not on the island of Patmos."

"I am completely enraptured by what I am seeing and by the peace of this place. I feel like spending the rest of my life here," said the PM.

"I feel the same myself," said the Archbishop. "That is why I asked if we are on the island of Patmos since this place is an imaginary island. By the way, does the island of Patmos exist?"

"Archbishop, if one of your priests or subjects were to ask that question, what would be your answer?" asked the young man.

"I know of Patmos in the Aegean Sea," said the Archbishop, "but I don't know if it is the same Patmos the Bible refers to."

"Whether it is the same Patmos or not, how does that improve your relationship with Me?" He asked.

"Sir, it is only a matter of interest," said the Archbishop. "Like Patmos, this island is under the sea, or rather ocean as You said. We've just crossed the sea to come back here, and I remember how we came through a tunnel under the ocean on our way to this island."

"I talked of relationship with Me, and you are talking of interest," said the young man, smiling. "Which is more important, the island of Patmos or Me? Draw close to Me and I will show you great and mighty things that you do not know. What you've seen so far is nothing compared with what I want to show those who love Me." As He said that, they sighted the roof of the lone house on the beautiful island.

"I want to ask you a question," He said.

"We are listening, sir," both of them said.

"Since you love this place, and since you are in a unique position to transform your country into a place close to this, why couldn't you do it?" He asked.

"Prime Minister, I think that is for you," said the Archbishop.

"Why do you say that?" asked the young man.

"He is the leader of the country," replied the Archbishop. "He is in the best possible position to change the country."

"And you think you are not in a position to contribute toward that?" asked the young man.

"That is not exactly what I am saying, sir," said the Archbishop. "I am not a politician, and I have no power to make laws. That is what I am saying."

"Your appointment was political," said the young man. "And even if it was ecclesiastical as by a synod, as someone in authority, especially one in such an important position, you can influence political decisions. So, if you must give an excuse, find a better one."

"Ours is a secular and difficult society, sir," said the Archbishop. "If I say anything outside church matters, I would be reminded that I am not a politician. If I say something that is religious and does not favor some people, I will be criticized for being out of touch with reality."

"No, I'd rather say you are out of touch with Me," said the young man. "You are dragging your relationship with Me before the world into political conformity, hence you are afraid of criticism. Religion has no part to play with Me. I prefer relationship, and until you are in that relationship, you cannot represent Me or the people committed into your care." After a little silence, He asked, "PM, what is your own defense?"

"Sir, you know that there is no place on earth that is like this place here," said the PM. "No government can make its country as serene and peaceful as this place. This is only possible with God."

The young man stopped abruptly and looked at the Prime Minister straight in the eye, then smiled and said, "Is that so? So, you recognize there is God. Why then don't you call God into the problems of your country?" They resumed walking and were now very close to the house.

"Sir, I know there is God, but I don't know Him in person to be able to speak to Him," said the PM. "Secondly, we separated the Church from the State so that each arm would adequately focus on its area of jurisdiction for the collective good of all. Unfortunately, the church seems to be distracted by things of the world."

"I can't believe you are saying this, Prime Minister," protested the Archbishop.

"Gently, My children," said the young man. "We are not here to argue. We are here to reason together. Prime Minister, let's talk about the state side of things. What has your government done to make Britain a better place?"

"You know more than I do, sir, that I lead the most stubborn people on earth," said the PM. "I have only good intentions for them, but whatever I do, I get criticized right, left and center. The MPs are even more critical than the people. Nothing ever pleases them. But the press—O Lord, save me from the press. The British press is the worst poison I have ever come across on Planet Earth—brutal, foul-mouthed, manipulative, psychopathic, warmongering and all the negatives."

"Why is that?" asked the young man.

"I don't know. But nothing I do ever pleases the press," said the Prime Minister. "Besides that, the challenge You are putting before me is quite revolutionary, sir. And revolutionary ideas are anathema to our Parliament. If you remember clearly, that was the principal cause for the failure of Chartism. Chartism was utopian to our Parliament, so they killed it."

As the Prime Minister was saying that, they entered the house. Ignoring the Prime Minister's explanations, the young man said, "OK, boys, we are home now; you can sit down and relax for a little while, and we will continue our discussion afterward. We still have lots of food and drink left on the table, and they are there as warm as when we left them. Please satisfy your desires. I will be right back."

And with that, He walked out through the front door and soothing music again started playing. The two of them sat there gazing all around without uttering a word. Neither took anything to eat, but they did have a drink of fruit juice—the PM, orange juice and the Archbishop, pineapple juice—which they took from the dining table before going back to stay in the living room. It must have been about twenty minutes before He re-entered the room from the same door.

"OK, gentlemen," He said, "have you rested enough?"

"Yes," they answered.

"Have you eaten?" He asked.

"We are not hungry, sir; thank you," the PM replied, speaking for both of them.

"All right," He said. "I told you we are here to reason together and see how we can move Britain forward into that Promised Land. We have taken a walk in this beautiful park to refresh, and if you prefer that we stay outside and sit on one of those garden benches, you let Me know."

"We are OK here, sir," they both responded.

"We have taken a walk inside mainland Britain to see the state of the country," He said. "I know you regard mainland Britain as four countries or country of four nations, but please accept my use of a *country* as a singular noun for our purpose here. Call it whatever you like when you get back. If you have any questions about what we saw on our walk across Britain or on this island, feel free to ask Me at any time as we go along in our discussion.

"But please know that what we saw are true happenings in Britain. That is why I ignored the Prime Minister's question about where the children's freedom experiment was taking place. There are many more problems we did not cover, but what we saw is representative enough. And what we saw was a spiritual representation. You will not see those things physically when you go back exactly as we saw them here, but they are there.

"Now, something prompted your being invited here. The outcry against your country is great and very grievous and has reached Us. We are being bombarded day and night by Our children in and outside Britain to intervene. Some have taken the extraordinary step of calling Us to destroy the country. And We always listen and grant the desires of those who dwell in Our presence.

"However, We are very compassionate and long-suffering, and because of this, We feel it would not be right for Us to act without first listening to you or giving you a second chance. Our last stop in our walk in Britain was at that massive worship center, so big that if you had seen it with your naked eyes, you could not have seen the end of the crowd. Only a very small fraction of those people there live in Britain or are British. And among the British, there are people of all nationalities and ethnicities. But all these people are in one accord and of one mind.

"Now, We could have invited anybody in the country here, but We recognize, as you said, that yours is a secular state. So you as head of government have to be invited. On the spiritual side, We could have picked any religious leader. But in official circles and state ceremonies, the State recognizes Christianity and the Anglican Church in particular, as the official religion. Hence you, the Archbishop of Canterbury, were invited.

"Before we go further, I would like to show you a small film. Please be alert and take in all you can so you may ask Me whatever questions that may emanate from it. After that, you will go on the eagle flight. I will have to leave you so you can properly focus."

And with that, He walked out through the same front door again. Immediately, the electronic screen that had appeared to them before emerged from the same wall again on its tripod. It rolled toward their front as before and stopped. The screen was not divided, yet each was watching his own individual life story as if it were the only one on the screen. Neither saw the other one's story playing out.

They were each ashamed because they thought the other person was seeing what they were seeing about themselves—every single thing they'd ever done and every single word they'd ever spoken since they had learned to differentiate between their left and right to date, including things they had done or said behind closed doors. Even their thoughts that they had not acted upon were shown. And things they had long forgotten were not left out.

It was a very embarrassing and humiliating experience for both of them. They occasionally glanced at each other as if to see each other's reaction to some episodes. The film ran very slowly, yet it finished in a relatively short time, a much shorter time than they had spent eating. But to them, it must have lasted a whole day. Everything was vivid.

In the end, the screen rolled back on its own accord and disappeared into the wall. Then the young man re-entered the room. He asked them to stand up and take a short walk behind the house to ease their apprehension, as He could easily read their fallen facial expressions. A short while later, He invited them back in.

Inside, the two leather chairs had been replaced by three reading chairs, placed equidistant from each other around a circular reading table. On the table were three bottles of water and three glasses placed to the side.

"Welcome back," He said to them. "Please take your seats."

They each took a seat adjacent to each other, while He took the remaining seat facing both of them, who were a bit to His left and right.

"How was the film? Soul-searching, I suppose," He said. "Please relax. You are not under judgment. And don't worry about what you see or what your mate thinks of you. What you saw is personal to you; your mate didn't see what you saw. So you have no reason to be embarrassed. But tell Me if what you saw is not true. From your childhood through all your education and working life, was anything missed, or was anything added or misrepresented?"

Both of them sat and stared glumly at Him, unable to say a word.

Then He tried to encourage them.

"C'mon," He said, "cheer up. There is nothing to worry about. I told you, you are not under judgment. We are here to reason together, and we can't do so if you start like this. It is just necessary for you to know that nothing is hidden from Us, which should help you to be both objective and truthful in our deliberations. Feel as free as you were when we went out for a walk. Know that the plan We have for you and your country is for good and not for evil.

"Please, I want both of you to reflect on what you saw when we walked across mainland Britain. That is why we are here, not to discuss what you saw of your past in the film. We are not discussing what you just watched."

"Sir, it would be naive for us to pretend we can reason with You," said the Archbishop. "From the little I have seen since we arrived, there is absolutely no basis for us to reason together. You are on an entirely different plane from us. For as far as the heavens are above the earth, so great is Your wisdom above ours."

"Despite that, we can still reason together," said the young man. "It is more profitable for us to brainstorm the problems facing your country together, don't you think?"

"I think the Archbishop is right," said the Prime Minister.

"I mean, We look at the problems together," said the young man, "and think of how best to solve them. When you make a suggestion, I will relate it to Our ordinances and see how we can make them work in consonance. After all, parents and children do put their heads together in resolving problems. You say two heads are better than one, don't you?"

"Yes, on the human plane, but this is entirely different from the human level," said the Archbishop. "We are not qualified to be Your students, let alone brainstorm with You. Parents reasoning with their children is flesh to flesh; hence they sometimes get it wrong. But this reasoning here is of a spiritual dimension, and who knows the mind of the spirit except He who searches our hearts? I'd rather we just remain silent and listen to You."

"That would not be fair," said the young man. "I am reasoning with you on the human level, and it is only fair that you make your opinion count. Besides, the onus of implementation of whatever we discuss here rests squarely on both of you."

"All things bright and beautiful divinely made for the benefit of man are manifested on the human level," said the Archbishop, "yet some of them fail because of human reasoning. Perfection comes only from the fountain of wisdom. We are Your pupils, and our contribution is to accept Your instructions. It is a rare privilege."

"I wouldn't say instructions," said the young man. "I would rather say suggestions. If it were a matter of instructions, We wouldn't have called you here, because you already have Our instruction manual. Our basis for a relationship with people is free will, and free will is better reflected in suggestions than in instructions. So I make suggestions, you make suggestions, and we arrive at a conclusion. That is a civilized way of reasoning together. So, shall we reason together?"

"Well, yes!" The Archbishop agreed, yet remained skeptical.

"Is the Prime Minister with us in this?" asked the young man.

"I am not so sure, sir," replied the PM. "The reason is that I don't seem to see anything wrong with our country, so it will be difficult for me to make any suggestions. The best thing is for You to tell us what is wrong and show us how best to deal with it."

"I agree with the PM," said the Archbishop.

"I am surprised you say you don't see anything wrong with your country," said the young man. "Even after all you saw during our walk?"

"I speak as a human being at the human level," said the PM. "That is not to say all is perfectly well with the country. Perfection can never be attained at the human level. Everything is relative."

"Sir, tell us what You have for us," said the Archbishop. "You invited us, and we are here to hear why You invited us. If we have questions, we'll ask."

"I have brought Myself down to your human level," said the young man, "and all we are discussing here is at that level. If everything were OK with your country at that level, then your citizens wouldn't bombard Us with so many complaints, which We receive all the time. We are here to discuss some of these complaints and find solutions. Know that these complaints are not necessarily during your tenure alone, as indeed is the case with those things we saw during our walk, but they reflect many years of British society and British leadership across the political spectrum. We will only discuss a very small number of points resulting from those complaints. We will talk about the spiritual side as we go along, so, Archbishop, don't think you are excluded; you are not an observer.

"Please feel at ease as much as possible because We are not in the habit of apportioning blame or guilt, for none is righteous. That is the only way you can make effective contributions to our discussion here." But both the Prime Minister and the Archbishop were already quite nervous, virtually frozen in their seats as they listened.

"There is a complaint of general indiscipline in society," said the young man. "There is a bitter complaint of government denying parents the right to discipline their children, and of lack of discipline in schools. A child's formative years are in the home and school, where the character is molded. Those are the two most important places basic discipline is infused in the individual; miss it and you miss it forever. What are your suggestions on how to rectify this?"

"I'd rather You suggest Yourself," said the Prime Minister.

"I have no suggestions that will be different from Our laid-down ordinances for a problem-free society, rejected by your governments," said the young man.

"Sir, as You well know," said the Prime Minister, "it takes time and experience to draw up a policy, and asking us for suggestions here and now may actually worsen the situation You want rectified."

"Asking for suggestions does not amount to policy formulation," said the young man. "The problem with politicians is that everything is policy-oriented. That gives no room for flexibility, especially when all policies are PC driven. Political correctness, or PC as your people term it, seems to be the main problem with your society; it has become a constant in all the complaints We receive."

"Sir, we didn't simply introduce PC policies for the fun of it," said the Prime Minister. "Ours is a democratic government. With a population of more than sixty-six million people, we cannot possibly satisfy everybody. So while we listen to everybody, we can only embark on what the majority wants. We rule by majority."

"Yes. You can't satisfy everybody," said the young man, "but it is not true that you yield to majority opinion. For instance, you were in Parliament during the tuition fee riots some years back. Were the voices in that debate those of minorities? Your government often silences the voice of the majority in preference of its own policies."

"I am sorry, sir," said the PM. "I should have said that we do what we think is right for the people, and in doing so, we go by majority vote of the MPs. Since MPs represent their constituencies, their votes count for their people's voices."

"It was the people's vote that put you in power, not the votes of the MPs," said the young man. "Albeit theirs may have made you the party leader. And when you talk about what you think is right for the people, you amaze Me. Who asked you to think for the people? And who made you a better judge than the people between right and wrong? You are not speaking like a Prime Minister."

"I really don't know how to explain it, sir," said the PM. "I don't rule the country alone; I haven't got any veto power over any issue. Ours is collective governance."

"Tell Me again," said the young man. "Every party has its own policies, which largely reflect the leader's personal agenda. It is for this reason that Prime Ministers are eager to have a parliamentary majority, for easy passage of any bill on the party lines and for defeat of others. So the truth is that MPs represent their own party or their own interests most of the time. Any representation of the people is secondary and without commitment."

"Believe me, sir, our policies represent what the people want," said the PM.

"You mean the people prefer to be misrepresented?" asked the young man. "You mean they prefer the present decay and insecurity? But the complaints We get indicate the contrary."

"Sir, the truth is that these people just want to be left alone to do what they like," said the PM. "They only show their anger when they fall victim to the ills of society. Any sympathy and grief when the same happens to others is superficial and short-lived. At least You know us more than we know ourselves. Ours is the most difficult people to deal with, the most hypocritical people You can ever think of."

"It has not always been like this. What happened?" asked the young man.

"Sir, I don't really know," replied the PM. "To be honest, the problems did not start with me; I met them. And some of them have lasted for as long as I can remember—in fact, before I was born. I am trying my best to solve as many as I can with our limited resources."

"So you think!" said the young man. "It is amazing that while citizens of other countries, right in their own countries, are fervently praying for your country, many of your own citizens just remain unconcerned about what is happening."

"That is what I was saying, sir," said the PM. "That is what they want; hence they are not worried."

"I don't think so," said the young man. "Some don't care because it gives them the freedom to behave as they choose. Others are simply tired of complaining and choose to be silent because the government criminalizes them for complaining rather than listening to them. However, I must remind you that you are here because of the cry of many of them, among whom are those who love Us, so We cannot ignore their pleas."

"Sir, in fairness to the PM, he is trying," said the Archbishop. "This century is different from any we have ever known. Population growth, multiculturalism, globalization, human rights issues, terrorism, failing economies and unrealistic and unreasonable expectations make twenty-first-century governance very difficult. It is very difficult to balance all the forces at play in such a way to satisfy everyone and provide for peace."

The young man smiled and said, "You really make Me laugh. Which country do you think is free from all these problems? None, although the magnitude varies from country to country, and there are those problems that are self-inflicted. But I'd rather we talk of the problems in your country and leave others out."

"Sir, but we can't live in isolation," said the PM. "Comparing ourselves with other nations helps us to know how we are faring. It helps us to improve on our standards."

"You are not here on behalf of any other country but your country," said the young man. "So let's start with your country and only make reference to other countries when necessary as we go along."

"OK then," said the Prime Minister.

"Sir, You know everything," said the Archbishop, "and we can't really argue with You. But in a society of so many ethnic groups such as ours, it is difficult to compel people of different cultures and nationalities to adopt a culture alien to them in an effort to provide for peaceful and orderly coexistence."

"You are still running away from the truth," said the young man. "Britain's ethnic mix is not the highest in the world. You've certainly heard people express the common notion that Britain is the sick man of Europe. That is not just the European view but is the view of the world, that Britain is *the sick man of the world.*

"But British people don't want to erase that image, because it takes honest leadership to do that. And Britain has no such leaders. Leadership is based on values. It is not about forcing people to adopt your perceptions of life or what you think is right for them. A good leader must have values, values based on goodness—goodness that is natural and humane."

"Sir, times are changing and so are values," said the PM. "When I was growing up, I never thought that what is happening today could ever happen, so we need a new approach to tackling today's problems."

"We are coming to that, but it takes leadership to develop a new approach based on the right values of life," said the young man. "Solving problems with the wrong values increases the problems. But let's talk about leadership first. The problems in Britain are not peculiar to them, but the leaders' response is either denial or piecemeal—and that is the real problem.

"No British leader is bold enough to talk about true British values or even the human values that are common to all peoples of the earth. They do not want to lose votes or face criticism, and that makes leadership opportunistic—acquiring power at the expense of their cherished values or whatever is left of those values."

"Sir, Britain is changing very fast," said the Archbishop. "All manner of people live there now. As a result, just as the Prime Minister said, values are changing. We are modernizing to accommodate these changes."

"I am sure you know I can't be deceived," said the young man. "Names and slogans mean nothing to Me because I see the real thing encased within each name or slogan. Modernism could be a malapropism when leaders entrench their own foibles within a society and brand their modernization. It is a term employed in political comedy by leaders who lack values. The question is, what is wrong with tested old values that necessitated your modernizing agenda?"

"If You were not who You are, I would say You don't understand," said the Archbishop, "Migration resulted in people's bringing their gods, different things that constituted their gods, corrupting our values and our society. This is the problem of multiculturalism. And it was the same problem in Israel of old during the reign of kings when the people mingled and intermarried with foreigners—the Hittites, the Perizzites, the Jebusites and the rest of them."

"You all have the same authority view," said the young man. "I call it authority view because it is only those in authority who share that view. The ordinary people see it differently."

"Sir," said the Archbishop, "let me quote a statement by one of our journalists to convince you that ordinary people share our view—that is the effect of migration and multiculturalism. He said, 'Majestic London has become a stinking bog of base humanity swimming in the filth of depravity. Britain has embraced and absorbed all the filths of its immigrants, tolerated every excess, accepted every philosophy, encouraged every abomination and swallowed every imported vomit.' So, you see, it is not only those in authority."

"A few minutes ago, the Prime Minister spoke of his dread of the press," said the young man, "a clear indication of how powerful the press and, thus, many journalists are. So a journalist is not an ordinary citizen and cannot in his lofty position see things as ordinary citizens see them. However, this journalist was honest enough to admit that London, and therefore your country, has become a stinking bog of base humanity swimming in the filth of depravity as against the Prime Minister's denials. What do you say to his accusation of your encouraging every abomination? You can only encourage what you love or see as right. What is your response to that damning indictment that can only be due to lack of true leadership?"

"What we said is the truth, sir; we are not hiding the truth," said the Archbishop. "At least I am not alone in that view."

"What is the ratio of foreigners to the indigenous population?" asked the young man. "What is the principle of democracy? Who controls the government and its policies? What is your concept of modernity—positive or negative?"

At these questions, the two men were frozen in silence as they sat tongue-tied for a while before the Archbishop, casting an apologetic glance at the young man, muttered a response. "Foreigners are in the minority, sir," he said.

"The principle of democracy is based on the majority. English people are in control of the government and its policies. Modernity is positive."

"Good. Do you accept that modernity can also be negative?" asked the young man.

"Yes," answered the Archbishop.

"OK, that means your country cannot blame foreigners for its downward spiral," said the young man. "If anything, it is foreigners who have held your country back from the precipice and prevented Our wrath. When we took a walk through mainland Britain, we saw a herd of sheep without a shepherd. We saw what freedom had done to those children and to their drunken parents in the pub. We saw what went on in the worship center, and the protestors tearing down everything in their path. Most of the people we saw there were not immigrants."

"That is true, sir," said the Archbishop. "But our indigenous population also makes up a greater percentage of believers in this country."

"While that is true," said the young man, "remember that the ratio of their population compared to the ratio of immigrant believers to their own population makes your own ratio very small. But I appreciate them; they are the ones who remember and value all We have done for them through their forefathers when those generations walked with Us.

"They do not overtly seek dubious rights and freedom from responsibility, nor do they engage in the intellectual glamorization of evil to amuse themselves. Why do your people take absolute pleasure in their own destructiveness? It is to avert the great evil I see in the air that we are here. And you are hesitant to help avert it."

VIII.

Back in London that Sunday morning, with the time being twenty past eleven, a phone report came through to the critical incident room of a sighting of the PM riding a bicycle in a street at South Ruislip. South Ruislip was one of the nearest villages to Northolt. The Prime Minister was known to be an avid bicycle rider before becoming Prime Minister.

The result of the phone call was the massive deployment of the security forces there, who sealed off the whole area and the adjacent villages—the whole of Ruislip Manor and South Harrow and up to the nearest part of Ickenham. It was a massive manhunt, and the airways were abuzz with radio messages. The entire area was subject to a near state of emergency. More roadblocks were mounted, and everybody in the street was stopped and searched, while at the same time, a house-to-house search was conducted.

The report proved to be a hoax because, after all the siege, a man was at last found relaxing in his living room with his newspaper in a house along Bourne Avenue. He had a striking resemblance to the PM. A brief interview showed that the man had just returned from Sunday Mass at the local Church of England—St Mary South Ruislip, on the Fairway—on his bicycle.

IX.

Back at the remote house on the mystery island, the argument continued. "When I spoke of London as a city rich and poor at the same time," said the young man, "I was talking of a people blessed but who rejected their blessing in favor of all sorts of curses they brought upon themselves. I was talking of London rotting away despite its affluence and grandeur, dying of its own corruption. How did your country become a stinking bog of base humanity swimming in the filth of depravity? How? Archbishop, do you remember John 3:19?"

"Yes, sir," replied the Archbishop. Then He quoted the verse Himself: "And this is the condemnation, that the light has come into the world, and men loved darkness rather than light because their deeds were evil."

"Yes, men chose darkness in preference to light because their deeds were evil. This is what is happening. The quality of a nation is dependent on the quality of its leaders. A nation is evil when its leaders are evil. So I want us to focus on leadership because that is the problem with Britain—nothing else.

"Now, since you are not ready to make any suggestions, and because I have nothing to add to our original template for living, which you rejected, let Me ask you a few questions, drawn from issues raised in many of the complaints We received." There was a hushed silence. After a while, looking them directly in the eye, He broke the silence.

"Indiscipline has become the bane of your society because of the lack of any moral guiding principle, Prime Minister, can you tell us why this is?"

"I don't know," replied the Prime Minister.

"Think of discipline in the formative years of the individual person," said the young man. "I earlier talked of the home and school environments. When a child is properly trained, it is difficult for him to depart from the ways he was trained when he grew up. What do you think?"

"That is correct if only there are no external influences from the society, such as peer pressure," said the Prime Minister.

"A largely disciplined society can only exert positive influence, not negative," said the young man. "And a disciplined society results from disciplined homes and schools. Now, when the government's political correctness goes against discipline in the home and school, the only hope left is religion, and when religion is taken away from schools, all hope is lost because discipline is a by-product of good religion. I want the Archbishop to help us answer the question of what happens if there is a breakdown in religion."

"I will try," said the Archbishop with some measured hesitation. "But do help me if You see me struggling. OK, let me explain by saying that the fear of the Lord is the beginning of wisdom. If we understand this, then we understand everything. But we can't get this understanding if we lose sight of God.

"And we can easily lose sight of God if we don't promote religious activities in the community that enhance our vision of God. A breakdown in religion leads to a breakdown of law and order because, without the fear of God, there will be no law and order. The absence of law and order leads to anarchy. Therefore, religious study is something the government should encourage and make compulsory in schools."

"Good effort," said the young man. "This is what I want—for each of us to contribute to the discussion rather than Me doing all the talking and you doing all the listening."

"Sir, we are here to learn from the Master, not to interrupt," replied the Archbishop, "knowing full well that whatever You say is the truth."

"Useful interruptions, questions and suggestions are part of learning," said the young man. "Don't you agree?"

"I wholeheartedly agree," said the Archbishop. "But the awesomeness of this place demands one to be very quiet, only eager to listen and hear."

"That is good, but you have been invited as active discussants," said the young man. "And being active discussants helps the learning process as it is harder to forget your own contributions than what someone else says."

"That is very true, sir," said the Archbishop.

"I also want you to know that hearing is not enough," said the young man. "Acting on what you hear is very important."

"Absolutely," said the Archbishop. "That is why churchgoing is necessary because there is a close correlation between going to church and the heavenly vision—as it is in heaven, so on earth."

"Excellent," commended the young man.

"I have a question," said the Prime Minister.

"Beautiful; this is what I want," said the young man. "Ask your question."

"The Archbishop talks of churchgoing and making religion compulsory in schools," said the Prime Minister. "Which of the religions should be made compulsory when there are so many religions? Can the government force people to go to church or other worship centers?"

"You yourself have always maintained that this is a Christian country," said the Archbishop. "So the Christian religion should be made compulsory in state schools. Then faith schools should be made to teach their own religious faith in their schools."

"That would be dangerous," said the Prime Minister, "because there are some religious extremists who will radicalize young people."

"I disagree," said the Archbishop, "as there are ways of monitoring what goes on in schools. I mean, if prayer houses are monitored, why not schools?"

"The truth is that no one has legislated against religious knowledge in schools," said the PM. "RK is still being taught at schools."

"Yes, in some state schools, but not all," said the Archbishop. "But even in the schools where it is taught, it is being taught not in the way we know it. What is taught is anything but religion."

"What of Churchgoing?" asked the Prime Minister.

"Churchgoing helps you to be grounded in the heavenly vision," answered the Archbishop. "And the heavenly vision is God's purpose for man on earth, which the church teaches. It is how God ordained for goodness and peace to reign on earth." The young man was nodding His head affirmatively as the Archbishop explained. "We lose sight of God and the essence of life when we stop thinking about God," the Archbishop continued. "And then we stop seeing things the way God sees them. The heavenly vision is necessary both to find fulfillment in life and to build a better society."

"The reason I ask is that there are people who don't believe in God," said the PM. "And the government can't force people to worship God."

"True, you can't force people to worship God, but you can create an atmosphere that encourages it," said the Archbishop.

"Not believing in God does not exclude anyone from the right way of life," said the young man, "for no one denies nature—and nature speaks volumes of God's presence. Nature is full of God's goodness, which is bestowed on everybody, including those who hate God. So, tell Me what is to be done to restore faith and hope—faith in God and in your country?"

"Sir, we are trying our best," replied the Prime Minister. "Our people have faith in our leadership."

"That does not really answer My question," said the young man.

"Sir," said the Archbishop, "the moral problems are so deep-rooted that it is almost impossible to do anything except that being who You are, nothing is impossible."

"It is not about who I am," said the young man, "because I already set out My plan for man—for good and not for evil. It is for man to follow My plan."

"Well, we haven't been very good at handling things," said the Archbishop, "but the politicians will always argue that their efforts are the best."

"You tend to blame politicians all the time," said the Prime Minister. "Yet we don't act alone, as we take advice from well-meaning people, especially the church."

"Well, as I have been saying," the Archbishop said, continuing his argument, "the government went against the church by taking religious instruction out of schools. That is taking people's most important asset in life away from them. That robs them of any sense of value and also of hope. When the odds are down, it is hope that keeps one going—hope that nothing is new under the sun and that nothing is permanent, hope that anything that has a beginning must have an end because nothing lasts forever."

"That is correct," said the young man. "Your hope is placed in your values, and your values are found in your belief system. It is your belief system that either entangles you or frees you. It is your belief system that gives you identity and motivates you to go the extra mile in the hope that you—"

"We are a very hopeful nation, sir," the Prime Minister said, interrupting. "We have faith in our systems."

"Good!" said the young man. "You have qualified the faith you have. Experience has shown bitter disappointment for those placing their hope or faith in humans and their systems. I am the only basis for faith. Without Me, there can be no faith. Listen to this: When wealth is gone, little is lost; when health is gone, something is lost; when character is gone, all is lost; but when God—the only basis for character—is gone, there is no longer any basis for life. God is the only basis for hope and recovery and for the rediscovery of self and society. God is the hope for living, I hope the Prime Minister is listening."

"I am, sir," said the Prime Minister, shrugging, "but—"

"No nation can survive that takes its eyes off God," continued the young man. "There can be no vision and direction without wisdom, for wisdom is the principal thing. And the Source of wisdom is God, who created everything in His wisdom. Wisdom produces understanding; understanding gives vision; vision gives direction; direction gives purpose; and purpose demands action that leads to a solution. So there can be no solution when the Source of wisdom is shut out. But Britain has shut out God. Britain has forgotten where her strength lies and who the Source of her power is. It is good to remember that no stream rises above its source."

"Sir, I honestly think I am the wrong person to confront on these issues," said the Prime Minister. "I have no hand in all this. I grew up to know this country to be a secular state. And I took office while it was still a secular state."

"Yours is not alone," said the young man. "A great number of the world's countries are secular, but their secularity did not necessarily turn their eyes completely away from God. Whenever there is a problem, they know where to turn."

"Remember I told you we don't know we have any problem," said the PM. "Maybe that is why we don't know where to turn."

"Remember, too, that I told you that only you, the leaders pretend not to know you have problems," said the young man. "As you can see from the comments of one of your journalists, there are serious problems."

"Sir, part of our problem is avid secularism," said the Archbishop. "Our governments have progressively become more secular and have stampeded our people only in the secular direction. That is why the church is toothless."

"I completely disagree with you, Archbishop," the Prime Minister objected. "Although there is a separation between State and Church, or religion, each part is expected to play its part in working together to improve society. If there is any failure, both have failed."

"It sounds all right to say it is a separation of State from religion," responded the Archbishop, "but what we see in today's Britain is the aggressive denouncement of anything religious. The government is the lawmaker and consults no person and no organization before making any law. Yet they force everybody to obey, whatever the consequences. The government is insensitive to people's opinions or their plight. That is what is causing problems."

"You can't say that," argued the Prime Minister. "There is always a long period of consultation with people and organizations before any law is passed. There is never any unanimous agreement on the outcome of such consultations, so we always go by the majority.

"The same goes for the church, where so much disagreement among the leaders prevents them from ever presenting a common front on any issue. So we go by the opinion of the majority of their leaders."

"Gentlemen, let's not debate on consultation or no consultation," said the young man. "The truth is that governments have often acted in a way that resulted in minority and individual gains at the expense of the majority. But what we are seeking here are solutions, not blame. However, we need to know the problems in order to apply the right measures that will bring solutions, especially as you say you don't know of any problems."

"Honestly speaking, sir," said the Prime Minister, "we are not the worst country in the world."

"That is true, but there are reasons why your case is different," said the young man. "Your country has never been like it is today. Policies always reflected the foundational basis on which your country was established until the fading years of the twentieth century when all this became completely eroded. What happened?"

"People simply blame the government for all sorts of things, including their self-inflicted problems," said the Prime Minister. "My government has done—"

He was interrupted by the young man, who continued His analysis in a quiet, accommodating voice. "Very frequently political leaders talk of a road map in their efforts at finding solutions to problems. Yet not the least of the problems has been solved in that the only true road map to any solution is found in God.

"Now tell me, what is the purpose of so much legislation rushed through Parliament in the last few years to nail righteousness to the grave and to chain those who do not want to follow the crowd to the grave? Where is the vaunted freedom in all those laws?"

"Sir, they were meant to protect people from unnecessary harassment by people who don't share or agree with their way of life," said the PM.

"You don't make any law simply for the sake of it," said the young man, "or else it would result in injustice. Laws are made to enforce the right way, the natural way of life, not to compel people to endorse any way of life. If people should endorse any way of life, then laws would no longer be necessary. Nature itself has set boundaries, and if laws are made against such boundaries to please some people, then those laws become an offense.

"Are you not aware, for instance, that people lived in harmony when such natural boundaries were adhered to without any contrary laws made? People naturally knew what was acceptable and what was not and thus kept within the boundaries. This is how any civilized country with multiethnic, multicultural and multifaith groups is supposed to be if a good measure of peace is to be attained."

"Sir, without laws, there would be mayhem," said the PM. "Laws help to provide for respect and orderliness in society."

"That is true," said the young man. "Laws are necessary for orderliness, but not to further the PC agenda. We laid down the foundations for law, primarily scripted on people's hearts, and secondarily as natural ordinances with cause and effect. What I am saying is that today's laws are deliberately enacted against God's ordinances to criminalize the godly. Many of today's laws are opposed to natural laws. That is why they are causing problems." He paused briefly with His gaze fixed on them, moving his eyes from one to the other. Then He continued.

"We have complaints that the Cross of Jesus Christ has become a criminal offense in Britain, with many people preferring the Union flag to the Christian Cross. Prime Minister, what is your response to those who say people are perishing for lack of vision because of this antagonism to the Cross?"

"That is their problem," said the Prime Minister. "Perhaps they don't know the meaning of vision. Vision is foresight; it is the ability to project into the future and map out programs and strategies for a better future. And we have this in abundance. As I speak, we have policies and programs for the next 15,

25 and even 50 years. As for the Union flag and the Cross of Jesus Christ, I can't say anything."

"Why not?" asked the young man.

"Because I don't want to pontificate on a purely theological matter," said the Prime Minister. "And the reason I say this is that the Christian Cross has always generated acrimonious division. But more important is the fact that public opinion indicates that Britain is no longer a Christian country. Much energy and many resources have been expended on this issue in the country. There is nothing I am going to say here that will make a difference."

"OK, but what is your own opinion against public opinion?" asked the young man.

"My opinion is to be on the side of the people," said the Prime Minister, "because as a democracy, my government gives the people what they want."

"So you agree that Britain is not a Christian or a religious country?" asked the young man.

"If a former Archbishop of Canterbury says it is a post-Christian country, who am I to disagree?" answered the Prime Minister. "The foundation of the British state is Christian in principle, but today Christianity is rather obsolete; its appeal has waned almost to complete oblivion."

"So then, how do we revive the religious spirit?" asked the young man.

"That is what I am saying: it is beyond redemption," said the Prime Minister.

"Well, this is mere polemics," said the young man, "because defining a country as Christian or not does not necessarily make that country godly. God is a Spirit, and any relationship with Him must be in spirit and in truth. Now, any vision not linked to the Cross and appraised on the divine purpose would be too melioristic and bound to fail. That is why despite your projected vision, your people are perishing as rightly observed.

"The loss of vision or having the wrong vision is one of the worst things that could ever happen to any group of people. It is the loss of vision that leads to loss of direction. It is the loss of vision that results in legislating against the good of a nation and against the things that exalt a nation—against morality, against righteousness, against holiness and against godliness. It is lack of vision that promotes the things that divide the people rather than the things that unite them."

"Sir, I am tempted to think You are talking like this because You don't live on our planet," said the Prime Minister, "or else You would've known what the earth is really like."

"Please don't be tempted to think that way," said the young man, "because I live everywhere and I know the earth better than you do, for I formed it. Besides, I have brought Myself to your level, the human level, on Planet Earth."

"Yes, but You probably don't have the practical experience we have," said the Prime Minister.

"You really don't believe I know and feel the earth better than you do?" asked the young man. "Well, we are discussing the points raised by your people, who not only live on earth but also live in the same time and the same society as you. So don't talk like one lacking vision." There was a prolonged silence and a tense atmosphere in the room.

Then He continued: "It is lack of vision and direction that leads a nation to the abyss. Hence the Union flag is more important to you and your nation than the Cross of Jesus Christ, as is rightly pointed out. Your people have forgotten that without the Cross, there would be no Union Jack. Is it any wonder that some diehard religionists want to shred the Union Jack, even though they have nothing to do with the Cross?

"When there was no such ungodly legislation, there was no threat to the Union Jack. And why can't there be such a threat when even religious leaders have lost the moral authority to lead, abdicating their responsibilities in the quest for fame and glamour and loving the easy life? Archbishop, what have you to say?"

After a short while, without any response from the Archbishop, He continued.

"It seems you both are unwilling for us to reason together, particularly the Prime Minister. Therefore, the only choice I have now is to offer some advice on how to move the country forward. I love your country and don't want any of you to make the same mistakes many of your past leaders made. That is why you are here, to receive vision. I don't want your people to perish.

"However, your choice is your choice. I am never in the habit of forcing people against their will. Were it not so, your people would not have been craving for so much knowledge—the wrong knowledge—while rejecting the right knowledge from the very Source of knowledge, the knowledge that leads to true wisdom. Prime Minister, I suggest that you avoid at all costs the politics of division and distortion. Try to introduce a new style of governance, a responsive governance. Your politics must not be faceless; it must have a soul." He paused again briefly, then continued: "Please do not allow any political theory to appeal to you more than the gospel of Jesus Christ. As the leader of your country, you must endeavor to be all things to everyone to accommodate them."

"No one can be all things to everyone," said the Prime Minister. "That is just impossible. How can I really explain anything to Your satisfaction?"

"You are not expected to explain anything to My satisfaction," said the young man. "That is why I arranged this meeting, to hear you and see how I can help. But you don't seem even to be willing to listen to Me, let alone learn."

"I am willing," said the PM. "It's just that You haven't placed Yourself in my position—I, being a mere mortal, whose power is limited—not like You, who is an angel or some spiritual being with the awesome power to do whatever You like."

"I know your position, for I willed you into that position—which you may not know," said the young man. "And that is why I am here to help if only you would open up a bit and seek My help."

"Well, sir," said the PM, "why it is difficult for me is that most of the issues You are raising are unknown to me. For instance, in terms of political theories, I don't think of them in relation to the gospel of Christ. I am not a Bible pundit, and I don't know the gospel of Christ. So it is difficult for me to make an objective analysis and to compare the two.

"Naturally, what you don't know doesn't appeal to you. I have only heard that the Bible teaches morality and goodness. But we live in a world of difficulties, a world of contrasts and mysteries. We live in a world of problems. We live in a world where people do not often agree on anything, least of all what constitutes morality and goodness. We live in a world where one man's choice can affect nations. So it is not really what appeals to the leader or to any individual that matters."

"What matters then?" asked the young man.

"What matters for me," said the Prime Minister, "is what appeals to the people. As I said before, we serve the people. So it is really not about any political theory. The people's free choice of what constitutes their welfare is my political theory. The day the people choose the gospel of Christ as what appeals to them, we will enforce its teachings and guidelines as the basis for our national conduct. We had an Islamic political party that lasted sixteen years and was defunct by the middle of the first decade of the present century. We have a Christian political party that is still in existence. Nobody can stop them from taking office if they win any election. We have a democratic system where the people themselves choose what they want and who leads them."

"Very good," said the young man. "Let us approach it in another way because we are not here to argue but to reason together. Part of reasoning together is understanding the issues. Defending the status quo gives a semblance of argument, and that will not help our purpose. But before we get to the alternative approach, let Me quickly say this, not to blame or denigrate you, but as a learning process for you.

"A leader of many communities of people who wants his people to live in harmony will endeavor to understand them to be able to unify them. Part of that is studying their ways of life. And that is made easy by having advisers who have in-depth knowledge of those specific areas in governance. Anything short of this is an indictment of the leader and his political adviser and also smacks of a lack of working relationships with the experts and representatives of the various communities.

"For instance, since the Archbishop's appointment is political by way of some political endorsement, it is expected that the government recognize the community he represents and seeks his informed opinion on matters affecting that community. And by *that community*, I mean all religious groups who should be working together.

"Besides, members of Parliament of various faith groups ought to work with the Prime Minister in enlightening him on issues affecting their communities and adequately representing their people in Parliament, thereby making the Prime Minister relatively knowledgeable in the areas of the people's needs. This is what I mean by being all things to everyone."

"Sir, we have a good working relationship," said the Prime Minister.

"That doesn't seem to be the case," said the young man, "not with the two of you arguing right here in My presence. But anyway, as I was saying, your country has a history intricately linked to religion, and secularism has not changed that, nor has the assertion that it is a non-Christian or a non-religious country. I use *religion* here for lack of a better term that you could easily understand. Everybody expects any British politician, irrespective of ethnicity, to know the history and politics of Britain, from ages past to the present, and all the various political theories that ever existed in the developed world. And no other politician is better placed to know that than a first-class Oxford politics graduate at the pinnacle of his political career.

"But neither my assertion here nor your response addresses the simple point raised. It does not require knowledge of the scriptures. All that is required is to look at whatever political theories you know of and examine how they have affected people's lives, how long they have been relevant to people, and what good they have been to societies.

"Then think how these compare with the gospel of Christ, which has had an enduring legacy, positively affecting millions of lives throughout the world for centuries. It is constant irrespective of region, culture, or ideology. There is hardly anyone on earth today who has not heard of the gospel of Christ, whether they believe it or not, so it is easy to make such comparisons. So think about it and draw your own conclusion. Know that I am always ready to help."

"Well—" said the Prime Minister.

He was cut short by the young man, who continued with His statements: "I plead that you don't allow the Devil to establish his kingdom in your country. It is a very terrible thing to happen to any country; don't forget what we saw in your country during our walk. Resist the Devil and he will flee from you. But you cannot resist the Devil on your own strength. You need My presence, but I don't force Myself on anyone. Another point I wish to plead is that you do not allow anything to take precedence over truth, justice and ethical standards."

"Of course, that is standard for any leader," said the PM. "That is the core principle on which any government or institution is established, at least in the UK. And this is what we are fighting for, for the rest of the world to emulate."

"That is very good." The young man smiled. "Let's analyze this in a way that sheds light on the true concept meant by invoking these terms, so that our answers, in addition to addressing the issues raised, will help us to regard these terms according to their true meanings and enhance their proper future applications.

"You say you practice this principle in your country. Now, before you start fighting for the rest of the world, are there party policies and programs that are politically expedient so as to take priority over any of these three factors?"

"Not at all, sir," said the PM. "Not that I know of, and certainly not in my government."

"Archbishop, do you agree with his response?" asked the young man. "Can we say that of the church in the United Kingdom?"

"Sir, in all honesty, I have areas of disagreement with politics and with the government," replied the Archbishop. "I can only speak for the church here. As far as I know, there is no deceit of any kind in the church in the United Kingdom."

"Hmm, have you ever heard the word *compromise*?" asked the young man.

"Yes, sir," they both replied in unison.

"Does it mean anything to you?" He asked.

"Yes, sir," they both replied in unison again.

"Have you ever compromised on anything, such as your belief, your values, your position, or your relationship?" the young man asked.

"I have had to compromise on rare occasions on very difficult situations," said the Prime Minister. "It was the only amicable way out of a quagmire. And in politics, it is difficult not to compromise. In fact, I would say compromise is the soul of politics."

"You are right in saying you've compromised," said the young man. "Compromise corrupts truth and justice, and both the state and the Church have had several areas of untruths and injustice. But the purpose of the question is not to judge either your honesty or your weakness. It is to let you know that compromise is a form of injustice, and injustice reflects untruthfulness, which is unethical.

"But aside from compromise, blatant lies, deceit, injustice and unethical practices are rampant in your society. They are seen as legitimate means of governance, whether by the State or by the Church, or any area of human involvement, and this is unacceptable. Sticking to the truth and refusing to compromise in public office is only difficult when the leadership itself is based on deceit and falsehood, or when the foundation of the society itself is rooted in falsehood.

"I know you don't understand. Let Me explain. Many political parties want to be the ruling party. During election campaigns, many party leaders sell some untruths to the electorate, promising what they know they cannot deliver. They make all kinds of efforts to woo communities that do not share their visions. They water down any of their policy areas that are unpleasant to such communities, so as to placate them and win their votes. In effect, they speak what the people want to hear, what appeals to the people and will sway their opinions and garner their votes. The candidates temporarily jettison their individual values and occasionally sidetrack their party lines just to win votes. Once they assume office, they use deceptive phrases and political jargon to deviate from, alleviate themselves of and ameliorate their campaign promises. Am I right?"

A hushed silence was all that He received for an answer, and after a brief moment, He continued.

"In the case of societies rooted in falsehood, things such as untruths, injustice and unethical practices are the rule rather than the exception. There are underlying principles made to simulate truth and fairness, but these are mere whitewash. Over a period of time, people believe them and accept them as genuine things, but they are misplaced principles that wreck societies. They result in bitterness, acrimony, vengeance and instability.

"In many cases, they originate from defective government policies that are not corrected by successive governments. There comes a time when any government that spots them can no longer correct them because society is already embedded in them and would fight against any government that tries to stop them. This then constitutes a normative culture of that society. This is more pronounced if such policies encourage laziness and indiscipline because man by nature is lazy, deceitful and rebellious.

"Now, can truth, justice and ethical practices be achieved in any society?" He paused, raised His head and looked at them intently, as if expecting an answer, but they maintained a calculated silence.

"To a great extent, yes," He said, "when a society entrenches the standard of righteousness. The reason is that truth and justice are based on a conceptual framework that draws from God's commandments, pure and unaltered. Yes, I need to qualify this, because humans are prone to gross misinterpretations to suit their selfish purposes. That is the reason you interpret the systems you have as fair and just.

"Now think: is it possible to speak on the origin of species based on any theory other than that of Charles Darwin? No. Similarly, there can be no truth and justice without the overwhelming presence of reverence and fear of God. The same goes for ethical standards because ethics draw from the natural order of things as ordained by God. Ethical standards are moral standards, and only divine laws can designate the yardstick for measuring moral standards, not anything specified by man."

"So, is Darwin's theory of evolution by way of natural selection accepted in heaven?" the PM asked excitedly.

"What is that to you—whether or not it is accepted in heaven?" replied the young man. "How does that solve the problems in your country or ensure your own salvation?"

"I only ask because many Christians don't believe in Darwin's theory or in evolution," said the PM.

"The problem with the present generation is that it worries about and is troubled over many things," said the young man. "But only one thing is needed, which only a few have chosen, and it will not be taken from them."

"Does that mean that Christians are right?" asked the PM.

"Prime Minister," said the Archbishop, "listen. Jesus was performing miracles, healing people, setting them free and feeding multitudes miraculously, yet the leaders of the people asked Him to show them signs—a mark of their unbelief. Like them, you too are seeking signs. Scripture says an evil and adulterous generation seeks signs. Don't you understand? Please pay attention to what He is saying."

"But He said we could ask questions," argued the PM.

"Yes, and He answered your question," replied the Archbishop. "It was simple enough."

"It is easy for you to say that; I have never read the Bible," said the PM.

"This is not the Bible," said the Archbishop. "This is simple English. At any rate, the Bible is there for you to read."

There was a brief silence before the young man continued.

"So, as I was saying, truth and justice are the ethical foundation for any good society. The rebellious attitude in humans repels any efforts being made to do anything. However, if there is the knowledge of right and wrong, and an inherent attitude cultivated from childhood to do what is right, then truth, justice, law and order, ethical standards and all good qualities of human nature become the people's culture.

"They become everyday standards and practices that exalt society. The one and only way of doing this is through godliness. But when morality and the fear and reverence of a higher authority, as in religion, are taken away from society, and law and order virtually expunged from the home and schools, then you create anarchy and kill that society.

"The people will have no God, no respect and no fear of anything. And without this, there can be no truth, no justice and no standards of any type. Any law made outside of these principles cannot be justified. No matter how you say it, if it is unjust, it is unjust.

"Euphemism has no place in law, nor does any form of lingua gerrymandering portray a thing less evil because the government says so or because of the caliber of people involved. Such only serves the purpose of deceit. When a government loses an election because of problems it created, but the party criticizes the next government for difficulties resulting from efforts to solve the initial problems, it is injustice."

"That is politics, sir," said the PM.

"Of course it is politics," affirmed the young man. "But is it good politics? Is it not politics laden with injustice? Good politics is the means by which a country is run well. If politics is characterized by untruths and injustice, then the country is not run well. Unfortunately, through political deceit, the people of your country have become so alienated and distanced from the government.

"A nation fails when politics fails. Good politics is not the absence of problems or faults; it is the absence of people with integrity and vision. Vision and understanding as from the Source of wisdom. Good politics entails openness, honesty and sincerity in running a country.

"It is listening and hearing the people's heartbeat, alleviating their problems and allaying their fears. It is making them feel listened to, loved and cherished. It is giving them equal opportunities to develop and providing channels of responsibility so they can contribute to the common good. It is placing the interest and welfare of your citizens above anything else.

"I see you shaking your head, Prime Minister. Your mind is saying, *No leader can satisfy all these conditions or satisfy all his people.*"

"But You know this Yourself," said the Prime Minister.

"Yes, I agree with you," said the young man, "but I tell you one thing: it is not the inability to satisfy these conditions or satisfy all the people that leads to failure. What leads to failure is misplaced priority by leaders, and that is bad politics. They know the right thing to do but will not do it. They prefer to do that which satisfies their personal and party interests. They prefer wrangling with other politicians and political parties over attending to the needs of the people. Governments and leaders fail because there is no place for God in their lives and in their programs. And that is a problem because governments are run by humans—and We know the nature of man. We know what is in the heart of man. If the home front is not well-run, what then is expected at the international front? What are your foreign policy objectives? Do they reflect truth, justice and ethical standards?"

"Sir, our foreign policies and programs are very humanitarian," said the PM. "We are always among the first countries to provide urgent help where needed, in terms of both human resources and material resources."

"Well done," said the young man. "Your compassion is very much appreciated. Foreign policy is not all about your help to others. But even in the help you render, are there any elements of injustice?"

"None, sir," replied the Prime Minister.

"Are there conditions?" asked the young man. "Because sometimes conditions result in injustice. Imagine if We were to give conditions for Our blessings; not many people would qualify. But We provide for all despite their rebellion against Us. So are there conditions that reflect infraction of ethical standards in your giving?"

"No, sir. If anything, we fight for justice for those who cannot fight for themselves in other countries."

"This is the second time you have made mention of fighting for a cause for others," said the young man. "There are many ways of fighting a cause—negotiation, intimidation, incitement, outright war, etc. But My interest is not in any of these. It is in justice, fighting for a just cause. What is your definition of a just cause?"

"A cause that is just," said the Prime Minister. "I mean, just by international law."

"The problem with your definition is that international law is never really international," said the young man. "Law and order, and justice, has always had a conceptual framework that is regionally cultural. When international law reflects a predominantly regional judicial framework, it is only international on paper. That is why there are major problems and differences between nations despite international law.

"This is why some countries regard some pressure groups as terrorists while others regard them as freedom fighters. Besides, individuals and groups oftentimes interpret justice according to their own perceptions or selfish interests. That is why simply declaring one is fighting for others generates a lot of skepticism, which I don't want us to go into because it is unending. But one important thing I plead you avoid is deliberately provoking unnecessary hostilities to your country."

"How?" asked the Prime Minister.

"When we took a walk through mainland Britain, we saw the leader who was busy killing everything in a pond. That pond represents weaker countries, and the man throwing things into it represents the leaders of your country. Instead of the leaders and the government addressing the problems at home and giving quality leadership to their people, they are busy seeking offense and destruction of other countries. The absence of their leadership provides their citizens the opportunity to be lawless and reckless. The wise learn from experience. Pride goes before a fall. You must avoid the sin of pride at all costs."

"But how?" asked the Prime Minister.

"Do you have corruption in your country?" asked the young man.

"Yes," said the Prime Minister. "The parliamentary expenses scandal was too glaring to say there is none. And there will always be pockets of corruption and lawlessness even in high places, but by and large, ours is about the least corrupt or least lawless society in the world. Besides, criticizing foreign governments is nothing new. It is part of international politics and our way of getting even with others for their unjust criticisms of us."

"You are supposed to be a leader of the free world," said the young man, "a pacesetter. Leaders and pacesetters set good examples."

"Sir, I think by criticizing them, we are actually helping them to improve," said the Prime Minister. "We are fighting for the rights of their ordinary citizens. Keeping silent in the face of evil is encouraging them to go even further in wrongdoing."

"That is true," said the young man, "but to criticize others for the same thing that you are doing is injustice. First, correct your own attitude before pointing an accusatory finger at others."

"Such warnings are nonbinding, sir," said the Prime Minister. "It's just making them know the outside world is watching, just as they too watch other nations."

"It is much more than merely watching each other," said the young man. "It can become binding. For instance, there was the issue of a Foreign Secretary who forced the redrafting of the constitution of some overseas islands during his tenure. At every turn, you British are wont to defend your position by referencing democratic rights.

"So why do you deny the people of these islands their democratic rights to decide their own constitution and their own future? How come the only thing that offends the average British parliamentarian, as always, is a reference to righteousness? These are not only moral issues but ethical issues, which you said you uphold."

X.

"Once more, sir, I would have said that were not true if You weren't the one speaking," said the PM.

"Tell Me it is not true," said the young man, "and then explain why, out of hundreds of pages of documents making up the constitution, the only parts your Foreign Office finds offensive are those that make reference to traditional Christian morality? The same problem is found with all the constitutions of these islands, except those that are already excluded. And your present MPs are still fighting for the downgrading or total absence of godly principles everywhere they can reach."

"Oh, you are talking about Cayman and St Helena islands, I guess," said the PM.

"Yes," replied the young man. "In the introduction, the Cayman Islands' revised constitution says, 'It is a God-fearing country based on traditional Christian values, tolerant of other religions and beliefs', and adds that it 'is a country in which religion finds its expression in moral living and social justice.'

"Any nation whose fundamental principle of society is outside this scope is on a roller-coaster to anarchy. And only such countries find offense with such noble expressions of articles of faith. Similarly, the updated constitution of St Helena, Ascension and Tristan da Cunha was criticized because of its strong emphasis on Christian and family values.

"The British government actually went so far as specifically threaten the leaders to drop any reference to Christian values from their constitution or face withdrawal of British subsidies. If I may ask, does the word *Christianity* or *morality* offend your people? Does reference to God offend you? Why do you so much hate God and His ordinances? What is the reason for such aggressive atheism?"

"Sir, the islands under consideration are British overseas territories," said the PM, "and as we know, Britain is a multifaith society."

"I am not talking of faith now but of God and godliness," said the young man. "And if I may ask, who made Britain a multifaith society? The people in question are four thousand miles away from Britain, and Christianity is their dominant religion, so the argument about multifaith Britain is untenable. Besides, although the islands are British territories, they have their own constitution based on what they want. Their choice should be respected. Isn't that the essence of democracy?"

"Sir, most of these things happened before I came to power," said the PM. "It was those obsessed with the lopsided modernization agenda and new everything—new this, new that, new appellations to their party name—who, in their craze to modernize, fed the populace with the wrong doctrines of life. And when you throw in a word of caution, you are regarded as being out of touch with reality."

"You were in Parliament when some of these things happened and you never voted against them," said the young man. "But more important is that your government has not differed from any of the previous governments. Government policies in these areas have always remained the same, only coating them with a new lingo and presenting them on a different platter.

"Like your predecessors, you have caused bad blood in the international community for the same reasons the constitutions of these islands was criticized. Are these British territories too?"

"Sir, I may be the Prime Minister, but I don't have the sole prerogative of dictating policies and governance. Most of these things you are referring to happened years before I became Prime Minister. The Prime Minister at the time of the Cayman Islands issue, who happened to be a Christian himself, argued in terms of religion and morality, saying, 'Suggestions of a moral decline in this country are nonsense,' because, as he put it, 'It would depress people unnecessarily, trash Britain's reputation abroad and fail to deal with the problem in the only way that works.'

"However, he never suggested the only way he knew that worked or why he failed to implement his idea while in office. Instead, he added, 'The suggestion of moral decline would result in the wrong analysis, which would lead to the wrong diagnosis and then to the wrong prescription.' He saw it as *good politics but bad policy*, but never explained his reason for thinking so."

"The problem is with your people's interpretation of terms," said the young man. "Politics cannot be good when the policy is bad, because it is the policy that is at play in ordinary citizens' lives. Bad policy is bad governance and bad politics."

"Sir, governance is always at the mercy of political expediency," said the Archbishop, "irrespective of how it affects the populace. That is our experience, and although they know it is wrong, they always justify their action with the phrase 'It is the right thing to do.' But I have come to know that they only use that phrase when they are doing the wrong thing and want to avoid criticism."

"Maybe it was the right thing for them at that time," said the Prime Minister.

"That phrase has always been used by all British governments, including yours," said the young man. "A politician and serving minister once labeled members of a coalition party in the government in which he was serving as *ideological descendants of those who send children up chimneys* and called politicians of another party *childish fantasists*. Your governments are always fantasizing about successive chimney experiences for your citizens. And such chimney policies are driving citizens crazy and depressing them unnecessarily."

"Sir, that is what they are, the politicians: fantasists," said the Archbishop. "They fantasize about their reputations, about the nation's image abroad, about all that does not add anything to the well-being of our citizens. It is all about their personal image. Instead of finding solutions to problems, they fantasize all sorts of emotional problems and use sentimental terms to deliberately trick the people into thinking they care."

"Archbishop, we are in this together, you know," said the Prime Minister. "You can't wash your hands of it. Remember that when the State fails, the Church has failed. So stop putting all the blame on politicians."

"Please, I didn't bring you here to cause any friction between you," said the young man. "You must learn to work together to improve society. The government must listen and partner with faith groups. The purpose of the spiritual is to help improve the physical, and that includes the social. I cannot emphasize enough the need for the spiritual to be firmly embedded in the national consciousness. While We love to see everyone live a righteous life, this is not for the mere sake of seeking righteousness or holiness. No, it is for the good of society at large that people have a consciousness of good and evil, and repulsion toward evil and repercussions for choosing it."

"Sir, what you are saying will involve a completely new national direction," said the Prime Minister, "a process of national reorientation."

"Yes, toward what is good and right," said the young man, "and what is noble and humane."

"Sir, we are so entrenched in our way of life," said the Prime Minister, "that the earth will have to shake for us to be able to do that."

"Your entrenched position has not always been like that," responded the young man. "It took a gradual process. In the same way, this new orientation must take a gradual process. It must start with the family and must start now. What you have in Britain cannot be called a family unit, at least by Our definition of family.

"A family must have specific values embedded in the consciousness of every member. Old-tested family values must be revived through strong emphasis and government programs to promote a strong family life. A disciplined family is a disciplined society. A disciplined society makes for easy governance."

"That is very true, sir," said the Prime Minister. "How I wish some of my senior cabinet members were here."

"What matters is that you are here," said the young man. "That is enough to set things in motion. The relationship was a central theme of creation and marriage. Marriage was supposed to be a relationship of love, sacrifice and honest selflessness.

"Governments are in place to regulate society. They are there to prevent changes that are detrimental to society. They are not there to misuse legislative powers to enforce changes that satisfy their members' personal interests. The ways and examples of people in government who have no stable family life should not be allowed to take hold as a national norm."

"No, that cannot happen, sir," said the Prime Minister. "Our national statistics are not that bad."

"That means you don't know your national statistics," said the young man. "The Office for National Statistics figures, which have not been updated for quite a while in this area, say the ratio of married people is less than half the adult population. Unmarried but cohabiting are 34 percent, and single parents are 26 percent, with 49 percent of them separated and 51 percent never married. Only 23 percent of children live with both parents. More than sixty-seven thousand children are placed under local authority in just one year—when their parents are still alive. I know the present rate to be far higher than these figures, but I have to quote from what is available to you. What does that say about family life in your country?"

"Not good, but sometimes statistics are wrong," said the Prime Minister.

"Wrong or not, governments work on statistics," replied the young man. "Those statistics do not reflect what family life was intended to be. Parents and teachers must be given pivotal roles in developing young people for a better society. Fathers must be made to take responsibility for their children. The nature of your social security system is part of the problem and needs urgent review. A free-for-all society is no society. People cannot just live the way they like and expect society to be good."

"Sir, that is an untouchable area," said the Prime Minister. "Even the church is against us each time we try to address the social security problem. We have been severely accused of being inconsiderate and out of touch. Ask the Archbishop."

"I am not talking to you alone," said the young man. "The Archbishop, the church and every segment of society have their roles to play. There must be a departure from the past. The government cannot and should not take over all the roles of every segment. This brings enormous problems as it violates people's rights to play their part in national development. Families, schools and institutions should be allowed to play their part in nation-building."

"My Bible tells me that except the Lord builds the house, they labor in vain who build it," said the Archbishop. "Let's hope that this time around the government will listen to the church."

"They have to," said the young man, "because the Lord only complements the efforts of the builders. I earlier spoke of the need to listen and hear the people's heartbeat, of giving them equal opportunities to develop and of providing them with channels of responsibility.

"Democracy is no democracy if it is only applicable to elections. The people's heartbeat is their voice, and the Prime Minister spoke of listening to the voice of the majority. Various social surveys in your country indicate that the majority of your people are not happy. They are tired of the way things are;

they want changes to the way things are done. And the government's paying money in search of happiness testifies to that. You must depart from the way previous governments used democracy to deceive your people. For them, it is democratic when it suits their purpose. That is why your brand of democracy is destroying your country."

"But it is the same thing that is practiced in the rest of the democratic world," said the Prime Minister.

"Any government not listening to the genuine worries of its citizens," said the young man, "will have the same problems you are having. You should not fail because the rest of the world is failing. And where there are many clamors, know what is right and what is wrong. And encourage this in people by strong family policies, because everything starts from the family unit—developmental attitudes, love, responsibility, vision, creativity, notions of wrong and right, etc."

"Sir, you seem to be going back to the issue of family time and again," said the Prime Minister. "We can't really force people to marry or not to marry, or tell them how to raise their children."

"No one can force people to marry," said the young man, "but you can encourage it by deliberately formulating pro-marriage and family-friendly policies and programs. As it is now, government policies are anti-marriage and anti-family life; instead, they promote singleness, single parenthood and cohabitation. The issue of raising children needs special attention. As we noted earlier, the easiest and quickest way to societal breakdown is for the state to take away the power of discipline from parents and teachers, and plonk down education. It makes children unruly, unteachable and irresponsible."

"Sir, it has not always been that way," said the Prime Minister. "People are becoming extremely wicked, including parents. Children are the most abused people on earth. And we do whatever we can to protect them. But that is not to say we've taken away the right of parents and teachers to discipline children. We've only prescribed methods of discipline to minimize abuses."

"For restraining his eleven-year-old daughter," said the young man, "from running into a busy road while she was having a temper tantrum, a man was banned by his local Derbyshire council from seeing her, and the girl taken into care. Can you tell me in this incident who is abusing whom? If the child had been knocked down by a vehicle, the father would've been accused of negligence, and the child still would've been taken away if she had survived.

So either way, he is wrong in the eyes of the state. This type of prescribed discipline you put forward is what causes isolation and aggression, which leads to many problems for the child, the parents and the society."

"That was an isolated case, probably due to human or system error," said the Prime Minister.

"Isolated or not, you can see that your prescribed methods are not working," said the young man, "so you need to change your methods. Whom a parent loves, he disciplines. Likewise, a government that loves its children disciplines them. A disciplined child is a disciplined adult, which means a disciplined society. But it all starts with the family. A dysfunctional family is a dysfunctional society."

"Sir, whatever we do, we are expected to satisfy human rights requirements," said the Prime Minister. "It is not like we just do things without consulting anybody."

"We have talked about human rights before," said the young man. "Human rights are good but must not be at the expense of common sense. Common sense must be restored and must take precedence over any rights."

"If only people could understand relationships, there would be fewer problems," said the Prime Minister.

"That is why I keep emphasizing family life," said the young man, "because that is where the relationship begins. Get the family right and every other thing falls into place. Get it wrong and society suffers. Bad family life, bad society. It is what is causing all the anger and destruction.

"A bad family life results in a bad upbringing, and this negatively impacts community life. Oftentimes, innocent people are the victims of a bad family life. Yet the government is deliberately discouraging good family life. Many local councils are encouraging various forms of singleness. For instance, some are offering a 25 percent single-person discount in council tax, and various other forms of incentives for singleness that lead to family breakdown."

"Sir, family breakdown happens in every country," said the Prime Minister.

"That is true," said the young man. "But as I said before, you wouldn't like to perish because others are perishing. I am not telling you this to disparage you but to warn you that these are no normal times. When people now align themselves with and praise the works of evil and ridicule any goodness in others, you know that the Devil has taken over your country.

"In the area of foreign policy, you must know that no nation has the answers to the world's problems. And no nation has been appointed to speak for the rest of the world. Offer genuine help where you can.

"There is so much to talk about this, but I have given you the main hints. You must reconstruct Britain if you are to have some semblance of human society. And the starting point is the family. If you should forget any of the things we discussed here, one important thing you must not forget is the issue of the family. Tested family values must be reintroduced at all levels. The family is the life of a society; without it, there is no society.

"Understand that there is a difference between abuse and discipline. Know the right place to draw the line. There is also a difference between human rights and injustice. Again, know where to draw the line. You are called to make a change and provide hope for your people, but I must warn you that change doesn't come easy. You must know that change is not a destination and hope is not a strategy; you politicians have a penchant for misinterpreting and misrepresenting things. Once more, remember that love and forgiveness are essential to a healthy society. Leaders must draw from a deeper well, and where can they find that well? In God alone.

"Now, to summarize our discussion, you must not allow pride in any form to dictate your leadership in your personal, political, or spiritual life, both at home and abroad. Unforgiveness is both a disease and a sin. Patience, forgiveness and listening to alternative viewpoints make up the hallmark of true leadership. And you must listen to every segment of society, every community, no matter how small, because they are all your subjects. You must be sensitive to the people's yearnings and respond with wisdom, but wisdom is a very rare commodity. That is why I am always available to help if only you could call on Me.

"Please, I appeal to both of you: turn your nation's clock back to where you stopped seeking God, for I am still your hope from now to the end, your shelter from the storm, the only home where your defense is sure. Let Me be the foundation of your life, your society and your country.

"Finally, My children, please don't in the least think that I have been too harsh or that I brought you here to be grilled. I could have gone about our meeting in many different ways that would be more pleasant to you, but I chose this way so you would know how serious these matters are."

After a short silence, He said, "It is now time for you to go on the eagle's flight. Then you will be on your way back to your people as soon as you come back from the flight."

XI.

He bade them rise and led them outside to the front of the house, where they saw two giant white eagles waiting. He made them mount the eagles and told them to freely ask questions whenever they had cause to, saying that He would answer them.

As He turned to go back to the house, the eagles rose majestically into the air, rising above the roof and heading toward the rear of the house and through the fields, initially ascending gradually, but soon picking up speed once inside the clouds and soaring away to their preordained destination.

Despite the very high speed of the eagles, the Archbishop and the Prime Minister felt no gust of air tilting their mounted position, so they were not scared or rocked by simply sitting unstrapped to the eagles' backs. They only held on to a tuft of feathers around the back of the eagles' necks but felt quite secure as if in an enclosure.

Both the ascent and the cruise were very exhilarating, and their flight path was a spectrum of such indescribable beauty that it made a rainbow a toddler's paintwork. As they sailed through a vista of beautiful clouds, vibrant splashes of color made for an exciting viewing experience.

Wave after wave, the clouds slowly streamed the skyline in their full majesty, each displaying endless galleries of indescribable colors and producing such incredible splendor. Psalm 19:1 came to the Archbishop's mind: "The heavens declare the glory of God, and the firmament shows his handiwork." He was now experiencing the vivid greatness of that psalm.

Their pleasure flight lasted for what could have gone for thirty minutes as, all of a sudden, they flew into total darkness, pitch-darkness; they couldn't even see the shadow or outline of the eagles. They could see nothing, only the inky blackness. The air in the place felt heavy and oppressive, with an attendant chill that fought to take their breath away. In addition, they felt a scorching thirst.

As if this were not enough, there was a sudden continuous loss of altitude. The eagles seemed initially to be free-falling uncontrollably, tumbling and spiraling down very fast in the darkness. Their two riders lost their grip but surprisingly did not fall off their backs, or suffer any vertigo even as they twisted and tumbled. From tumbling and twisting, the eagles went into a straight nosedive at an extremely high speed that was extremely uncomfortable with heavy G-force displacement.

Suddenly, the eagles jerked to a stop, standing straight. The two men imagined they were in a tunnel and smelled strong dampness, decay and putrefaction. They were very scared. The place was dead silent and seemed to be even darker. The darkness was deadly and nauseating. It was not the mere darkness of the complete absence of light but was also the darkness of an internal nature that seemed to have taken the life out of them.

It created an emptiness in them that greatly craved to fill, creating an avid yearning they couldn't understand and couldn't ignore. It was emptiness so deep that it defied definition or description. Their fear was heightened by the fact that they did not know if they were still there together or were alone. Each longed to leave there as quickly as possible but had no power to command the eagles. Then they heard a loud cackle of gruesome evil laughter that seemed to reverberate all around. Then the whole place went dead silent again.

Suddenly, there was a cacophony of sounds—noises that chilled the spine. They heard echoes of loud wailings and yelling from a very far distance as people in terrible pain and agony, but they could not say where from. There were sounds like the breaking of bones, the shearing of cracked parts, noises of falling walls and the crushing of people.

Sometimes weird sounds of demons and unearthly beings brawling echoed in the distance. Sometimes it was swishing sounds like waves of turbulence in the sea, or of a strong destructive hurricane, or of thunder and heavy rain, or of the sizzling of hot iron and the crackling of fire. The wailing and sounds seemed to vibrate from all directions as if echoing from the walls of a tunnel. Sometimes they sounded very distant; sometimes, very near and loud.

Then gradually it was as if their sight were penetrating the darkness, and they were seeing dimly through the pitch-darkness what looked like a molten sea of volcanic lava pitching high up and then spilling down. They could see in gray silhouettes what looked like a multitude of people in the molten lava about to be drowned, crying loudly for help.

There was this choking, burning pungent smell and all the sounds and noises they were hearing now seemed to be centered and coming from the place. Both men shivered at the sight and were choked with fear and as stiff as dead. They were unsure if this was real or if they were hallucinating. They wished they had not asked for the eagle flight.

The smell of death pervaded everywhere. For the first time in their lives, they perceived that death had a smell. They screamed with fear, but they couldn't even hear each other. The chill had gone, now replaced with sweatiness from the gooseflesh of choking fear.

A short while later, the eagles seemed to have lifted up, but instead of ascending, they were descending as the ground seemed to have suddenly receded and they were sky-high, far above the clouds. The two men were not sure whether to be glad when the eagles took off, as they were unsure of where next they were headed, possibly a more sinister place.

But they were greatly relieved when, after less than what could have been a five-minute flight, they suddenly landed right in front of the house, in the very spot where they had taken off, with the young man right there waiting to receive them.

At first, they found it hard to see, having come into such brightness after the terrible darkness and squinted rapidly for some time before they could see clearly. And He spoke to them. "You are welcome back. Did you enjoy the flight?"

But they were both mute. They had seen things beyond words and were yet to fully recover from their shock and fear. It was a traumatic experience that had taken their breath and speech away, one they hoped never again to have. The emptiness they had experienced and the darkness had erased all the pleasures and splendor of the first part of the flight.

The young man ushered them into the room again. He made them sit, while He walked away from the room, allowing them a couple of minutes' rest to regain their composure.

Shortly after, He re-entered the room, smiled at them and asked, "Did you enjoy the flight? Were you at any point scared? The avid emptiness you felt in the dark is symptomatic of the separation from God—just a tiny sign of it. It symbolizes spiritual death. Your experience was two-dimensional, but none of them least reflected the magnitude of the true picture after your spirit exits your body. The picture of where you want to be depends on how you live your life—resulting in being forever separated or forever united with God.

"You will now be going back to your country and to your families, but don't forget what we have discussed here and what you have seen. You have the opportunity to change the course of history.

"Know that there is no excuse for failure. Your country needs you now as never before. Your people are obstinate and rebellious, and you will have many detractors, but you must not be afraid of them. You must not be haughty either. Know that from dust you came and to dust you shall return." He paused momentarily, then said, "Now ask what you want."

"Sir," said the Archbishop, "I ask for wisdom."

"You have asked wisely," He replied.

"To succeed in this assignment, sir," said the Prime Minister, "I need Your presence, Your whole presence, wherever I go."

"You have also asked wisely; just do not be afraid," He replied.

"One more thing, sir," said the Prime Minister.

"Yes?" asked the young man.

"Sir, you must help me stem the power of the press," said the Prime Minister. "Every government is afraid of the press. Mine is no exception. To be honest, our majority is more of the voice of the press than of the people. The press has the power to seat or unseat a government, and every Prime Minister dreads them."

"When you have My presence, you have everything," said the young man. "Because even in your weakest and darkest moments, My power is real and strong. I have promised that to you and, indeed, to all who diligently seek Me."

He made them rise, and they walked outside to the front of the house, where the same two horses that had brought them were waiting. He walked over to them and hugged each of the men passionately for a while. As the men mounted the horses and turned to go, He smiled and waved to them and bade them goodbye. He stood looking at them as the horses turned and set off.

The horses followed the same route they had taken on their outward journey. It was almost nine o'clock at night when the two men arrived at Northolt Airfield. The horses suddenly disappeared after they had alighted at the airfield, and the men found themselves seated in the same car that had brought them. They were driven back to Central London and to Downing Street by the same chauffeur and outriders.

The whole airport was full of officers, yet no one had seen the horses arriving or the car departing. From the mysterious house to the airfield and all the way to Downing Street, both men remained absolutely silent.

Chapter 20
Mystery Over, But...

In London, the clock was ticking away, and neither the security services nor the government had the faintest idea of what to do. They had exhausted their resources and ideas and still remained clueless. As it were, they simply waited for events to take their turn, whatever turn that would be.

It had been three days since they disappeared, and nobody had seen them on their way back from Northolt Airfield. No one, not even they themselves, could say how they had gotten out of the car that brought them back. All that the security officials knew was that they suddenly saw the men in their midst inside the large conference room at No. 10 from where they had disappeared.

No car had been seen driving to either the normal parking lot or to Downing Street, yet people were around at the time—yet suddenly, they saw the men in the conference room. Officers at the parking lot suddenly saw the car sitting in its space, without any occupants and without seeing how it had come, when it had arrived, or who had driven it there. The alarm was promptly raised upon the car's reappearance. And the more important reappearance of the two men was simultaneously relayed to the authorities.

The Met commissioner, the first Secretary of State, the Home Secretary, the Chancellor and the Defense Secretary were the first to be alerted about the reappearance of the Prime Minister and the Archbishop. Quickly, a few senior government officials assembled, this time not in the COBRA room but inside one of the conference rooms at No. 10. The urgent task before them was how to break the news officially and what should be included in the press briefing.

One important gray area was the fact that the men had been found at No. 10, which could mean either that the whole episode was a hoax or that some mysterious forces were at play. However it would be viewed, it was necessary for the government to break the news as quickly as possible. The whole world was still in suspense, unaware of the turn of events, and waiting for news of any breakthrough. It was an uncomfortable time for the first Secretary of State, who had the arduous task of addressing a press conference with very limited information concerning the reappearance of the two men, without a comprehensive situation report of the circumstances.

By 10:40 p.m., a press briefing was promptly given in front of No. 10. It was very short and directly to the point, only detailing the fact that the men had been found in No. 10 and were unharmed and were apparently in their right state of mind. They were to undergo some medical checks nevertheless, and not until after that would they be allowed to speak to the press.

Once the news was out, TV screens all over the world were littered with news flashes and breaking news. Activity in the press camps already in Downing Street suddenly increased, with every journalist jostling for a vantage point outside No. 10, hoping to be the first to capture sight and snaps of the two men whenever they emerged. But the journalists were in for a very long wait.

Meanwhile, the two men were taken to a room at the Berry Wing section of the Cabinet Office building, which was also on Downing Street. They were taken from the back of the building, completely secluded from the reach of the press and whisked from there by helicopter to Maudsley Hospital in Denmark Hill, South London, the best national hospital for neuropsychiatry, where a team of specialist doctors, experts in their chosen areas of specialism, conducted thorough medical examinations of both their physical state and mental state. It was past midnight when they were allowed to sleep. The following morning, more tests were conducted, and then the men were allowed some rest prior to debriefing and counseling.

Later in the day, with an all-clear bill of health, they were subjected to debriefing and counseling conducted by two renowned clinical psychologists. They were then taken back to No. 10 and subjected to further questioning in one of the many conference rooms there, being asked for an account of what had happened to them, as those present now had not been with the counseling psychologists when they narrated what happened to them as part of their counseling.

This time, the two men's wives were present, having been brought out from their protective hiding places. Also present were the first Secretary of State, the chancellor, the Foreign Secretary, the Home Secretary, the Defense

Secretary, the Archbishop of York (second highest in the Church of England hierarchy) and the Metropolitan Police commissioner. Both men narrated how they had found themselves driven to Northolt Aerodrome and taken by horses to an unknown place where they claimed to have met God. They spoke of all that had happened while there and how they were taken back by the same horses. They responded to all the questions thrown at them with a crystal clear sense of sanity, insisting that they were telling the truth.

But all present could make no sense out of all they said. They did not believe they had actually met God. Even the Archbishop of York was skeptical. They were convinced that the two men had had some evil encounter and must have been taken hostage and deluded by some extraterrestrial being. Most of them bluntly refused the men's argument that they were in their right minds, that they knew exactly what they were saying, and that it was the truth. But their listeners could not fault their comportment or the ease and sequential flow of their story. The more panicky part was what was to be presented to the press and the world.

After listening to their story, the group left both men and went to another room, where they deliberated on this for quite a while before deciding on what to present to the world press. Again the first Secretary of State was mandated to make the press statements.

At precisely half past one o'clock in the afternoon, Jo Baker, the first Secretary of State, gave a very short press conference, telling the world that the British Prime Minister and the Archbishop of Canterbury had been taken hostage and were confused by some mysterious forces. She added that they had been taken in for examination, as they were not in a stable condition to give a press conference or perform their duties and wouldn't be until certified fit and free from external influences. The first Secretary of State was more or less effectively covering the PM's duties.

About twenty minutes after the press statement, the Prime Minister and the Archbishop emerged outside No. 10, and the press went haywire. Like a swarm of predators, the world press suddenly burst into a frenzy at their appearance. The vigil was over as countless camera flashes and dozens of microphones jostled for words from the two men. They stood side by side as the Prime Minister spoke. He debunked the first Secretary of State's statement about their mental state, claiming they were in their right states of mind and able to function in their official capacities.

The Archbishop was all the time nodding to affirm the Prime Minister's statements. The Prime Minister did not restate the whole story as he had done during the counseling session but, instead, gave a brief synopsis of what had happened, repeating their claim to have met God.

It was usual for the press to ask questions at the end of such a press conference, but the two men made it clear at the end of their story that they were not prepared to ask questions. Many questions were thrown at them, but they refused to answer any.

Instead, all the Prime Minister said in response was that they had been invited by God for leadership coaching and with that, both men simply walked back into No. 10. Knowing the same skepticism that attended their meeting with senior government officials and the Archbishop of York would be repeated here, they felt it was pointless trying to convince people who had already made up their minds.

As expected, the audience was very skeptical. Most did not believe it. They thought the story was too bizarre to be true and felt that the two men needed psychiatric treatment to be able to return to normal life. Even those who believed them had some doubt, not being fully convinced. But no one doubted that the two men had had some mysterious encounter.

Soon after the press briefing, the Archbishop and his wife were driven home to Lambeth Palace, where it was felt he would *recover* faster. And there he summoned a meeting of some senior Church of England clergy in London for six o'clock that evening. There he explained the reason for the impromptu meeting, which was for them to hear from him directly rather than from the press.

He again narrated the same story as they had heard in the press, explaining and trying his best to convince them that it was real and that he was not under any illusions. In the end, once again even among the clergy, there was divided opinion as few were convinced and many remained unconvinced. Some advised the Archbishop to be sent for further counseling, while others offered to pray for him.

The counter-press briefing by the Prime Minister and the Archbishop was an embarrassment to the government, and attempts to compel the two men to undergo further counseling were strongly rebuffed by both of them. That night the Prime Minister and his wife had fewer than two hours' sleep. He was too excited to be able to sleep and spent almost the entire night talking to his wife.

He was explaining and convincing her that he was in his right frame of mind and that he was speaking the truth of what had happened, also telling her of the urgent need and his resolve to chart a new course, both in his personal life and in governance, pleading her unflinching support and promising to resign rather than carry on with the old system. He had heard from the Master of the Universe, and nothing was going to change his mind.

He remembered the emptiness and the unfathomable darkness he had experienced during the eagle's flight. Those were things he could never forget. He reasoned that it symbolized both the complete wretchedness and emptiness of a life without God, irrespective of power and material wealth.

"I don't want to experience what I saw during our eagle's flight. That is enough for me not to take my relationship with God lightly," he had told her.

The following day, Parliament reconvened. It was almost a full house, with the Prime Minister taking his rightful place in the House chambers, to the chagrin of those who secretly wanted him committed for having dared to make reference to God publicly. The Prime Minister's Question Time the next day, Wednesday, provided an opportunity for mockery and deliberate provocation.

It was the first time British politicians showed that they were no different from people of less civilized nations, as the whole session was turned into acrimonious bickering over the sanity of the Prime Minister and his ability to lead the country. The speaker had no small problem trying to maintain order, while the Prime Minister displayed unimaginable decorum and equanimity in the face of deliberate provocation. He answered all their questions briskly and directly to the point, even smiling and injecting humor into his answers.

From that first day in Parliament, he started singing a different tune on legislative issues bordering on governance, becoming increasingly uncomfortable with and antagonistic toward the status quo. He tried to convince the House of the need for a change of direction. He tried with all his wits to introduce morality into the national debate and attempted to change legislation that was offensive to faith groups, but the British Parliament proved a hard nut to crack. There were calls for his impeachment, but he didn't have to give them room for that.

His resolve was cast iron enough to remain unbending. He had made up his mind to serve God in or out of Downing Street. He chose the latter, and only two months after the encounter, he resigned but remained a parliamentarian as a trusted representative of his local constituency and his new faith group. He had seen enough and had been warned enough. And his wife was solidly behind him, both of them clinging to their newfound faith and religion with great tenacity.

But before these events, on the first weekend after the mysterious journey, the Prime Minister went back to Chequers to be alone. There he embarked on a period of soul-searching. He reflected on life and contemplated on many issues of life, asking questions about nature, about Creation, about one's place in society and about society itself. He had several questions for God but never got any answers.

He had not deliberately set out to fast but found he had no appetite for food. He prayed in his own little way, having never prayed before, and sought God as best he could. For the first time in his life, it dawned on him that he was absolutely nothing without God and deserved not to be accorded any recognition by Almighty God, and so shed great tears—tears of joy and repentance.

Suddenly, he became very hungry for God. Getting back to No. 10, he convinced his family of the need to join a local church and started checking out churches to find which agreed with his spiritual hunger.

His family became active members of a local church, attending church services on Sundays and becoming fully involved in weekday church activities. They regularly attended seminars and conferences both within and outside their denomination. The Prime Minister saw himself as Christ's ambassador, honored many invitations and spoke several times at many conferences and in different countries.

His new dynamism went beyond church attendance and participation in church activities. He had a real personal relationship with God, daily spending quality time in His presence and soaking himself in His Word. In no time, he started championing the Christian cause in and out of Parliament, becoming a big voice for Justice for British Christians, which he had joined and for many Christian NGOs.

And despite all manner of criticisms and name-calling, he remained steadfast in expressing the Christian views in several articles in major newspapers. He saw his new calling as God-imposed, something in which he had no choice.

The Prime Minister was cautioned on a number of occasions, and taken to court three times over his writings and pronouncements, but he remained unrepentant and was acquitted of any wrongdoing in all court cases. He was equally involved in litigation against various infringements of Christian principles and Christian rights.

The Prime Minister's conversion had little impact on the nation. Many people were drawn to Christianity because of his testimonies and his tenacious defense of Christian principles. Everyone, including his detractors, knew that his newfound faith and zeal were not ordinary.

The Archbishop, on his part, was full of enthusiasm and eager to reform the church but wanted to make haste slowly. So, unlike the Prime Minister, he was reluctant to offend any member of the church with any quick radical reforms. He was even more reluctant when each time he raised an idea or made any suggestions, he was ignored or met with serious resistance either by individual bishops or by the synod.

The erstwhile Prime Minister, fired by his newfound passion, visited the Archbishop frequently to encourage him. He kept reminding the Archbishop that it was much easier for him as the leader of a church to reform the church than for himself as a Prime Minister to reform Parliament. Everyone knew the stand of the church on all issues and that a greater proportion of members would readily support reforms that promoted Christian ethics, he assured him.

But the Archbishop was too slow to act, too passive and afraid to confront and address the lukewarmness of the church. He was still very much a laissez-faire Christian leader. Soon the euphoria died down, and both he and the church remained as they had been.

When the erstwhile Prime Minister saw that their theophanic encounter had not changed the Archbishop, he resented his peer's complacency and temporary cut-off from him. That singular act changed everything. For some strange reason, after the Prime Minister's last visit in which he told the Archbishop that he was disappointed and would stop visiting him, the Archbishop suddenly lost his peace and became restless and thoughtful.

He remembered how he had felt on his way to No. 10 on that fateful day when he disappeared with the former Prime Minister. Gradually, he became more determined to find ways to introduce reforms, finding that the more he tried, the more his peace returned.

However, his new vision was at odds with the modernist theology of some leaders of the church, who vehemently fought to kill it before it had time to take root. The Archbishop's wife had always supported him in whatever he did.

When the church opposed his efforts at reform, she advised him to resign, saying, "If your eye offends you, pluck it out, for it is better for you to enter heaven with one eye than to have two eyes and go to hellfire."

After much pressure from her, he stepped down. His determined supporters were few and were disappointed at his resignation, but knew he was fighting a formidable opposition. He found life outside Lambeth Palace more peaceful and more fulfilling in his engagement with various but less high-profile church activities.

He was not as active or as vocal as the ex-PM but was active enough in lending weight to Christian offensives toward Christians' regaining their rightful place in society.

Chapter 21
The Audacity of Faith

It was the seventh year of the Jericho Wall marches. Jay's Justice for British Christians (J4BC) constituted the core group of the Jericho Wall Marchers. By now the erstwhile Prime Minister Tim Lane had become the head of the United Christian Joint Action Front (UCJAF). Together he and Jay teamed up to organize a special seventh-anniversary celebration, which was scheduled to last for seven days in the seventh month of the seventh year.

Although their very first march started in March of the first year, they decided to hold the anniversary in July because they wanted everything to be 7-7-7, with seven being a very significant number in the Bible: the number of spiritual perfection, the number of the covenant and the number of completion.

A program of events for the celebration included marching for seven days and holding a three-day conference on the last three evenings. The theme of the conference was *Britain: A Festival of Restoration—God Among Us*, to celebrate the enthronement of God as Lord over Britain. Two gospel artists and two preachers were invited from within the country, and one preacher was invited from the continent, to support the in-house team for the three-day conference.

The Emmanuel Evangelical Church was where the Parliament marchers always met before and after their marches, while the nearby Emmanuel Center was the scheduled venue for their three-day conference, which would conclude their anniversary celebrations.

Both the church and center were closely linked and shared the same premises located on Marsham Street, in the South West One area of Westminster, just a five-minute walk from the Houses of Parliament, Westminster Abbey and Big Ben. The Emmanuel Center was a renowned conference center with a good public address system; a number of multichannel audio mixing desk gates, LCD projectors and laptop computers; and a number of roaming, line and lapel microphones, with front projection screens and so forth.

To have a large turnout, it had been arranged for the marches to be held on Saturdays and Sundays instead of a straight seven days that would include weekdays. The marches were thus spread out to start on the first Sunday and end on the fourth Sunday of the month. The conference was to run in the evenings of the last weekend, from Friday to Sunday, the last marching day. Conference time was 6.30-10 p.m. each day.

In May, two full months before the anniversary's first march, a strange thing happened. It had been five full years since the divine encounter involving the former Prime Minister and the Archbishop, and the seventh year of the Jericho Wall Marchers starting their monthly march. It was early in the month, and the late afternoon sky was clear and bright.

In the South East area of England, small pockets of people were gathering here and there, looking up to the sky. Faintly appearing through the thin wavy pockets of blue and white clouds was what looked like a small disc, in the size and shape of a discus. The full outline of its shape was obscured in parts by the clouds. It was an object of curiosity that drew people out of their homes and offices and temporarily halted commercial activities and indeed many activities.

Some reports of its sighting also filtered in from other parts of the country, including the Midlands. The gathering of people greatly increased after the BBC and evening papers went public with the observation. Rumors started flying everywhere. Some said it was an unidentified flying object (UFO); some said it was an asteroid; some others said it was a fragment of a failed space probe or some satellite fragments falling from space; and still, others said it was a spaceship carrying extraterrestrial entities from other planets to spy on the Earth.

Astronomers at the Royal Observatory in Greenwich, London, set their instruments to work. Their instruments, however, failed to pick up the object. Other observatory posts in the country also tried but failed. By the third day, more astronomers from other countries with sophisticated equipment came to complement the local efforts, but all failed to capture the object.

Meanwhile, every new day, the object was becoming more conspicuous and discrete in outline. London, mainly, had become a beehive of media activity. People started rumoring that the end of the world had suddenly come. With the intensity of the heat and brightness of the sun in this late spring season, some people rumored it was likely a precursor of a solar superstorm—an explosion of protons and plasma from the sun that would destabilize the earth, following global warming.

A solar superstorm had last occurred in 1859. Every day the object was looming larger until it could be seen from everywhere in mainland Britain. As it became larger, so it seemed to become closer to Earth, but astronomers could still not capture it in their instruments, and so unable to make out what it was. Even the International Society of Meteorology couldn't make out what it was. But it could be clearly seen with the naked eye. It looked rocky and mountainous and had now changed from its initial discus-like shape, looking a bit more flat and less convex.

By the twenty-first day, the object had gotten so large and so close that pilots were afraid to take off. But once they took off, they found that the farther they climbed, the higher the object rose, maintaining equidistance from their altitude, as seen from the ground. But the object never appeared on their radar, only through their windshields, and was also unseen once they left British airspace. However, the fact that the object eluded their radar made the fear of possible collision very real.

By the twenty-eighth day, it had become so large that its circumference covered almost the entire British skyline. Although there was daylight, the object cast such a dull shadow that the sun's rays that managed to pierce the clouds became very hazy. The air became humid and hot, staying that way. By now the object had become visible to the people in the north, necessitating a press gathering in Manchester.

Real fear descended on Britain. Flights were suspended, including military flights. People started panicking, and some started running to neighboring countries. Workers were taking emergency holidays to temporarily leave the country. Deliberate absenteeism was becoming rampant. With the suspension of flights, international rail stations and seaports became busier.

Tourism grounded to a halt as foreign visitors already in the country cut short their visits and prospective visitors canceled their arrangements. There were warning alerts by nations all over the world to their citizens to avoid going to Britain. Foreign embassies were temporarily closed down.

Stockpiling of food through panic buying by individual families emptied the shops.

By the fortieth day, the situation was worsened by the rapid slowing down of local produce distribution, which adversely affected sales. Although imports remained the same, distribution was slowing down because of staff absenteeism, and the risk of running short of food and drugs was becoming a possibility. It was as if nature wanted to impose sanctions on Britain, but shortages were avoided given the short time the whole episode lasted, with emergency aid shipments from foreign countries having been avoided.

However, as a precautionary measure, the central government set up distribution strategies, including the possible use of task forces, through local councils for easy and effective food distribution should it become necessary, with a network of well-organized distribution centers.

The fear that the mountainous-looking object could fall and crush everything on the ground sent jitters through every mind. People were scared stiff; stepping outside was a frightening necessity. Those who braved going to work only did so out of the fear of losing their jobs and salaries, and in the belief that what was bound to happen would still happen irrespective of where they chose to be.

Staff strength of most offices had drastically reduced and many businesses operated minimally, while some small-scale ones closed completely. Streets were partially deserted and vehicular traffic was at its lowest rate in almost a century. Other nationals working in Britain left in haste while they still had the opportunity.

Britain had been brought to her knees without anyone's raising a voice or a finger against her. Her pride and power had been reduced to absolutely nothing. An ominous cloud of uncertainty and trepidation hung so stiffly in the air that one could literally grab it with one's bare hands. The certitude of death was as sure as breathing and stared nakedly at everyone. It was no longer a matter of if but of when. The Irish Republic and the Northern Ireland suddenly became swamped with people from mainland Britain. Within continental Europe, Calais, France, became the main exit point to other places.

Meanwhile, in Britain, power blackouts were becoming a frequent occurrence, and gas and water supplies were becoming erratic, as workers and maintenance crews thinned down every day. By the forty-ninth day, what looked like cracks—irregular lines marking a potential chipping-off of huge fragments—became clearly visible on the object. It now appeared very rocky and irregularly segmented.

At the center of one of the innermost segments appeared a faint and incomplete outline of a human face. It had a pair of eyes or something resembling such, that were very faintly visible. Other features of a face were conspicuously absent. In a matter of days, the *eyes* had become very visible and seemed to be open most of the time.

The seldom blinking was in the manner of an owl—probably once every minute, each time very sluggishly. People were afraid to look at the *eyes* as they appeared to be fiercely penetrating and intimidating. Soon, for those who dared to glimpse, it was noticed that both *eyes* were wet with tears. The tears in each *eye* gradually formed a small droplet that got bigger by the day.

At one stage, they looked as big as a medium-sized chicken egg, but no one was sure how big they were because no one could say exactly how far the object was from the ground. The paralyzing fear greatly increased with the uncertainty of what was going to happen next. Every discussion and movement was becoming hushed as if to avoid the object's noticing.

In the first few days of the appearance of the object, there was a COBRA meeting of senior government ministers that lasted less than thirty minutes. Its purpose was to decide emergency measures and how to respond to the problem. The problem was the first of its kind, and there was absolutely nothing to guide the members' deliberations.

There was the suggestion to launch a surface-to-air missile to blast the object, but there were many factors against such an attack. One was the fact that no one knew how high the object was from the ground or whether the missiles could actually reach it.

The second was that no one knew if the object was destructible since no one knew what it was or what it was composed of. Third was the fear that even if it was possible to destroy it, it would in turn wreak havoc on human life on the ground by way of falling debris. The fourth was that no one was sure what the breaking of it, if such a thing were possible, would unleash on the earth—chemicals, germs, unknown pandemics, etc.

There were many other suggestions, but all these ended in futile arguments with unrealistic expectations. So the meeting ended as quickly as it had started. Few other such meetings that were held ended the same way. Bullish, tough-talking British politicians had been utterly subdued. Like the London

Assembly, Parliament, out of fear, went on a temporary recess. A few MPs and some cabinet ministers took unscheduled holidays overseas to temporarily escape for their safety.

The Prime Minister was forced to call for prayers for the nation, but before that, churches, mosques, temples, synagogues, gurdwaras and other worship centers had intensified their prayers for the country. For the Christian church, a series of prayer meetings were organized by many churches, day and night. There were also interdenominational meetings held at various locations.

The number of attendees at churches and many worship centers was becoming fewer as many faith groups were afraid to step out. Most people resorted to praying in their homes, while prayer centers suddenly sprang up in many estates and neighborhoods, organized by local people of particular faiths.

By the sixty-third day of the sighting of the object, the facial outline had enlarged greatly and the *eyes* had become bigger, with each of the tear-like drops as big as the size of a rugby ball. But for the same reason—the distance from the ground—nobody could say how big they really were. Each teardrop tapered from the *eye*, getting progressively slimmer toward the attachment point. Each was precariously suspended by a small attachment to the *eye* and seemed delicate, about to drop off. People were fearfully anticipating the imminent fall of the tears.

The eighty-fourth day of the sighting was like any other summer day except for the silhouetted sun casting a dull shadow. In the current season, the day was mundane and as ominous as ever, except that it coincided with the last Saturday of the Jericho Wall marching anniversary. The appearance of the strange object in the sky did not stop the marchers, though it initially reduced their numbers. However, despite the fear, which hung in the air like thick smog, many Christians from various churches responded to the open invitation to attend the marching anniversary. That greatly swelled their numbers, especially in the last three days.

Their celebration had started from the first weekend of the month and was now on the penultimate day, the sixth day, which was the last Saturday of the march. Kojo was with the City Hall group, while Jay and Tim Lane were with the Parliament group.

July was generally free from weather problems, but, rather unusually, the weather forecast for the day had predicted that fierce winds of up to eighty miles per hour would sweep across many parts of the country. Saturday was a work-free day, but a few people still went to work, and many people, fearing imminent food shortages, still went out attempting to increase their stockpile. There were also others out and about for sundry reasons. But generally, the number of people out in the streets and public places was far fewer than at normal times.

Because of the prevailing situation in the country, most renowned annual events for that summer had been canceled, notably among which were the Gay Pride Parade, the Wimbledon tennis tournament—both of which were normally held in July—and the Notting Hill Carnival, which was held in the last week of August.

As part of the anniversary celebration, the Jericho Wall marches were made to commence by one o'clock in the afternoon on the marching days instead of their usual three o'clock. The City Hall marchers added talks or speaking intervals to their normal schedule of marching, praying and singing, while the Parliament marchers held their own talks, at the end of the day's march, at the Emmanuel Evangelical Church because of their long marching route and lack of a sheltering assembly point along it.

That Saturday marching had just begun, and normal daily activities within the bounds of the current situation in the country were going on, when suddenly everything changed. The forecasted fierce wind was at its peak of 80 mph when, at exactly 1.40 p.m. local time, the right tear-like drop detached and landed with a terrifying sound as it crashed to Earth, falling straight onto City Hall, the seat of the London government, leveling it to the ground and leaving a massive crater.

What looked like the size of a rugby ball in the sky proved to have the shape and twice the size of City Hall—a massive weight of solid concrete. The teardrop disintegrated on impact, grinding City Hall to mere particles and sending chunks of debris flying everywhere. The crashing sound was so deafening that people thought the world had come to an end. People reported hearing it more than two hundred and fifty miles away. Many buildings in London shook as if by an earthquake.

The crater left in the ground combined with the debris of the crashed City Hall, which, along with some of the affected immediate surrounding buildings, was picked up by the gale force wind to form a massive dust storm, which began racing at a sudden accelerated speed of one hundred and eighty miles per hour with ferocious monstrosity, leaving a trail of destruction in its wake.

People caught up in this sudden massive hurricane were blown miles away to their deaths. Within minutes, the dust cloud had enveloped the atmosphere to a near-total darkness.

The few vehicles that were on the roads were tossed away like empty plastic toys and crashed far away from where they had been flung off. Big high-velocity swirling vortexes of broken pieces of debris from City Hall and other affected buildings crashed against more buildings, many of which in turn crashed their own debris against others. The ripple effect went far and wide. Power lines, signposts and trees were at the mercy of the wind and roads were blocked by falling debris. Many parked vehicles were moved, crashing against nearby structures. The Jericho Wall marches were in full swing at both venues when the explosion happened.

At the time the tear-like drop landed on City Hall, the Christian marchers there were gathered on the lawn for their speaking interval as one of their leaders preached. The sound of the impact immediately sent everyone around, including passersby, scampering for safety. There were a few pedestrians in the area and a few youths who still braved the ominous climate to engage in their usual bicycle riding stunts around the London Bridge/City Hall area.

But the marching group at their assembled spot was immediately overshadowed by a pillar of thick white cloud. They too tried to run for safety but were prevented by the pillar of cloud, which, though thick and white on the outer wall, was as bright as a midsummer day inside. An invisible force had made the outer edge of the cloud an impregnable wall so that none could enter or leave, yet they could walk about inside it and could see through it.

All the devastation did not touch them, and the crater's outer margin ended at the edge of the cloud. There were always some people, including tourists, who out of curiosity or in mockery, or simply for the fun of it, or for some other reason, joined the Christians in their marches and prayers, fully or partly. That day, those who joined their group and were on the lawn with them during the speaking interval escaped death.

Everyone within the grounds of the building, including those on Tower Bridge and its environs, were all struck dead. Those who had gathered for the speaking interval sat there inside the cloud, initially afraid and clinging tightly to one another, but soon realized a miracle had just happened. Then suddenly they broke into song and started dancing and praising God.

The Parliament marchers were on their rounds, singing and praising God when the tear-like drop hit City Hall. Suddenly they were enveloped in a similar cloud all along their route—from Milbank, through Lambeth Bridge, to Lambeth Palace Road and on to Westminster Bridge. There was always a long throng of people walking in one general direction.

Those in front were just entering Westminster Bridge, while the last segment was almost exiting Milbank when City Hall was hit. All the flying debris either landed ahead of or behind where they were, including within the rectangle of their marching route. They could see wave after wave of debris killing people and destroying things very close to them.

Ordinary people, none of them members of their group, who were caught up with them as they walked along on their designated route were untouched by the destruction going on. Even those walking in the opposite direction but caught up in their midst were spared. Accordingly, those who initially weren't part of their group all joined in marching with them rather than continue their own journey, to keep safe.

A big chunk of debris blew a massive hole into one side of the Houses of Parliament, the wall by the side of the Thames River, but that was the only damage to the building. A great many buildings everywhere in London were affected and not just the Southwark area, where City Hall was located. As the dust storm raced to other parts of the country, so did the destruction extend everywhere. The greatest miracle of God's mercy was the Shard.

The Shard, with its eighty-seven stories and standing at three hundred and ten meters high, was reputed to be the tallest building in Europe at the time. It was located at 32 London Bridge Street and directly overlooked London Bridge train station.

The Shard, which was within the proximity of City Hall, about five minutes' walk away, despite the smaller buildings in the area being affected, was completely untouched. As it was built almost entirely with glass panels and housed many facilities, including a power station, three restaurants, a hotel and many residential apartments, retail units and offices, it would have resulted in carnage if it had been hit.

Tower Bridge, which was within a stone's throw from City Hall, was also spared. But heavy chunks of concrete that fragmented from the droplet on impact caused devastation to buildings as far away as Docklands and Canary Wharf, and also miles away in all directions. All the buildings on the same premises as City Hall were either partially or fully destroyed. But like the Shard, the nearby Guy's Hospital was completely untouched. Although many people were afraid to venture outside, many collapsed buildings killed a great number of their occupants, and emergency rescue missions were practically absent.

At exactly the same time the London blast occurred, the left eye's tear-like drop detached and landed on the world's first industrialized city, Manchester. Unlike the droplet that landed as a solid mass in London, parts of the one that landed in Manchester broke off midair before landing. The main body landed on bare ground, in a public recreational park and dug a big crater that sent vortexes of spiraling debris everywhere.

Chunks of heavy debris from the impact and parts broken off midair landed in different places and on several buildings. Beetham Tower took a direct hit from parts falling from the air. With forty-seven floors, and at one hundred and sixty-nine meters in height, the Beetham Tower was the second-tallest building in the United Kingdom outside London at the time.

It housed two hundred and nineteen residential apartments from levels 25 to 47, sixteen of them being penthouses. Six of the top-floor penthouses were either fully or partly destroyed, with eight fatalities and various levels of injuries for a number of residents.

Below the apartments was the four-star 279-bedroom Hilton hotel and its very popular thirty-third-floor Sky Bar. The bar was hit on the side by a chunk of debris that caused only minor damage. The tower usually emitted a loud howl in windy weather which was heard over large parts of the area. And with the rising vortex, the howl increased its loudness to a frightening level for people who were already traumatized by fear.

Manchester Town Hall, one of the high-rise buildings in the city, received a direct hit as well but was only partially damaged with no fatalities. Heavy flying debris caused large-scale destruction and damage to several buildings, vehicles and infrastructure, with the ripple effect going far and wide. Thousands of buildings, including low-rise ones, had their roofs blown off and their windows damaged by the high speed of the wind, which also gusted at one hundred and eighty miles per hour like the London wind and smashed everything in its path.

As had happened at City Hall, a crater left on the ground in the park became a ready source of heavy dust particles, creating an avalanche that refused to decrease in intensity. Within an hour of the blasts, the whole country was covered by the dust storm and its trail of destruction. Clouds of dust, thick and dark, reduced visibility to less than two hundred and fifty feet. Surprisingly, no rain accompanied the wind.

As the dust swept across the ground, people indoors were afraid to look outside, let alone step outdoors. No one was sure if any living thing outside was still alive. Wave after wave, the dust cloud continued to surge, whether from the craters dug by the impact or from an unknown source was a matter of conjecture—but it raced everywhere, in one direction and then another, throughout the country. Fireballs erupted from the severe impact of materials and gas explosions in various buildings, and floods spilled forth from burst water pipelines, to complete the cycle of devastation.

This was July when sunset wasn't until about nine o'clock at night, but now in the afternoon hours, the day was dark gray and dim with an invisible skyline, hidden by dust and clouds—a day of gloom and doom. Social outdoor activities at this time of year were usually at their peak, but the fear that gripped the country saw public places deserted. It could have been total annihilation if there were no foreboding of an impending doom that restricted outing.

Being Saturday, many offices were closed, but the few workers who had gone in were trapped in their offices. Those in their homes remained at home, and those in various enclosed spaces remained there for fear of dying outside, although some buildings held no safety for their occupants. Everybody alive was now indoors, save the Christians trapped on their marching grounds and those caught up with them. Many of those indoors were forced into emergency prayers of some sort, including those who never had prayed all their lives.

Roads were blocked by fallen trees and debris, and movement was impossible, except on foot, which had to take a staggered form to avoid obstacles. Most marchers always went to the marching venues on public transport because of a lack of parking spaces in the areas. The few who drove close by that day on pay-and-park bays were not sure if their cars were safe, let alone able to function for the drive home.

Now, the number of invited Christians who joined the march, and more importantly, the number of ordinary people caught up in the midst of the marchers, especially those with the Parliament marchers, whose route was very long, increased greatly. Although both marching groups were supposed to walk to the Emmanuel Center—their scheduled conference venue—they were now afraid to move. The lead segment of the Parliament marchers was just linking up at Westminster Bridge, coming from Lambeth Palace Road, when the blast occurred. But the pillar of cloud in front of them created an enclosed space in front of them to walk in.

As they walked into the space, the cloud shifted and kept shifting continuously, thus leading them. The last segment of their group was closer to their starting point, having just linked up with Lambeth Bridge from Milbank at the tail end of their starting position, but couldn't run back because of the restrictive pillar of the cloud.

So they stood still and moved when they saw the segments in front moving forward since they could see inside the pillar of cloud, it was very bright. This was despite the near-total darkness outside. The pillar of the cloud led the first segment through Westminster Bridge and Parliament Square and onto Methodist Central Hall, instead of the Emmanuel Center and the other segments followed. Like the Parliament group, the City Hall group was also led by the white cloud, which was creating a shaft of rays a few meters ahead of them, guiding them on their route to the Methodist Central Hall as well.

Both groups sang great worship songs as they went: "We are marching in the light of God. We are marching in the light of God," and so on. It took both groups quite a long to arrive at the hall because of obstacles on the roads, but the Parliament group arrived first, being much closer to the venue. However, the last segment of the Parliament group arrived only a few minutes ahead of the City Hall group.

The Methodist Central Hall was only approximately a five-minute walk from their original venue. It served as a Methodist church and a conference center and had an art gallery and an office building. It was formerly the headquarters of the Methodist Church of Great Britain until the turn of the century. It was strategically located at the corner of Tothill Street and Storeys Gate just off Victoria Street, near the junction with the Sanctuary and facing Westminster Abbey.

With twenty-two rooms for conferences, meetings and seminars, it was about the best place for them. With more conference facilities than the Emmanuel Center, and with its large Great Hall seating close to two and half thousand people at a time, along with having a large balcony and seminar rooms seating four hundred and fifty each at a time, it was an excellent place, especially for the increased number of the groups of people.

Getting there in the midst of the pillar of the white cloud that now guided them, the Parliament group, who were first to get there, were not surprised to find the doors firmly locked. They were not expecting anyone to be bold enough to attend to any knock on the door but were sure the Spirit of God, who had led them there, would make a way.

So they knocked, and truly the door was opened for them. They went in and found there were a few people, mainly staff who had been stranded there. They told their story and told them their mission. The people were surprised that anyone could be bold enough to be in the streets at this time but were very happy to receive them.

On arriving at the Great Hall, the Parliament group was unsure of the fate of the City Hall group. They could not contact them as communication networks were all down and out of service. As soon as the last of their group arrived, they started praying for the safety of the City Hall group. It was only after this group arrived that they started deliberating on what to do next.

Some suggested bringing the evening conference forward since the main speakers had accompanied them in the march and were there with them. Some advocated its cancellation for that day because of what had happened, asking everyone to think of how they would feed all the people. Others disagreed, saying what had happened should reinforce the need for the conference.

In the end, they agreed to have the conference, but only after considering the issue of food, namely how they would find food to feed the throng with them. It was almost six o'clock in the evening, and people were hungry. With no one had expected to be stranded at their marching venues, only a couple of them had brought small dinner packs for their children, which were absolutely nothing to the now more than five thousand people present, among whom were some children and pregnant women.

Out of inquisitiveness, some youths wandered into the kitchen on the lower ground floor to find that there were still some food items left in the kitchen. The marchers always fasted on marching days, and on this anniversary celebration, they had been fasting throughout the marching period, including the non-marching days, only breaking fast after six o'clock in the evening. Now they had not eaten anything since morning and were trapped.

But the organizers were more concerned about the children among them. So they took the small dinner packs volunteered by members, and they added them to whatever was in an edible form found in the kitchen—bread, biscuits, cereal, fruit, etc., along with drinks—and fed the children, then the younger teens and the pregnant women.

Among the marchers were members of the public who had gone in search of food items to buy for their families and had gotten caught up in their midst. There were no markets as shops were closed, but there were fresh food items found in the kitchen which were handed over to those who, at the request of the leaders, volunteered to cook.

This food was initially served to the youths and women in very small quantities so it could go around. But God was merciful, for as they served, the food did not diminish; it was as if it was self-replenishing, which enabled them to eventually serve everyone to full satisfaction, though there were no leftovers. It was a sheer miracle.

The issue of where to pass the night was a difficult one. So after dinner, they asked the people to have some rest and assemble in the Great Hall by 10.30 p.m. for the conference, which was not scheduled to start until 11 p.m. With the Great Hall not being spacious enough to accommodate everybody, they moved some people to other conference rooms.

Most of the conference rooms already had their own LCD screens, and these were linked to the projectors in the Great Hall, where all activities were centered. They rearranged the seats in the Great Hall to accommodate as many people as possible with only three of the seminar rooms taken up as overflows during the conference. Although the power supply was erratic in many areas, and there was a total blackout in some. Their new venue had a permanent power supply throughout their stay—another miracle.

The organizers of the marching anniversary had not expected the foreign invited speaker to attend their conference because of the fear that had gripped the country. So they were surprised to see the speaker, a renowned evangelist, Josef Reinhart, show up on Friday, the first conference day, which was a day before the tear-like drop blast.

There were no flights to the UK, but he had flown from Germany to France's Lille Airport, where he had boarded a light aircraft to the nearest French airport to London, that is Dunkerque Airport, in Marck and hired a taxi that took him the seven-kilometer journey to Calais, where he boarded a ferry to Dover, located east of London, England.

At Dover, he rented a self-drive car to London—a distance of approximately seventy-six miles or one hundred and twenty-two kilometers.

The two invited speakers within the country already had turned up for the Friday conference, before things got worse on Saturday. They had all joined the groups in the Saturday march and were still with them at the time of the blast.

After the conference, which lasted till 2 am., they all went to sleep. They had separated themselves into different groups and allocated rooms to different groups, with women staying in separate rooms from men and little children sleeping with their mothers. The Great Hall was solely occupied by the men. Some slept sitting on chairs in an inclined position, but the majority slept on the carpeted floor after stacking the chairs to create space.

Elsewhere that night, people were afraid to sleep, unsure if they would wake up the next morning. The high-pitched swirling noise of the wind was enough to frighten anyone awake. All through the night, the dust still spilled out like volcanic lava and sent ripples of deadly emissions across the country. The fire was still being ignited in some places and raging uncontrollably.

While both the London and the Manchester gusts met up at approximately the middle of the country, most of the south was covered by the London dust storm, while the Manchester dust storm progressively covered most of the north and Scotland. No one knew for sure what was contained in the dust, what the tear-like drops were composed of, or what they may have unleashed into the atmosphere—deadly chemicals, viruses, etc.

The waves that reached Scotland were equally devastating in the southernmost part of the country but grew progressively feeble toward the north and caused less damage there. Visibility was equally poor but progressively improved toward the northernmost part.

By the following morning, the billowing dust cloud had reduced in intensity and the accompanying darkness had lightened, so people could see relatively more clearly. It was then that those who dared to peep through their glass windows saw death and carnage in the streets. Dead bodies were strewn all over the place. Mangled pieces of metal, broken pieces of furniture, and sheared fallen trees were strewn everywhere.

On Sunday morning, the marchers held an interdenominational service in the Great Hall. It was during this service that an altar call was made, especially for the benefit of those who had been caught up in the midst of the marching Christians who wanted to invite Christ into their lives. About two thousand people gave their lives or recommitted.

Fear of stepping outside, Christians in their homes left many church doors unopened. Many people did not know of the cloud protection given to the Jericho Wall Marchers on their way to the Methodist Central Hall. Some of those who lived in the area and had seen them along their route to the hall were not sure if the cloud protection offered to them served as blanket protection for all Christians, so no one wanted to take the risk of stepping out to church. Everyone was sorely afraid to the point of morbidity. Yet the homes held no security as the roaring wind was still threatening and damaging many homes with fallen trees, crashing metal and fallen power lines, which ignited fires.

After service, the hall was turned into a carnival of some sort. Breakfast was not expected, if only for the fact that whatever food items were in the kitchen had been cooked and consumed the previous evening.

However, out of sheer inquisitiveness, some teens had wandered into the kitchen and found the whole place filled with fresh supplies—biscuits; baskets of loaves of bread, cereals, assorted fresh fruits and various fruit drinks; bottled water; bags of fresh potatoes, including potato chips; bags of parboiled rice, beans, macaroni, spaghetti, etc.—with assorted ingredients for stew, gravy and soup, along with spices and various types of fresh meat and fish.

They reported their findings to the older people, who, in turn, told the organizers. Children and vulnerable adults were served eggs—fried and scrambled—with bread immediately after the church service, while the rest fasted.

After a short break, the carnival of worship started. As decided, the meeting was less of a speaking engagement and more of a time of praying, singingv dancing, the people's fear-driven away by the joy of worship. They had breaks at intervals to refresh and interact with one another. Children and youths played various improvised games. The youths turned their sessions into a musical jamboree.

The atmosphere inside was electric, in complete contrast to the tragic events outside and despite their not knowing of the fate of their loved ones outside the venue. Their joy was spontaneous and unexplained, as if of a source above and outside them. It was as if God had appeared physically in their midst. Outside the hall, the pillar of white cloud remained, surrounding the building.

By that Saturday evening, the day of the eruption of the dust cloud, most transmission and aerial communication facilities had been disabled. Many radio and TV channels in the UK had gone off-air. Most journalists representing various foreign media organizations had withdrawn from mainland Britain before the City Hall blast. Those still within, and the local press journalists who on the day of the blast were indoors, were lucky and made no attempt to step outside, as those caught up in the hurricane outside had met an untimely death.

Many of those trapped inside broadcasting houses or press offices simply remained there. There was no feedback from reporters to broadcast or print. But people needed to know what was happening outside their immediate vicinity.

Most Christian events were usually filmed officially by the organizing groups, or unofficially by participants with their own cameras or mobile phones. Some members of the Jericho Wall Marchers always filmed the marching events either to enjoy replaying it for themselves or to play it for family and friends as a means of drawing them to future participation.

A few of them had been filming the marching activities when the City Hall blast occurred. After the initial shock, some of them continued filming. They turned themselves into amateur photojournalists and field reporters. Their clips of happenings in the streets around the marching venues and generally within the reach of their cameras, and the goings-on within and around the Methodist Central Hall, were shared on social media.

Their audiovisual media on the events in London became the primary source of news for the rest of the world's radio and TV channels. Nothing was coming from the rest of the country, as people simply couldn't venture outside.

Meanwhile, Christians all over the world were praying for Britain. No one was sure if what was happening would be restricted to Britain or would spill over to other countries. But that was not why Christians were praying for Britain. Britain's agnosticism and atheistic offensive against Christians and godliness had become an open secret to the rest of the world, one that clearly needed divine intervention.

Also, before now, requests for prayers from various Christian organizations in Britain such as Justice for British Christians had resulted in Christians all over the world praying for Britain. So prayers were intensified.

Chapter 22
The Lord Reigns

The Jericho Wall Marchers were supposed to round off their anniversary celebration that Sunday with their final march before the evening conference. Events, however, dictated a variation from their original arrangement. That fact notwithstanding, after morning service and the carnival-like celebrations, which lasted till 3 p.m., some of the leaders suggested they go and complete their march.

But there were strong objections because of the debris lying everywhere, including along their marching route, and the fear that gripped everyone. Some saw it as testing God after they'd been miraculously rescued, which amounted to a sin. The arguments for and against carried on for a while. Eventually, the idea was abandoned. Instead, they decided the evening conference would be turned into a full-night vigil. So they had a short praise and worship session and went back for dinner and rest, with instruction to be back by 10 p.m. for the vigil.

The vigil was not a night of silent waiting on God. It was a night of prayer, worship and spiritual warfare. They kept the original theme of the conference, which was *Britain: A Festival of Restoration—God among Us*.

There were only two preaching sessions during the night vigil, but the speakers did a good job of eulogizing the goodness of God and His matchless power. They spoke of several instances where the enemy seemed to be on the verge of victory, only for God to overthrow them and turn the situation around. There was a lot of praying and praise worship.

At the end of a segment of one of the praying sessions, the person leading the prayers announced that they were to undertake another march despite the obstacles and their earlier decision not to engage in any further marching. He said he had seen a vision of them marching completely away from their normal route. Instead, they were marching through Whitehall and Downing Street. He said the vision was very vivid. In the vision, they marched along a route that completely encircled Downing Street and Whitehall offices, from the Methodist Central Hall through Broad Sanctuary to Parliament Street, then through Whitehall to Downing Street.

At the end of Downing Street, they turned around and walked back to Whitehall, continued on Whitehall to Trafalgar Square, turning left onto the Mall, left again onto Horse Guard Road and then left again onto Great George Road to Parliament Square.

When he said this, there was dead silence in the hall. Everyone could sense some measure of resentment in the air and rightly so. But whatever resentment they had, no one spoke out openly against the plan. So it was agreed that they would give it a trial in the daytime. The night vigil concluded by five o'clock in the morning, and then they went to sleep or whatever form of it each individual had.

By one o'clock that Monday afternoon, those in the overflow joined the assembly in the Great Hall as prearranged for *the Great March* as they termed it. Before the march, while still inside the hall, they embarked on another round of intense worship and exhortation, pleading for God's intervention.

In their exhortations, they reminded God of His awesome power and all He had done in times past: the miracle of the Red Sea, the Jericho Wall, Jonah in the belly of the fish, Meshach, Shadrach and Abednego in the fire, Daniel in the lions' den, Peter in Herod's prison, Paul and Silas in prison, Paul's shipwreck in Malta and so forth. They reminded Him of His promises.

After a full hour of exaltation, they left the children behind, together with the pregnant women and anyone who felt too feeble to participate. The rest gathered at Parliament Square, from where they started their march, singing, "Ah Lord God, Thou hast made the heaven and the earth by Thy great power… Nothing is too difficult for Thee," and several other faith-building songs. They followed the route as detailed during the night vigil.

It was an arduous slow walk, but they edged on. When they got to the entrance to Downing Street, the iron barricades collapsed and fell on their own accord, and they walked through, trampling them underfoot, rejoicing and singing, "For He has broken the gates of brass and cut the bars of iron in asunder." They stayed for quite a while at Downing Street as they sang, and as they left Downing Street, they changed their song to the following:

All the nations of the earth,
praise the Lord who brings to birth
the greatest star, the smallest flower.
Hallelujah.

Rebellious Britain, praise the Lord, hallelujah.
Let every Briton praise the Lord, hallelujah.
London and country, praise the Lord, hallelujah.
Dusty windstorm, praise the Lord, hallelujah.
All the nations of the earth,
praise the Lord who brings to birth
the greatest star, the smallest flower.
Hallelujah.

So they continued singing as they marched back to Whitehall. As soon as those in the forefront linked up with Whitehall and turned left in continuation of their predetermined route toward Trafalgar Square, an amazing thing happened. The obstacles on their route just ahead of them started clearing away on their own accord as they approached.

The same wild wind that had caused the devastation suddenly became organized along their route as if specifically channeled with such power and force that it pushed all debris to both sides of the road. Large fallen trees and their sheared branches, mangled metal pieces of vehicles and heavy chunks of bricks all cleared and properly aligned along the edge of their route, while other roads remained clustered and obstructed.

It was a wonderful sight to behold. They were overjoyed and gave each other high fives as they quickly passed the news to those behind. Now they could dance, and they did not allow the opportunity to slip them by for the rest of their route. Some youths among them walked back to the hall to pick up musical instruments from the church and to their amazement, the routes to the building also cleared of their own accord of all obstacles.

So they ran instead of walking. The two gospel artists invited to perform at the last two conference nights were absent, having been prevented from attending by the sudden disaster that had occurred before they had time to leave for the conference. So youth choir members of individual churches in the marching group rolled out the drums from the Methodist Central Hall Church to celebrate the wonders of God as they rejoined the marching and played their hearts out. Instead of the pace of walking increasing now that the roads were clear, it slowed because of dancing and rejoicing.

They continued, edging their way forward toward their starting point at Parliament Square. As they approached from Great George Road, the entire square was suddenly cleared of all its debris, including all the surrounding roads that defined the square. They got to the square and walked around it seven times.

It was a long line that would have joined the leading and the trailing groups into one continuous ring of people, but they deliberately maintained a short gap between them to be able to accurately count the number of rounds. At the end of the seventh round, they amassed on the lawn inside the square gave a loud shout of "Hallelujah!" and continued singing and dancing.

As they shouted "Hallelujah!" another amazing thing happened. Both the shroud of white cloud around them and the destructive windstorm with its dust cloud suddenly disappeared, and a beautiful shaft of sunrays crafted the square with majestic splendor—but only in the square. Now was the real dancing as they turned the square into a glorious carnival of worship.

Those of them who had turned themselves into field reporters, filming with their cameras and mobile phones, went to work right from inside the Great Hall even before the start of the marching. Once more they shared on social media their clips of all that was happening on their route down to the square—the singing and dancing, the clearing of rubbish, the sudden disappearance of the dust cloud and the sudden replacement of the white cloud with the beautiful sun rays.

The whole world was glued to their TV screens as the Methodist Central Hall and Parliament Square became the center of the world, the focal point of Christian synergy and the hub of media outlets to the world, as TVs replayed social media clips.

While the carnival of worship continued at Parliament Square, things started to happen. Firstly there was a big hissing sound of a massive swirling wind. The wind then started losing its strength and started slowing down. Then the dust particles started thinning out, and the dull grayness of the cloud started disappearing, making for much-improved visibility. The clearing of the dust cloud started from all around the square and spread outward 360° to the rest of London and the rest of the country, sweeping across Manchester and all the areas the blast there had affected. As the dust cloud cleared, the beautiful sun replaced it. Whatever was the source of the furious dust wind and the dense smog had simply dried up.

From their homes and hiding places, people could see outside more clearly, but no one dared step outside. And this was not just in London, but the whole country. Those who still had electric power within the country watched unfolding events at Parliament Square from sky channels and from all available channels in the rest of the world.

After more than an hour of praise and worship at the square, the group moved back into the Great Hall to formally declare the victory of good over evil, with much celebration—singing and dancing—to conclude their marching anniversary celebration.

Tim Lane, the erstwhile Prime Minister, in his final speech, challenged Christian leaders to boldly stand up for the Christian cause and stand firm in their commitment to God. He appealed to politicians worldwide to uphold moral principles and religious freedom within their respective domains. Jay gave the vote of thanks, but before then, the only foreign invited guest at the ceremony, evangelist Josef Reinhart, was given the honor of making the final closing remarks. As they clapped when he mounted the rostrum, he asked them to repeat the following psalm after him, which they did:

Cry out with joy to God all the earth.
O sing to the glory of His name.
O render him glorious praise.
Say to God: How tremendous your deeds are.

Before you, all the earth shall bow.
They shall sing to you, sing to your name.
Come and see the works of God,
Tremendous his deeds among men.

He turned the sea into dry land.
They passed through the river dry-shod.
Let our joy then be in him.
He rules forever by his might.

Come and hear, all who fear God.
I will tell what he did for my soul.
Blessed be God who did not reject my prayer
Nor withhold his love from me.

When they finished reciting the psalm, he beckoned them by a wave of his hands to sit down.

"My dear people of God," he started, "once more I thank you for counting me worthy of being part of this great celebration. On my arrival, I was asked why I dared to come to a place where everybody was running away. My response was that I am a soldier of Christ. Only soldiers go to where people are running away. As soldiers on a conquering mission for Christ, we are the only people who can step out without fear and without harm.

"What just happened proves that. But it seems many of us are only just beginning to realize the awesome power God gave us. What we are witnessing right now in this country is the manifestation of the power of God in the believer. This is the culmination of seven years of prophetic marching prayers you've undertaken in storming heaven with your pleas on behalf of this country.

"In Exodus, God said, 'I have heard the cry of my people in Egypt by reason of their taskmasters.' That means although He knew the sufferings of His people in Egypt, He did not act until they cried out to Him. Until the prodigal son made a deliberate decision to go back to his father, the father could not respond to his needs. Paul cursed Elymas and he became blind. Jesus cursed a fig tree and it dried up.

The Bible is replete with God's response to the call of His people. Someone once said, 'Faith is to believe what we do not see, and the reward is to see what we believe.' That is what we are experiencing here and now. Until you cry out to God in prayer, you are hindering His power in you, and I dare say until you cry out to Him, you are not a Christian, because a Christian is one who is Christlike, and Christ was given too much praying; in fact, He did nothing without prayers. And not only did He pray, but also He acted on His prayers.

"And if Christ, being God, can pray, then who are you not to? But there are prayers and then there are prayers. There are prayers that don't ruffle an ant—prayers that make the Devil smile. You don't confront a roaring lion with such prayers. But there are prayers that put the Devil to flight, prayers that force God's hand and provoke His presence in battle, and fire prayers that produce remarkable results. I dare those who were mocking and jesting when you started your Jericho Wall march to come out and laugh now.

"I have preached firepower evangelism for decades in various parts of the world, with great impact in Africa and South America. Europe has trampled on God's Word and compassion for too long and is only just beginning to pay the price. God uses the foolish things of the world to confound the wise. That is why people could mock your prophetic march. For who would've thought that a symbolic march could bring a country to its knees?

"Using the simple things to confound the wise is the reason why, in all the wisdom of Europe, it took the weakness of colored immigrants to set this country on fire for God. God is a respecter of no person. Volunteer yourself and He will use you. What just happened confirms that our God is a consuming fire. And we rejoice at the awesome manifestation of this fire.

"We rejoice not just because of the sudden end to this tragedy but also because our God is always in control, and because He wants us to rejoice always, knowing that in His hands is victory. It doesn't have to take a tragedy of this proportion to prove the existence of God, but unfortunately, that is how the world, and Europe in particular, wants it.

"The hand of King Jeroboam withered when stretched against the righteous indignation of the man of God. Let all those who hold political power and all who constitute their Bethel altar, who come against our righteous indignation, be warned. What just happened has exposed their weakness. So fear them not for the fire of the Holy Spirit is real.

"It must flow through the church of Jesus Christ like blood through the veins. God's people on fire and the church as a whole on fire: that is what will win our lost generation for Him."

With that, he stepped down from the rostrum, with a prolonged outstanding ovation by the audience, before Jay mounted the rostrum for his vote of thanks.

By five o'clock that evening, every place was clear, and the only shadows that could be seen were those cast by the sunlight. The rocky object had gone, and a summer-like beautiful skyline was all that adorned the troposphere. It was a dramatic end to a deadly mystery.

It was a new day, bright and beautiful, blessed and glorious. It was the day of the Lord among us. The people went out of the Great Hall to start clearing the roads. It was devastation on a scale they could not handle, but they wanted to let the people know that they were safe to step outside and embark on the massive task of reparation. They started clearing debris with their bare hands, but it was no use.

So they went back to their Great Hall temporary residence. The following day, those whose homes were nearby and who could venture it walked home. The rest who couldn't, especially those from boroughs/counties farther away, remained in the Great Hall. Meanwhile, the group leaders were appealing to people through radio and television, which had now started functioning again, to step out and help clear the streets, dispelling their fears.

The participants who had gone home were asked to take the lead, and many of them actually brought their families outside to assure their neighbors. It was not until two days later that the government operating only inside No. 10, using junior noncommissioned military officers, decided to test the safety outside. From there, the military, the police and volunteer groups were all called to help clear the streets and roads. They also carried out mass burials of the dead.

Two weeks after return to normalcy, the Prime Minister invited the Jericho Wall Marchers to a state banquet in appreciation of their help in bringing the darkest chapter of British history to a dramatic end.

Epilogue
Mission Accomplished

One year after this divine visitation, Jay Wilson relocated to Jamaica after being offered a professorial seat at the University of Kingston, Jamaica. Six months later, Kojo Agyei was promoted to chief executive officer of his parent company and was posted back to the head office in Accra.

Even after their return to their respective countries, they remained friends and kept in contact through phone and occasional visits. Kojo had always wondered why he was posted to London and how he was able to endure living there, a place he hated so much. Similarly, Jay had often questioned his reasons for staying behind after graduation, when he could have easily gotten a job in Jamaica. It was not until after they had returned to their countries that they realized they were on assignment to God.

But the fire of the Spirit to take the gospel to the entire world was still always aflame in them. They promoted Christian life and values all over the world and often met at international Christian gatherings. Tim Lane (the erstwhile PM) also kept in contact with them and often met with them at international Christian gatherings. He remained a high-profile promoter of Christian values and an indomitable fighter for the Christian cause throughout the UK for the rest of his life. His indomitable efforts in promoting peace, tolerance and godliness throughout the world were rewarded with an appointment as a peace and goodwill ambassador of the United Nations.